The Transformative Potential of Small-Scale Entrepreneurship

Small Business and the City examines the power of small-scale entrepreneurship to transform local neighbourhoods and the cities they inhabit. In their evaluation of the factors that help small businesses survive and thrive, the authors highlight the success of a Canadian concept which has spread worldwide: the Business Improvement Area (BIA). By encouraging small-scale entrepreneurs to pool their resources with like-minded businesses, BIAs become sources of urban rejuvenation, magnets for human talent, and incubators for local innovation.

The book also analyses the policies necessary to support urban vitality, describing how cities can stimulate and support locally owned independent businesses. Through inspiring accounts of examples of urban transformation, *Small Business and the City* introduces a new "main street agenda" for the twenty-first century city.

RAFAEL GOMEZ is Associate Professor of Employment Relations at Woodsworth College and the Centre for Industrial Relations and Human Resources at the University of Toronto.

ANDRE ISAKOV is currently the Manager of Park Planning and Design with the City of Coquitlam, British Columbia. Previously, he was the Community and Economic Development Officer for the Village of Harrison Hot Springs and the Executive Director of Business Improvement Areas of British Columbia.

MATT SEMANSKY is an award-winning journalist based in Dartmouth, Nova Scotia. His work has appeared in publications such as *This Magazine*, the *National Post*, the *Halifax Chronicle Herald*, *The Coast*, and *Marketing*.

RAFAEL GOMEZ
ANDRE ISAKOV
MATT SEMANSKY

Small Business and the City

The Transformative Potential of Small-Scale Entrepreneurship

UNIVERSITY OF TORONTO PRESS
Toronto Buffalo London

© University of Toronto Press 2015
Rotman-UTP Publishing
Toronto Buffalo London
www.utppublishing.com
Printed in the U.S.A

ISBN 978-1-4426-4362-8 (cloth)
ISBN 978-1-4426-1209-9 (paper)

Printed on acid-free, 100% post-consumer recycled paper with vegetable-based inks.

Library and Archives Canada Cataloguing in Publication

Gomez, Rafael, 1972-, author
Small business and the city : transformative potential of small-scale entrepreneurship / Rafael Gomez, Andre Isakov, Matt Semanksy.

(Rotman-UTP)
Includes bibliographical references and index.
ISBN 978-1-4426-4362-8 (bound).--ISBN 978-1-4426-1209-9 (pbk.)

1. Small business – Canada.   2. Central business districts – Canada.   3. Cities and towns – Canada – Growth.   4. Urban renewal – Canada.   5. Community development, Urban – Canada.   I. Isakov, Andre, 1985-, author   II. Semansky, Matt, 1976-, author   III. Title.

HD62.7.G654 2015   658.02'20971   C2014-906733-X

University of Toronto Press acknowledges the financial assistance to its publishing program of the Canada Council for the Arts and the Ontario Arts Council, an agency of the Government of Ontario.

Canada Council   **Conseil des Arts**
for the Arts   **du Canada**

ONTARIO ARTS COUNCIL
CONSEIL DES ARTS DE L'ONTARIO
an Ontario government agency
un organisme du gouvernement de l'Ontario

University of Toronto Press acknowledges the financial support of the Government of Canada through the Canada Book Fund for its publishing activities.

For our parents
Juan Rafael and Dolores Gomez
Alex Isakov and Irina Korolyova
Patricia and Paul Semansky and Rick Warren

Contents

businesses, providing access to finance, offering business support programs to spur new business start-ups and innovation, and, crucially, recognizing the vital role small businesses play in building social capital in communities across Canada.

As such, there is no substitute for the kind of "bottom-up" study of economic development that Professor Gomez and his colleagues share on these pages. I hope this book is read widely by social and economic policy makers and elected officials at all levels of government. Coming as we are out of one of the most serious economic downturns in modern history, we must have an effective and joined-up national strategy to spur entrepreneurialism and new business start-ups if we are to sustain our nascent but still fragile economic recovery.

If Canada is to avoid the kind of social and economic dislocation that has befallen other countries, we first need to understand how building an economy around thriving small-scale entrepreneurship that produces tangible goods and services at the local level works to soften the blows dealt by the vagaries of the global economy. *Small Business and the City* is thus a ground-breaking indispensable step towards the goal of understanding the importance that our neighbourhood businesses and entrepreneurs play in maintaining the vitality of city living and our nation's economy.

Councillor Michael Thompson
Chair of Economic Development, City of Toronto
Ward 37 Scarborough Centre
City of Toronto

But economic growth doesn't happen in a vacuum; it takes vision and collective action. When I and a few local businesses began the process of forming the Wexford Heights BIA in the early 2000s, the long-term future of the strip was by no means a given. A lack of investment in both public and private infrastructure, fear of crime, and a lack of consensus and vision on how best to position the community within Toronto threatened to undermine its long-term success.

Through a series of BIA-led investments in the streetscape, marketing programs, street festivals, and community policing initiatives, the neighbourhood continues to be a lively hub of business and leisure activity, even garnering enhanced coverage in local media. A key element of this success is the number of new Canadians and immigrants who form the nucleus of entrepreneurs taking forward new business ventures in the ward. Undoubtedly, for Toronto and my ward, immigration is a vital demographic and economic lifeline.

But getting people and entrepreneurs to move to your city and community, as we've learned in Scarborough Centre, requires a focus on quality-of-life issues (good schools, parks, public safety) and amenities such as public transit. At a time when public finances are under threat, this is of course not an easy job, but one that nonetheless needs to be seen as a critical investment in future economic success. Bringing together public and private-sector players through BIAs is certainly one way of achieving this objective.

Small-Scale Entrepreneurial Success and the Dynamism of City Life

There is little question that a major part of the enduring vibrancy of Canada's major urban centres lies in the dynamism of its small firms. Whether it's a filmmaker in Halifax, an independent auto-repair shop owner in Toronto, or a bed-and-breakfast operator in Vancouver, these varied and small entrepreneurs contribute not only to the strength of local economies through their positive impact on local supply chains and labour markets but also to community development through participation in BIAs and support for a myriad not-for-profit organizations and charities.

In looking at the experiences of Toronto, Halifax, and Vancouver, however, it is clear that governments at all levels could do more to ensure the success of small businesses. This includes, among other things, offering competitive and fair tax rates across all city regions, carefully considering the impacts of planning and zoning decisions on small public characters such as small shopkeepers and local barbers enhance the social structure of local life. These truths are as valid today as they were in the early 1960s when she penned the classic *The Death and Life of Great American Cities.*[3] Indeed, Jacobs's ideas have been vividly extended right here in Toronto at the Martin Prosperity Institute in the work of Richard Florida and his colleagues, who have noted that cities tend to survive by acquiring and keeping human talent, which is in turn attracted by convenient and unique urban amenities. The capital and investment that follow can be traced back to human capital, which is itself determined by the quality of our main streets and city life.

My City, My Neighbourhood

This brings me to my own city of Toronto. Anyone searching for a case study substantiating Glaeser's and Jacobs's insights, need only look at the Kennedy Road Business Improvement Area (KBIA) and the Wexford Heights Business Improvement Area (WBIA), which straddle Kennedy Road and Lawrence Avenue East, respectively, two of the main thoroughfares in the ward of Scarborough Centre that I represent in the east end of Toronto. The community of Wexford, in particular, with its collection of small businesses, is the ultimate microcosm of Canada's economy, with virtually every sector represented, from financial and professional services to retail and manufacturing.

In a world seemingly dominated by chain stores and corporate fast-food giants, Lawrence Avenue East and Kennedy Road stand as unique bastions of independent entrepreneurialism and eclecticism. Defying mono-ethnic neighbourhood appellations, Lawrence East is at once the Middle East, the Far East, the Caribbean, Britain, southern Europe, and, for good measure, a bit of 1950s and early 1960s North America. Where else can one find Chinese food takeaways, Guyanese-Trinidadian curry shops, Lebanese bakeries, British pubs, and Greek delis on the same street block? The defining architectural form is the sometimes unfairly maligned strip mall. Unlike the vast parking-lot-dominated malls that would be built after the 1970s, Lawrence Avenue's are almost sixty years old (built in the 1950s and early 1960s) with design features reminiscent of the early Las Vegas strip. Yet these are not stagnant period pieces but dynamic and evolving structures reflecting the ebbs and flows of demographic change and economic transformation: from burger joint to used-car outlet to frozen-food store to bicycle shop to post office to organic grocery store, and so it goes.

Foreword

Despite the fact that Canadian politicians routinely sing the praises of small and medium-sized enterprises, too often the focus of economic development efforts is on attracting – at times with large tax breaks and subsidies – the "one" firm, big sports franchise, or retailer that can transform a city's economic fortunes with jobs and growth. While nobody would deny the value of inward investment, there is always the danger of ignoring the true driver of growth: our base of small businesses. As urban economist Ed Glaeser notes, places with greater numbers of small, independent firms and abundant new start-ups experience faster income and employment growth than cities with one or two major employers.[1] Although luring a big firm garners splashy headlines, statistically we know that growth is more reliably correlated with the number of smaller independent firms in your region.[2]

It's also useful to remind readers that many of Canada's big corporate players, such as RIM, Rogers, and Bombardier, were once small businesses themselves. Bombardier evolved from a small manufacturer of Ski-Doos in 1930s Quebec into one of the world's largest manufacturers of regional aircraft, mass transportation, and recreational vehicles. Meanwhile, Rogers Communications, founded by Edward S. Rogers, Sr, got its start as Radio Manufacturing Corporation Limited in 1925, selling radios with what at the time was cutting-edge vacuum tube technology. And RIM, at the dawn of mobile telephony in the 1990s, was just the dream of a Waterloo-based engineer and his business partner.

But it's not just about economics. Our small businesses and the locations they occupy on our many streets and avenues form an integral part of this country's social fabric and community spirit. We should not lose sight of Jane Jacobs's prescient observations about how self-appointed

Acknowledgments

A book such as this would not have been possible without the input of many hardworking individuals. In particular, the time provided to the authors by the many small business owners in Halifax, Toronto, and Vancouver whose activity and insights form the backbone of this book is gratefully acknowledged. In addition, the knowledge provided to us by devoted civil servants in all three cities who at various levels of government often acted as advocates for the small-scale entrepreneurs and the neighbourhoods they inhabit proved indispensable. We also are deeply indebted to our editor at University of Toronto Press, Jennifer DiDomenico, who believed in this project and allowed us the space and time to improve the manuscript. We are especially grateful to the artful and careful work of the managing editor, Anne Laughlin, and our copy-editor, Margaret Allen, at University of Toronto Press.

We are grateful to Infrastructure Canada and the Knowledge, Outreach and Awareness (KOA) grant it provided in 2007 to our study of business improvement areas (BIAs); to Ian Chodikoff and Dave LeBlanc for supporting our efforts to disseminate the research via the Fringe Benefits project and the Architourist column of the *Globe and Mail*, respectively; to Juan Gomez for his careful reading and many helpful comments on our manuscript; and a special thanks to Morley Gunderson and Melanie Brady for their gracious help in finalizing the manuscript.

We are very thankful to Kirsten Greer for her initial interest in this topic, her successful grant application, and her early work on the origins and impacts of the business improvement areas (BIAs) in Canada. We also thank Andrew Steinewall, Nicole Jones, Andrei Mazanik, Nathaniel Lewis, Mark Horvat, Ziyan Hussein, Salim Rachid, Tina Saskida, Jeremy Hopkin, Tom Sardelic, Anton Sardelic, Michael

Tamburro, Peter Hamilton, Peter Felice, Derek Law, Sep Radjpoust, Jessica Erskine, John Cross, Kevin Money, Alex Bryson, Richard Griffiths, Barbara Cohen, Viet Hoang, Umar Boodoo, James Gen Meers, Todd Harris, Peter Bouris, and Danielle Lamb for their research assistance work on BIAs and interviews of Toronto business owners in Crossroads of the Danforth, Roncesvalles, Cabbagetown, Bloorcourt/ Bloordale, and Wexford in west Scarborough (in east-end Toronto). We also thank Marc-Oliver Cote, Elisabeth Rivest (from Convercite), and Gazeleh Etezal for their work in Montreal and Toronto interviewing the heads of the various sociétés de développement commercial (SDCs) and BIAs. We would like to thank Michael Thompson, Ihor Wons, John Kiru, Bob Sysak, Jeff Somerville, John Nash, and Henry Byers for their help in identifying people such as Alex Ling (the co-founder of the first BIA) and neighbourhoods of interest in the cities of Toronto and Vancouver.

Rafael Gomez would like to thank his colleagues at the Centre for Industrial Relations and Woodsworth College at the University of Toronto and colleagues at the London School of Economics and Glendon College (York University) for the support and freedom that allowed him to devote his time to the research for this book. He would also like to thank Anne Gloger from the Storefront, Colette Murphy (formerly Metcalf Foundation), the members of People Plan Toronto, Kathryn Firth from the Cities program at the London School of Economics, and Alex Quito and Lorraine Gauthier at Work Worth Doing for their "brainstorming" help in the early stages of this research, and especially my wife, Trisha Orzech, whose moral support as well as organizational and logistical work at the helm of ThinkTankToronto made this research project a going concern.

During the process of researching this book Andre Isakov and Matt Semansky kindly agreed to provide their "bi-coastal" input. Their deep understanding of the underlying process by which the BIA movement works in Vancouver and Halifax, respectively, and their work in shaping it for the reader to consider means that the findings of this book are supported by the experiences of literally hundreds of entrepreneurs in cities across the country However, despite the diversity of contributions, we have decided to retain the first-person singular in the narrative, as we all believe that the reader will benefit more from an informal and personal style.

Andre Isakov would like to thank the friends at BIABC, Simon Fraser University, and in Harrison Hot Springs, Coquitlam, and the

Centre for Civic Governance at Columbia Institute. He would like to give special gratitude to family and loved ones for all their support and inspiration.

Matt Semansky would like to thank the members of the small business community in the Halifax Regional Municipality for sharing their experiences. He would also like to thank Bernard Smith of the North End Business Commission, Paul Mackinnon of the Downtown Halifax Business Commission, and Nancy Tissington of the Spring Garden Area Merchants Association for providing critical historical background as well as information about current conditions. Finally, he would like to thank the numerous journalists at the *Halifax Chronicle-Herald* and *The Coast*, whose work served as a guide to the city and the jumping-off point for much of his research.

SMALL BUSINESS AND THE CITY

The Transformative Potential of Small-Scale
Entrepreneurship

1 Introduction: Small Business and City Life

How do small, independent, locally operated businesses survive?

This book is a fairly involved answer to this seemingly simple question. In addressing this question it focuses on the emergence of business improvement areas (BIAs) and their relation to the quality of city life. It also centres on our desire to understand the source(s) of entrepreneurial success and the continued persistence of small business in what has increasingly become a hyper-globalized and corporatized world. Along the way it tries to figure out why such a simple question needs to be asked in the first place. The small-scale entrepreneur has clearly outlived the predictions of many learned economists and social thinkers. Joseph Schumpeter and Karl Marx, among several, assumed that independent entrepreneurs – the petit bourgeoisie of another time and place – would fade away with the rise of corporate hierarchies, technological innovation, and the increased scale of enterprise.[1]

The question of why small businesses have not only survived but also seemingly thrived in our major cities, where they still occupy a prominent place both physically (in neighbourhoods) and psychologically (in the minds of city dwellers), is therefore an interesting one for academics and students alike. It should also be of interest to a more generalized and informed group of readers, including policy makers, city enthusiasts, and, most importantly, urban residents and small business owners themselves.

What Do We Mean by Small-Scale Entrepreneurship?

In this book we make the claim that cities thrive when large numbers of small, locally based, and independently run businesses are given space to emerge and thrive. By "small" we mean not being so large that a business does not fit into the typical main street areas where urban commerce (both retail and professional) was originally intended to occur. By "local" we mean having a presence in a neighbourhood. By "independent" we mean that the effective ownership and control are not subsumed under a larger corporate entity. "Small" is a standard of fitting into the constraints imposed by urban living; "local" is a standard of rootedness in community; and "independence" is a standard of freedom to be unique and nonconformist in the delivery of services or the provision of goods. Applying this framework to what makes urban living unique provides a rich analytical framework in which researchers, practitioners, and policy makers can analyse and compare cities' economic development in terms of the health of their small, local, and independent business sectors. To this end, we first define small-scale entrepreneurship using the terms "small," "local," and "independent" in the context of urban regions.

The Importance of Being Small, Local, *and* Independent

A small business is one that perhaps remains small because of scarce resources, especially of time and money. It can be small in the sense of generating revenues of less than several million dollars. Small businesses can be small by choice – in that the owner of the retail store, restaurant, or dental office prefers not to expand in order to focus on customer satisfaction instead. Or, a corporate chain can use "small" locations as part of their business strategy (i.e., Starbucks and Tim Horton's mandate that locations cover a small footprint). Smallness can result from various features of urban design, such as the need for smaller retail footprints in the dense inner urban areas of older cities or in the strip malls of early postwar suburbs. For businesses, another aspect of being "small" is the extent to which ownership depends on paid employees for service delivery or production. Smallness might also signal a "strategy" of being close to the customer and having a focus on quality over quantity, as with a particularly good restaurant that purposely keeps its premises small. Customers may suffer long waits or shortages but tolerate this in order to receive a high-quality meal. Their success notwithstanding, these small firms may remain small not from necessity but by design.

"Local" in the context of a business rooted in a city describes a relative standard. The primary attribute of a local business is proximity to most local residents, and here the definition of "proximity" may vary. Certainly in older urban cores, the standard is walkability: "Can I walk in a few minutes to my local store?" If not, then the store is not considered local. The standard in a mid-century inner suburb may be "Can I drive in a few minutes to my local store?" The concept of "local" also implies that the business caters to local needs and is sufficiently rooted in the community to understand what those needs are and when those needs are not being met. Individual customers entering a local bank in an immigrant neighbourhood should receive more targeted, specialized, though not necessarily lower-quality, treatment than someone entering a bank branch in the financial district. Moreover, a truly local business treats individual users/customers/clients with respect, sensitivity, and privacy. Also implicit in the term "local" is the possibility of "customization" – such as the capacity to offer price discounts to those with less willingness to pay – and a reliance on trust to prevent arbitrary or capricious behaviour and enhance accountability. A local business is also, by design, more accessible than a non-locally based one because it is close by.

The "independent" dimension of small businesses in a city captures the extent to which the people who own and run the operation are tied (through legal ownership) to a larger corporate entity (i.e., a franchiser) or conglomerate. This dimension includes important aspects of scope for action, such as having an ability – either as manager or employee – to offer price discounts on the spot. Independence can also include the extent to which individuals who are part of a conglomerate and who manage an otherwise small, local operation have input into the day-to-day running of the business and into specific policies and strategies. Because "local" and "independent" might both be thought to imply a condition of being "unique" or "autonomous," it can be tempting to combine the two dimensions. But the qualities of being local and of being independent are different and require separate analyses. Whereas the local dimension focuses on the "geographic" setting, the independent dimension focuses on how much "discretion" the persons running a business actually have. A small business can be local (by being rooted in a neighbourhood main street) but lack independence, or can include independence but be decidedly non-local (the organic farm located an hour's drive from the city is a case in point). A bank whose retail operations are predicated on having many small branches located in cities could have a significant measure of "locality" but lack independence, since all decisions (concerning everything from the colour scheme to the music playing over the speakers) are mandated by head office. This distinction becomes particularly important in analysing how rooted these "non-independent" local players are in their neighbourhoods. Because they do not depend on an individual local business for the bulk (or even a minor portion) of their overall revenues, they are often willing to "exit" when conditions change (a property tax differential may be enough to induce flight). The small and independent firm is clearly more rooted in its neighbourhood, perhaps by desire but also by the lack of these viable exit options, which multinationals possess in abundance.

So, in short, any one of the qualifying elements calls for inclusion, albeit with less attention, in our study. That is, even a firm that may be locally owned and managed but is not small or independent (it may be part of a regional or national chain) has been shown to confer advantages on its host location that are larger (on average) than those of an otherwise similar firm without local ownership (i.e., the locally owned firm tends to stay rooted in the location where it was founded and employ more local residents). Likewise, a shop that is small and located along a main street shopping district imparts certain benefits regardless of whether it is part of a global brand whose ownership resides somewhere else. Indeed, this kind of firm, one with a universal brand, often can "legitimize" an area (i.e., in economic terms it can act as a credible "signalling mechanism" of neighbourhood safety and/or market desirability for other firms thinking of opening up a business in that area).[2] The strongest effect is clearly the one produced in the eyes of some consumers, which is why a small franchise can act as an "anchor" tenant for the neighbourhood's independent businesses. Once drawn to the area by this well-known tenant, other firms benefit from the resulting increase in foot traffic and exposure.

The Geometry of Small-Scale Entrepreneurship

The metrics of the "small," "local," and "independent" criteria therefore provide an analytical framework for analysing and comparing different urban regions in terms of the strength of their small-scale entrepreneurial sector and, to a considerable degree, their socioeconomic success as well. Following Hyman's (2001) "geometry of trade unionism," Budd's (2004) "geometry of the employment relationship," and Budd and Colvin's (2007) "geometry of dispute settlement systems," this analysis focuses on the "geometry of small-scale entrepreneurship" within a city.

As such, business exemplars are located in exhibit 1.1 based on the extent to which they are small, local, and independent. Exhibit 1.1 is an equilateral triangle reflecting the equal weight placed on each of the three attributes. The business names and relative locations in the exhibit will become apparent as the various businesses (some of which may not be known to a readership outside of Toronto or Canada) are discussed in the first part of the book. Disagreements over these locations are of course possible, as the major contribution of this three-dimensional framework is in providing a coherent basis for such debates. What we do feel emerges from the geometry of small-scale entrepreneurship is that there should be both a positive and a normative desire for urban areas to have sufficient numbers of businesses located at the centre of the triangle or G; that is, having a sufficient number of small, locally based, and independently run businesses is a predictor of economic resilience and viability. It is the "gold standard" by which to judge and predict whether one city is better positioned to withstand an economic shock than another.

Of course, it is also essential to understand the social and economic importance of large, national or international, non-independent, corporately managed firms. They have a role to play in the urban economic ecosystem, and we do not claim that their presence, in and of itself, is a bad thing for a city. Clearly not. However, as governments and the media tend to place most emphasis on these actors (how many headlines does the closing, opening, or subsidizing of a major corporate location garner), we feel that a tilting of the scales in another direction is in order.

Exhibit 1.1 is intended as a convenient tool for considering and comparing various configurations of small business types in a city. We recognize that more precise analyses require identifying and measuring specific components of being small, local, and independent. Table 1.1 therefore provides an initial deconstruction of the three dimensions, with some suggested metrics. Recent research (to be discussed in greater detail in Part II of this book) on urban growth has examined a number of these measures as important indicators of the performance of cities. For example, a study by Glaeser and Kerr found that a 10 per cent increase in average establishment size within a city region was associated with a 7 per cent decline in employment growth. That is, the larger the size of the firms in a city, the slower the overall employment growth. In the words of the authors, "an abundance of small, independent firms is one of the best predictors of urban [economic] growth." In one of the earliest studies of why San Francisco and Silicon Valley have been so successful, Anna Lee Saxenian observed that the

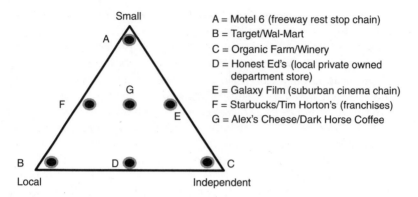

Exhibit 1.1: The geometry of small-scale entrepreneurship

region's abundance of small independent firms facilitated further entrepreneurship by developing a network of independent suppliers, venture financiers, and an entrepreneurial culture that lowered the costs of entry for new capitalists. Echoing this work is a study by Fleming and Goetz that asks, "Does local firm ownership matter?" The answer, based on an analysis of 2,953 counties in the United States that includes rural, suburban, and urban locations is decidedly "yes." The authors found that those counties with higher densities of small, locally owned businesses experienced greater per capita income growth, whereas the presence of large, non-local businesses had a negative effect on incomes.

Each of these studies, and other similar ones that will be discussed later in the book, indicate the value of being small, local, and independent. Previous studies, however, have not combined individual measures into broad metrics and an overall conceptual framework for comparing and evaluating why some cities and their small business sectors seem to thrive while others seem to dive. This lack of synthesis is perhaps why we still, as a society, seem fixated on the activities and behaviours of large, non-local, and non-independent firms. The question becomes, is this attention truly warranted?

Have We Been Backing the Wrong Horse?

As a culture of consumers seemingly willing to do anything to save a buck, we seem to have arrived at a time and place when whatever allegiance to and knowledge about our local shopkeepers we once

Table 1.1: Three metrics for measuring small-scale entrepreneurship

Dimension/Definition	Specific Measures/Attributes
Small "Small" means not being so large that a business does not fit into the typical main street areas where urban commerce (both retail and professional) was originally intended to occur.	– Number of employees – Revenues – Marketing strategy – Business space – Fit with urban fabric
Local "Local" means being present in a neighbourhood.	– Proximity to clients – Distance from closest neighbourhood residences – Catering to local needs
Independent "Independent" means that the effective ownership and control is not subsumed under a larger corporate entity.	– Ownership – Autonomy and discretion in operational matters – Ease of "exit" option if conditions get "tough"

possessed has been replaced by anonymous shopping experiences in an endless parade of big-box stores. Somehow, this most elemental of consuming activities, visiting your local main street shop, has come to require a remarkable amount of acumen, luck, and expert advice.

How did we get here? At what point did hipster magazines have to tell us where the best local burger or pizza could be found? Why is it that commercial districts built in our newest subdivisions have the same look and feel (regardless of context) and the same set of stores? Why do we need to "hunt down" authentic buying experiences? Why aren't they available on every city corner, as they once were? And why do we need urban "flâneurs" to determine where we should buy our new eyeglasses frames?

One answer is clear to anyone who has witnessed the process of late-twentieth-century urban planning and development. Many of our main street shopping districts have simply disappeared. With the advent of hyper-suburbanization, valuable (to the small-scale entrepreneur) and affordable commercial/storefront spaces have simply been erased from the landscape. In the words of Michael Doucet and Keith Jones, modern retail spaces with their huge lots and free car parks have not "just given the local competition a run for its money – they [have] eliminated it by design."[3] Finding and preserving spaces for small-scale entrepreneurs to grow is not only vital to the quality of our urban life; it is crucial in times of macro-economic turbulence.

History Repeats Itself, First as Tragedy and Later with More Tax Subsidies

For us the importance (and absurdity) of this situation became inescapable in fall 2008 when, during the onset of the financial crisis, governments around the world began bailing out the very culprits responsible for the collapse, which happened to be some of largest corporations in the world. With billions of dollars in taxpayer subsidies, established economic actors were once again saved with public dollars on the assumption (to some extent justified) that they had become "too large to fail."

This was not the first time such hefty sums had been funnelled towards established economic players in a moment of crisis. In 1981, not long after declaring in his inaugural presidential address that there were no problems of government that required fixing because the problem was with *government* itself, Ronald Reagan famously handed Lee Iacocca, then CEO of Chrysler Corp, a government lifeline to the tune of $1 billion (adjusted for inflation). Three decades on, Chrysler, which in the interim was sold twice to foreign car companies and bailed out yet again by four national governments (Germany, Italy, Canada, and the United States), nevertheless went on slashing jobs. From a peak of over 30,000 workers employed in Chrysler auto manufacturing plants in Ontario at the start of the 1990s, the company now employs just over 10,000.[4]

Why do governments continually back these money-losing players? Would the billions of dollars spent on maintaining existing oligopolies have been better spent on important local initiatives such as transit and clean energy in our towns and cities? What if these billions were simply given to consumers or small businesses to spend and invest as they wish? Whatever you may think of such a proposal, the point is we'll never know how such a strategy might have turned out because governments seem fixated, especially during times of crisis, on bailing out the same large and well-established economic players rather than in ushering in a new cohort of entrepreneurs.

Perhaps there is an unstated assumption on the part of policy makers that saving the giants of the economic food chain helps keep smaller players alive as well. We have all heard from time to time the news story claiming that every "Big 3" auto manufacturing job supports four others in the local economy.

But is this really true? Is every small business merely an appendage to a larger corporate giant? The image that this type of thinking connotes, if we are inclined to believe these statements, is of a local diner or coffee shop, where workers from the large plant up the road end up congregating between shifts. If the big plant closes or moves on, so do the local businesses that grew up around it.

Small-Scale Entrepreneurs and Cities: An Ecosystem View[5]

While the big-is-better world view may apply to the small one-industry town, it does not necessarily translate to a diversified economic region. In cities, where most of us now live or commute to, the economic role and influence of large economic actors is in some sense inverted from what we observe in towns and smaller urban environments. If the city is populous enough, it is large firms that are considerably more dependent on the health of small enterprises for their existence and survival than the reverse.[6] In the words of Christopher Kennedy, "the distribution of firm sizes in an urban economy has similarities with organisms in an ecosystem. As with a food web, there is a structural relationship between firms in an economy, with capital, goods and services generally *passed upwards* [my italics] through a structural hierarchy."[7] Note the direction of effects emphasized here; economic activity flows upwards (from small to large) not downwards (from large to small) in an urban economy.

As an example of this principle, take the city of Toronto. Most of its big employers are service providers (i.e., transport, finance, energy, and telecommunications) that are critically dependent on the city's small independent businesses for a large portion of their sales. Just think of how many UPS courier trucks, Bell mobility contracts, and TD credit lines would disappear overnight should the equivalent of a tsunami destroy the city's small businesses. Without the array of independent clients that cluster in and around cities like Toronto, most large-scale service providers would disappear. This is especially the case in Canada, where our major service providers (think media, banks, and telecoms) are regulated and effectively shielded from global competition.[8] In short, they rely almost wholly on locally sourced customers.

But if large businesses are not the key to small business survival, at least in urban centres, then what keeps our local independent shops alive?

The answer to that question is "us" – the urban-dwelling shopper – as evidenced by our continued loyalty to our local barbers, florists, and mechanics. Despite the omnipresence of big global brands, it turns out that we still buy lots of stuff from our independent local businesses, and for good reason. Whether you're going to a corner barbershop for a quick trim or getting your clothes dry-cleaned, there's a social aspect to the experience. People chat, linger, and relax in spaces where they feel "at home." Such is the success of corporate chains like Starbucks and Tim Horton's that they have adapted these ideas into requirements that none of their individual coffee shops become too big or exactly alike, lest customers lose their comfort and attachment to their local cafe and to the overall brand.[9]

Indeed, despite being a huge multinational employer, Starbucks has adopted a model of corporate growth that bears some resemblance to what we argue is the hallmark of small locally owned business. The company has mandated two things for its coffee-shop empire around the world: that the design and management of individual coffee shops (which they are loath to franchise and hence hardly ever do) must maintain essential features of the Starbucks brand but must also be attuned to the local neighbourhood wherever possible; and that the individual cafes themselves be no larger than 2,500 square feet. These essential features Howard Schultz claims to have "stolen" from his experience in Italy's small and largely independently owned and operated coffee bars and coffee houses, following a transformational trip to Europe in the late 1980s.

The lesson here is that much of what makes some of the largest firms perennially dominant, at least those operating in highly competitive sectors where barriers to entry are low and hence, one would assume, open to many upstarts, is that they have also preserved as many of the features of their small-scale origins as possible. These include the end-user focus and the maintenance of a loyal customer base.

What about Gentrification?

Sometimes the evolution of consumer spending habits and the ability of small local players to be the first to cater to these habits create tension in urban environments. People don't like to see wholesale changes to their neighbourhood overnight, yet this is what often happens when there is an active entrepreneurial culture at work in a city.

There is clearly some opposition to seeing lively urban commercial streets increasingly occupied by hospitality establishments and retail businesses targeted towards incoming gentrifying residents. While some urban main street shopping districts are indeed being converted from more diversified retailers to hospitality sector establishments, other streets are as lively and diversified as ever. As we shall see in Part I, some of this is owing to smart decisions by BIAs and their boards to pressure property owners into being more selective and patient about whom they choose as tenants, in order to preserve the fine balance characteristic of diversified commercial districts that serve a local resident population as well as out-of-neighbourhood customers.

Though it may seem obvious to view the urban main street conversions to bars, restaurants, and gentrified dining as a sign of a general weakness in small-scale enterprise, we believe the opposite is true – that this conversion is a sign of strength. The consumption patterns of a young-adult and mature market, as opposed to a middle-aged or very old society, are located precisely in hospitality sector offerings. To echo the argument made more than a decade ago by Professor David Foot in his book *Boom, Bust and Echo*, there are clear data showing that one of the greatest items of expenditure among those in the eighteen-to-thirty-four and the fifty-to-sixty-four age brackets is food prepared outside the home.

The trend is even greater if those same age cohorts live in big cities; demand in this case does indeed create its very own supply. At present the population in Canada is dominated by two demographic groups, boomers (born between 1947 and 1966) and their children (the "echo" generation born between 1980 and 1995). The transformation of some of our main streets into outdoor culinary districts speaks to the flexibility and vitality of small-scale main street shopping to meet the needs of these two large segments. The segment not spending money on hospitality services is instead bringing up kids and paying down a mortgage, and has little or no free time (there's living proof among two-thirds of the authors of this book) to enjoy a nice meal in the newest hipster restaurant. We're talking here about the thirty-five-to-forty-nine age group, the "bust" generation, born between 1967 and 1979, which occupies the relatively smallest share of the population/consuming public. And guess who's catering relatively less to them ... most businesses in Canada, regardless of their size!

Small Is (Still) Beautiful

The impression that small, local, independent business still matters is confirmed by a *Consumer Reports* survey of nearly 16,000 subscribers that rated independent local retailers as providing the "most satisfying" shopping experience of any retail group, including big name brands such as Wal-Mart and its warehouse club sibling, Sam's Club, which scored the lowest ratings in the survey.[10] When it came to service, independent retailers also earned the highest marks from shoppers, with most other well-known retailers posting the worst results. One of the reasons for the big retail chains' poor performance, according to *Consumer Reports*, was, in their words, the "level of interaction with sales help [or lack thereof]," with "78 percent of shoppers in large chains having little or no contact with any staff at all." The typical complaints centred on the difficulty of finding salespeople to help, especially "ones that seemed knowledgeable or even interested."

Tailored offerings and informed salesmanship are seemingly difficult for large enterprises to provide. At least when it comes to offering attentive personalized customer service, smaller businesses do appear to perform better.[11]

We caught a first-hand glimpse of this on a fact-finding trip taken early in the writing of this book to a friend's guitar shop in Guelph, Ontario (recently relocated to Waterloo, Ontario), about an hour west of Toronto. There, on a Saturday morning, in a small main street business location, people steadily made their way into the store. Although the store never became overly crowded, each person who came in purchased something before leaving. Some came from as far away as Hamilton and London, Ontario, to sit, play, and discuss their guitar purchases. There was lots of string picking, browsing, and trying out of guitars.

Mark Stutman, the owner-operator of Folkway Music, was never alone in his store even when the customers left the premises, presumably taking a break for lunch. He had knowledgeable staff on call to help with sales and guitar repairs. During these down times the employees and Mark bantered on about music while re-tuning some of the instruments sampled by customers. When the shoppers returned, though, I noticed something interesting that had escaped me earlier: how subtly but qualitatively different the shopping experience was when Mark rather than his staff dealt with customers. The attention to detail, the genuine customer follow-up, and, of course, the experience housed in Mark's hands – for Mark is also an expert *luthier* (repairer of guitars), with "folks" from as far away as Fort McMurray, Alberta, and London, England, sending him Martin guitars to repair and mail back – is simply not replicable by even the finest of employees).

This, by the way, was what Adam Smith also noted in his study of factories and shops that were run and managed by their owners. Smith, of course, was well aware of the advantages of size, which could drive down costs and allow an owner to sell more for less, enlarge his operation, and expand his market share. But he qualified his belief in "bigness" with what today may be referred to as an early statement of the principal-agent problem. According to Smith the attention of the manager when his own capital is employed is much more acute than that of the appointed trustee (i.e., the paid manager.)[12]

This is why we might expect to see a trade-off in service if all that shoppers ultimately care about is finding the lowest price possible. Like budget airlines whose service we may bemoan but still fly with, maybe this is where the net benefit of shopping at the large chain store resides.

Does the Lowest Price Ultimately Win Out?

Well, not exactly, at least according to respondents to the same *Consumer Reports* survey. Of those shoppers who asked for a lower price, 80 per cent of independent stores or small regional chains provided such a deal, whereas only 60 per cent of major retailers such as Sears or Best Buy offered customers any price break. I saw this as well when visiting Folkway. Though Mark and his staff impress on their customers that the guitars are priced to sell without fat-cat mark-ups, there is a sizeable consignment guitar component to the store. Mark takes the time to call individual owners to see if they wish to lower their price in response to a customer request for a price break. This kind of flexibility is impossible, almost by design, for a corporate retailer. They simply don't (or can't) haggle over prices.

To one degree or another, what these survey results and first-hand experience demonstrate is that the survival of small independent businesses is less surprising than the success and proliferation of large retail brand names. And this is where the connection between city and small business becomes slightly more obvious.

City, Suburb, and the Rise of the Power Centre

Most of us can distinguish town from countryside and urban from suburban forms. Yet, explaining how we tell the difference isn't always easy. One of the salient features of city living that is recognized by all is its reliance on local amenities. And it is here that the idiosyncratic nature of what an urban main street can offer local residents stands in sharp contrast to the predictable monoculture of contemporary retail development.[13] There is a chaos and a bustle that one notices along a traditional urban main street that is decidedly missing when the same elements are found plopped in an office park or power centre. Yet, that is where all the "new growth" in retail and commerce has occurred over the past two decades in North America. And not just in the suburbs but inside urban centres, too, through the conversion of industrial land to retail. In Toronto "approximately 60% of new format retail [box-store development] … is located on industrial zoned land."[14]

This "innovation in retail formats" has meant that shopping has moved from the main streets of the pre-war (1945) city to shopping malls in the early inner-burbs (built up between 1945 and the 1980s) to the box stores and power centres of present-day suburbia (beginning in the early 1990s to the present). Each transformation has meant larger and larger commercial facilities making it ever more difficult for independent operators to set up shop. As noted by Blais, "One power node in Toronto includes five separate power centres, three shopping malls, fifty-four box stores and almost 2.8 million square feet of retail space."[15] The same retail evolution has also made it very difficult to integrate shopping into walkable, interconnected neighbourhoods, given that the average power centre in Canada is set around a massive parking lot, has about 380,000 square feet of floor space, and occupies forty acres of land.[16] Clearly, under these conditions, a leisurely stroll to your local cafe is out of the question.

At least the covered shopping mall of the early postwar period, now located in the inner suburbs of most North American cities, allowed for small business entry and was located within walking (or short driving) distance of existing residential developments. Since the early 1990s, however, box stores have emerged to dominate the physical landscape and social habits of modern suburban residents. By extension, this has transformed life for a majority of citizens and small-scale entrepreneurs around North America. Without debating the merits of such a move or how it came to be, it does explain how, despite poorer customer relations, well-known brands can nevertheless dominate the retail landscape and alter the relationship we as consumers and residents have with our local environment. Though there are clear signs that this retail model has reached its peak (see exhibit 1.2), the suburban power centre of the late 1990s and 2000s has been built (by design) in a way that has kept smaller (and often newer, independent) local players out of the retail game.[17]

By way of contrast, the traditional early-twentieth-century form of urban living – based on a physical infrastructure built before the proliferation of individual car travel and extensive highway networks – is ideally suited to local independent ownership. Likewise, the small locally owned businesses situated along these main streets have come to define most of the well-known areas of our large cities. These are areas characterized by corner stores, local movie parlours, and main streets with shops at ground level and offices or residences above. Without them, city neighbourhoods would be just as indistinguishable as the countless power centres encountered when travelling around North America's contemporary suburbs. Main street urban forms provide history, meaning, and "emotions associated [with an] environment," whereas suburban-style power centres are spaces with an "absence of distinct meaning, a Non-place," in the words of Ute Lehrer.[18]

Exhibit 1.2 shows a recently shuttered big-box electronics store in a major power centre in the Greater Toronto Area. The company that owns the retailer is Best Buy, and it recently announced that it would be closing fifteen major stores and laying off a further 950 employees in 2014 on top of the 1,600 that it let go earlier in 2013. However, one of the company's turnaround strategies is to replace these mega-stores with smaller Radio Shack-style stores that are closer to consumers and where online orders can be conveniently picked up.

If one believes Jeff Rubin, author of *Why Your World Is about to Get a Whole Lot Smaller: Oil and the End of Globalization*, then this is not an isolated cyclical response to a bad economy but a sign of the future of retail. In a world where people are older, congestion more pronounced, cities becoming denser, and where time is scarce, the car is no longer king. As a result, windswept power centres will become ripe for reconversion. The future may even be here, given that many retailers, from Best Buy to the major banks, have placed a major bet on opening up scaled-down branches in high-density, mixed-use neighbourhoods to accommodate urban dwellers. The Bank of Montreal, for example, has announced that it will open up to fifteen "studio branches" across Canada and in the U.S. Midwest, where the company operates as BMO Harris Bank. In 2012, the firm opened six new micro-branches in Quebec, and it is investing an additional $15 million to open eight more "new and updated branches – all in recognition of changes in traffic patterns and customer preferences," a bank representative was quoted as saying.[19]

As this book goes to press there is word that the United States, through its vast shale oil reserves, will soon become a self-sufficient oil producer and thereby postpone peak oil predictions for several decades. Fine, but this only highlights an associated trend – increased frustration related to greater car use and congestion – which may well encourage staying close to home and using local amenities. More to the point, the demographic shift touched upon earlier also serves to encourage closer urban living. As noted by Andres Duany and colleagues,[20] people outlive their ability to drive by many years – decades, in some cases. As we age we also lose our desire and ability to drive long distances. The baby boom generation is now firmly ensconced in its late-stage working life and early retirement phase, which will likely increase the demand for closer, amenable urban options that are "walkable."

Where We Shop Defines How Well We Live

The association between an urban neighbourhood's sense of place and its locally owned businesses is amplified in North American cities like Vancouver, Toronto, and Halifax, since, rather than seeking recreation in central parks or hanging out in public squares, which North American cities decidedly lack as compared to their European counterparts, we spend the bulk of our time outside the home either working or shopping. Whether we do so along pedestrian-oriented streets that "feature small-format retail and services" or drive to "large-scale … single-use … parcels of land"[21] has a significant effect on our health, both physical and mental, and, as it turns out, on our pocketbooks as well.

A recent Pennsylvania State University study found that areas with small locally owned businesses of fewer than 100 employees have greater levels of per capita income and income growth than areas with larger non-locally owned firms.[22] In terms of health, an Ontario College of Physicians report stresses the dangers of hyper-suburban living based largely on our reliance on the car. Suburbanites are significantly less likely to walk for at least thirty minutes a day, and are correspondingly more at risk for heart disease and stroke.[23] And in a 2007 *Rand Health* research study, the links between where we shop and how we live were even more starkly identified. According to the authors, "Having four or more different types of businesses in a neighborhood increased the number of walking trips among residents." The authors speculate that this is probably true because of added convenience: "Residents are able to accomplish multiple routine errands in a single walking trip and thus may drive less."[24] Researchers also found that a

Exhibit 1.2: The future may not be looking as bright for big-box retail as we once thought. A recently shuttered Future Shop box store in a major Toronto-area power centre. *Photo by Todd Harris © 2014.*

greater number of four-way intersections in a given area – a feature of pre-Second World War urban design that was eschewed in favour of longer distances between intersections after 1950 – was associated with more walking.[25]

David Owen, in his 2009 book *Green Metropolis*, has described this as "built-in" sustainability. Pointing out that Manhattan consumes one-third the energy of a similar-sized suburban city or rural America, Owen boils it down to two essential features: people live/work within a smaller property footprint and they don't drive.[26] They walk, bike, hail cabs, or take public transit because it's the preferred way to get around town. This type of urban form has the largely unintended consequence of making smaller, locally established firms better able to cater to local needs. And the feedback loop is completed because residents/workers are less inclined to venture too far afield to have their needs for work and consumption met.

   Much of what we describe above seems perfectly suited to the urban core of a major North American city. But what of the suburbs, especially those built immediately after the Second World War with strip-mall-laden storefronts? It is arguably up for debate whether strip malls constitute "urbane main street development," but we want to encourage readers to take a second look at these urban forms. Given where they were built (the inner suburbs of large Canadian cities) and when (between the 1950s up to the early 1980s), they actually were perfectly suited to their environment, incorporating features – such as storefront angle parking, ramps instead of stairs, and low-rise architecture – that modern designers would now see as following principles of "universal design" (i.e., providing easy access to people with disabilities). We think what has given this retail development model a slightly bad rap has been the hyper-suburbanized form of development that has occurred from the late 1980s to the present. Cities like Mississauga or Brampton, located northwest of Toronto – whose growth took place much later than that of, say, Dartmouth in Halifax – have been victimized by the hyper-segmentation-of-use-model described by Christopher Hume in one of his *Toronto Star* columns as "location in-efficient living."[27] This has been the default urban growth model for the past quarter century, but this was not the rule in the modern suburbs of the 1950s.

   To be sure, transport was assumed to occur in a car, and city design was adjusted accordingly, with wider and more lanes for car traffic, but the rule was to drive a short distance through streets to your local shopping mall or recreational facility. Contrast this with the assumption of postmodern development, where a home is located in a segmented pod with other homes just the same and where residents are supposed to drive a non-trivial distance for even the most basic of amenities to a power centre kilometres away from home. On the way, you cross streets with only backyard fences as visual signposts of where you may be, since no strip mall or plaza is allowed to interfere with the separation-of-use requirement that keeps every human activity – from work, to play, to commerce – in its segmented and geographically distinct space.

The Premise(s) of This Book

Our hunch in writing *Small Business and the City*, fuelled as it is with insights about the organic and symbiotic nature of urban living and small business life, was that the best way to answer questions about the viability of small business and the authenticity of our feelings of loss when a local bookshop or record store closes was to go back to the very beginning, to the source of what sustains our thoughts and the realities of city life. We wanted to look at the supplying and demanding of goods and services at their most fundamental – that is, as a transaction between the owner of a business (who also happens to operate it with the help of a few employees) and the purchaser, who deals directly (though not always in person) with said owner-operator. What we try to do in this book is approach the question of small business as a naturalist might, through the wider lenses of anthropology, economics, geography, and sociology, as well as the narrower, more intimate lens of personal experience and observation.

Our starting premises are that, like every actor in a city, small, locally owned and operated businesses play an important part in an urban economic food chain or web and that their place in that web determines to a considerable extent what kind of city we live in. The fact that small businesses can at the same time be the most locally oriented and globally connected of institutions – one thinks back to the scene in *Godfather, Part II*, when a young Vito Corleone is seen hoisting his Italian Olive Oil import-export sign above a storefront in New York's Little Italy – has done much to shape the nature of urban life, both socially and materially, in what Doug Saunders has aptly called "arrival cities" like Toronto and Vancouver.[28]

Staying Put Instils a Sense of Local Culture, Loyalty, and Risk Taking

The prodigious power of our collective minds to foster and create "local culture" and our curious desire as residents of a city to simultaneously experience novelty and keep important connections to the past owe much to the capacity of small businesses to stay fixed in one location, even as the urban form shifts and changes around them. Some authors have argued that the very resilience of small business, in an era of highly organized corporate marketing machines, is testament to two important forces:

1. The power of regional "loyalty" in the face of economic incentives that may otherwise push consumers in the direction of the "cheaper deal"; and
2. The value of risk-taking on the part of the entrepreneur in the face of truly unknown future prospects – what economists refer to as "Knightian risk or uncertainty" (named after the economist Frank

Knight who distinguished between "risk" and "uncertainty").[29] Uncertainty differs from "calculable risk," which is made up of probabilities that are known ahead of time to a decision maker. Uncertainty is what Donald Rumsfeld famously referred to as the "unknown unknowns."[30]

It turns out customers, by default, are loyal and seem to prefer it that way, and that small-scale entrepreneurs often take the biggest risks primarily because they are not part of "footloose capital," able to shift operations whenever the going gets rough. Small-scale entrepreneurs typically are guided only by their business acumen and intuition rather than by corporate marketing models that produce calculable decision trees. They are true "Knightian" risk takers.

These last points are important since cities are made up not only of what residents are known to demand and want from their private and public actors but also of what is provided to them for the first time, seemingly "out of nowhere," by savvy local entrepreneurs or, as once was the case in Ontario, by innovative public actors as well. For example, who was demanding an Ontario Science Centre or an Imax theatre when they were first financed with public funds in the late 1960s and early 1970s? Henry Ford, at the time of his entrepreneurial leap into car production, rightly stated that if he had been solely guided by "what the market wanted" he would have produced a faster horse and buggy instead of the Model T.

The Need for Collective Provision ... or Why Urban Cities Differ from Towns and Suburbs

Cities are different from suburban fringes and small towns because – though all of them have to guarantee the basics of what Aristotle called the "good life," including clean water, a food supply, efficient waste-removal procedures, and ways to reconstruct and extend themselves – the basic questions of human organization assume a greater importance and new complexity in cities. This is especially true of big cities, as Christopher Kennedy has observed in his study of the world's great urban centres, which, unlike smaller or less dense agglomerations of people, require a steadily greater sphere of collective action. Note that this does not necessarily mean greater public action or centralized power to maintain urban order. Collective action can and often does consist in giving wider powers to private agents. But what "is undeniable and irreversible," as noted by the eminent surveyor of the rise of cities Sir Peter Hall, "is the steady growth of collective provision" of basic goods and services in large urban environments.[31]

Interestingly, a verification of this principle has been observed in successful cities around the world, starting in the late 1960s in, of all places, Toronto, where small independent retailers were the first to recognize that by competing among themselves they would collectively fail. They were the first to impose a mandatory business "levy" that would be collected by local governments and thereby prevent free-riding of the kind that always ended up sinking the voluntary marketing associations of old. Independent businesses would use their collective revenues for much needed local investments, area-wide marketing, and neighbourhood beautification projects.

This unique innovation of the last forty years, created by the smallest economic actors operating inside our largest cities, should be a topic worth examining, particularly since the real world of industrialists and politicians is now obsessed with the topic of creativity and innovation. These are, the experts incessantly tell us, the keys to economic survival. In a globalized economy, every day made more frenetic by new technologies, the nation or city that fails to innovate is destined to join the ranks of the economic has-beens, its old industries condemned to hopeless competition with the new plants and cheap labour of China and the developing world. And, as we now know, industry need not even mean industry anymore; as emerging economies take over manufacturing and do it more cheaply, it is essential for the developed nations of the West to shift out of mass manufacturing and goods processing into niche production, the service sector, and the processing and curating of information.

It is perhaps not so surprising, then, that many cities facing severe economic decline in the wake of the financial crisis – cities like Chicago, Detroit, and Buffalo – have placed a renewed emphasis on small-scale entrepreneurship – a term no longer anomalous or offensive – in the hope that it may provide the basis for economic regeneration, filling the gap left by vanished factories and warehouses and creating a new urban image that would make them more attractive to larger pools of mobile capital and increasingly mobile human talent.

So it matters that we try to understand how creativity at the local level comes about. It is much more than an academic question. Letting graduate students loose in organizations will not answer it, but a detailed look at what happens locally might do so.

Small Business in the Bigger Scheme of Things

Our ultimate premise is that the way we consume and purchase things represents our most profound engagement with the urban world. Daily, our purchasing decisions turn our habits into culture, transforming the anonymous world of city life into our own personal and shared existence. Locally owned and operated businesses have done more to (re)shape and (re)fashion the cities we know and love than anything else done at the local level by private action. Both the streetscape and the composition of our neighbourhood identity are determined by what lies open for business on our main street. We know that neighbourhoods left abandoned by local entrepreneurs end up having a higher incidence of crime, unemployment, and general social dislocation. The decline is out of proportion to the directly observed employment losses from the closing of a small business but is commensurate with declines in social capital that come with losing important "third spaces," which act as hubs of knowledge dissemination and informal social assistance. These windfalls are all generated by living in areas with a vibrant local culture that is more often than not provided by the small-scale entrepreneur.

Our shopping habits also constitute a relationship with dozens of other actors in our cities – the mail carriers, the local politicians, and all classes of city workers – with which local businesses and residents have co-evolved to the point where all fates are deeply intertwined. For example, a city with taxes set so low that it cannot meet the minimum requirements for street cleanliness and safety will soon lose its shoppers and entrepreneurs; likewise, a city that places too much emphasis on stability and safety will stamp out the creativity and "bohemianism" required to innovate and prosper.[32] Buying goods and services from locally owned and operated businesses puts us in touch with all that we share with our fellow city dwellers, and all that sets us apart from country living. It defines, we argue, that which is uniquely our own urban existence.

What is perhaps most sad and troubling about the evolution of commerce is how thoroughly power-centre shopping obscures all these relationships and connections of city life. To replace walking a few hundred metres to buy some basic groceries at the corner shop with driving several kilometres in order to enter your "local convenience store" is to leave the world of city living in a journey of social forgetting that is not only costly in terms of personal fulfilment and individual health but also bad for the health of our planet. Forgetting, or not knowing in the first place, what is lost when all our actions, including shopping, become depersonalized is a key consequence of an atomized model of consumption. If we could see what lies on the other side of the increasingly high walls of our mega-store parking lots, we would surely change the way we shop and would redesign our yet-to-be-built suburbs to suit a more organic and spontaneous form of living.

Still, as documented in our book, even in the most suburbanized environments small businesses stubbornly hang on, sometimes quite successfully, as in the somewhat eerily preserved vestiges of pre-sprawl main streets in current suburbs (e.g., Unionville in Markham and Streetsville in Mississauga), or more often and against even greater odds at the edge of larger power-centre developments.

Plan of the Book

This book is the outcome of years of interviewing, observing, reading, and thinking about the power of small-scale entrepreneurship to transform local neighbourhoods and, by extension, the cities they inhabit. In writing it, we have borrowed from our own earlier research where appropriate. We have used a mixture of empirical and theoretical analysis as well as case analysis, as exemplified in Part I, which presents three lengthy examinations (or case studies) of particular Canadian cities, each chosen to illustrate a particular theme (or a unique set of themes) that contributes to our understanding of what makes small businesses survive and thrive in large cities, and in turn, what cities can do (or stop doing) to foster and maintain the advantages flowing from independent local ownership.

What, we ask, has allowed this unique bastion of upstart capitalism to endure even as retail trends and urban forms have conspired against it?

This question is partly addressed in Part II of the book through our examination of a movement in which small businesses have joined together in order to promote their local neighbourhoods. Canada is the birthplace of the so-called Business Improvement Area (BIA), whereby small-scale entrepreneurs – by pooling resources with other like-minded businesses – have not only survived but emerged as a vital source of urban rejuvenation, acting as magnets for human talent and fostering local innovation in cities around the globe. These are important points to (re)state and document with first-hand examples drawn from our nation's most successful neighbourhoods and cities.

Part II therefore brings both the ground-level observations made in Part I and the findings from academic research into a better balanced perspective. The three chapters that make up Part II start with policies and ideas relevant for the growing movement of businesses that have united and formed associations designed to maintain the integrity of their streetscapes and to increasingly pressure local and provincial governments to promote policies that support local investment and job creation. The section then showcases the problems that arise with economic development when it focuses too much on big business (either as a cause of economic malaise or the source of economic vitality) and ignores the vitality of small locally owned businesses. The section ends with a discussion of what a "main street agenda" might look like if public policy were to take account of the ideas and stories contained in this volume.

The Individual Chapters

Such is the broad picture of the book's structure. As for the individual chapters, Part I, chapter 2, describes how the notion of collective action was applied by small businesses to create one of the past century's most impressive (but little known) innovations – the modern business improvement area (BIA). We also discuss the role that these relatively new agglomerations of (mostly) small, independent, and locally owned enterprises play in bringing about positive change that works to counteract the inertia accumulated in large established enterprises or public bureaucracies. An interesting point is the part the members of BIAs play in investing locally and also employing persons from the surrounding neighbourhood(s) in which they are located, helping both to make the city greener and more liveable and (crucially) to replace jobs lost in declining industries.

In chapter 3, Matt Semansky charts the voices of Haligonian businesses and city officials. The Halifax duality of being simultaneously too big and too small has informed the evolution of a city that simultaneously punches above and below its weight. The chapter captures the sense of pride among Haligonians that stems both from the city's top-dog status within the Atlantic provinces and from the fact that it does things differently from the Torontos or Vancouvers of the world. This mindset, Semansky argues, extends to the business world, where Haligonians excel at putting the fabricated hybrid-word "co-opetition" into practice. To cite just one example, local filmmakers have put the area on the cinematic map (and not only as a location stand-in) by working as a close-knit community and by lending moral and professional support to one another's projects.

In chapter 4, Andre Isakov approaches the challenges that local officials and businesses in the Vancouver city region must face in order to remain viable and competitive in attracting new visitors and customers with a "place-making" orientation. The chapter deals with the inquiries of urban geographers and sociologists into what makes urban localities prosper. Isakov's point of departure is the concept that, just as corporations distil what "they are about" by effectively "branding" themselves, so must localities, working in concert with the many small businesses that populate local neighbourhoods, begin to work together to highlight why one should shop, work, visit, and invest in a particular urban environment. In particular, Isakov notes that the primitive notion of a city location defined by what the local "tourist board" deems is its unique selling point, without effective consultation and buy-in from the local enterprises, leaves much of the payoff from such public marketing investments unrealized. However, the wide application of bottom-up place-making activity requires an imaginative rebalancing of the financial windfalls that occur as a result of local efforts to promote economic activity. Currently, many of these successful local efforts at place-making are hampered by a public finance model that favours provincial and federal levels of government at the expense of the small businesses and city governments that engineer these policies.

Chapter 5, which concludes Part I, relates some of the insights from the introduction to what small businesses are currently doing and at the same time "saying" about the city that once was said to operate like "New York run by the Swiss." Certainly no one living inside the civic boundaries of Toronto would say that about the city today, and yet it remains one of the most highly ranked (fourth out of 174 cities in 2011) places to live and conduct business by no less a "hard-nosed" authority than the Economist Intelligence Unit. The discrepancy between what "officialdom" offers up as the best of the city and what is produced at the local level by citizens and small-scale entrepreneurs is the puzzle that lies at the heart of the chapter.

Whereas Part I focused on the particular stories and specific geographic characteristics of our three city case studies, Part II takes a more policy-focused and macro perspective, attempting to place those field-level observations in a wider context. The work in Part II of the book therefore builds on the kinds of concepts highlighted above.

Chapter 6 illustrates the broad themes that emerge from our analysis of business improvement areas in three cities and also suggests concrete suggestions for all actors (e.g., business leaders, government officials, residents' associations) concerned with preserving and enhancing the functioning of BIAs. The chapter distils and analyses the results of first-hand knowledge, observation, and study, including surveys of business owners and insights from founders of some of the earliest BIAs. We start with a typology of BIAs and demonstrate how urban design is a key factor in determining the right mix of policies and objectives for small businesses with (or aiming to form) BIAs.

In chapter 7 we show how undue emphasis (both positive and negative) in economic development circles on the role of corporations has implicitly understated the role of smaller enterprises and the potential brought forth by the BIA movement. Large, publicly owned corporations in some major industries are indeed the most conspicuous type of economic organization, which is why some proponents of Western-style capitalism attribute economic growth and our collective wealth to these corporations. Conversely, critics of modern-day capitalism interpret their emergence as a reason for our current economic malaise. But the publicly held company rose to prominence too recently (from a historical perspective) to be the source of our economic well-being. Neither was it a fundamental cause of the decline in our economic fortunes, since the large corporation was a prominent part of the postwar economic system that for nearly forty years produced unparalleled economic growth and prosperity. Both critics and proponents appear to be missing something.

What should be noted instead in this debate is that corporate enterprises are the predominant users of capital and technology, but smaller, locally owned enterprises are the predominant employers of labour – a point often forgotten by countries mired in public deficits and high unemployment. And although larger organizations quite rightly have more money to spend on research and development, much innovation, even in modern economies, has actually come about through new ideas tested by enterprises organized on a small experimental scale, with little commitment to the "corporate status quo."

Take, for example, the experience of U.S. military and State Department efforts to produce workable drone technology in the late 1970s. In 1977, the Pentagon had almost given up on robotic planes. At the time, its most promising technology required thirty people to launch it, flew for just minutes at a time, and crashed at an alarmingly high rate.

Enter Mr Karem, an Israeli immigrant, who founded a company, Leading Systems, in the garage of his Los Angeles home and began work on a drone that would ultimately transform the way modern countries wage war. It was built in an intentionally low-tech manner, using plywood, home-made fibreglass, and a two-stroke engine of the kind normally found in go-carts. "I wanted to prove that performance is largely a result of inspired design and highly optimised and integrated subsystems, not the application of the most advanced technology," he said in a 2102 interview in the *Economist*.[33]

Mr Karem's drone, code-named Albatross, was developed by a handful of engineers, and could be operated by a team of just three. "Doing things with the absolute smallest team increases the chance that you're not going to screw up," said Mr Karem. "Nothing replaces highly talented people – white-hot passionate thinkers in love with doing challenging things." After a flight test during which the drone remained aloft for fifty-six hours, the research arm of America's armed forces funded Mr Karem to scale it up into a more capable drone called Amber. It, in turn, evolved into the modern Predator, which has adorned the cover of a 2013 issue of *Time* magazine.

Large, slightly disorganized urban environments are, it turns out, great places for small, local entrepreneurs like Mr Karem to set up shop, as they provide relatively quick and easy access to networks of talented employees and users. For this reason, both innovation and employment growth in a country are intimately linked to the health of its cities and its small business sector. Indeed we need look no further than Mr Karem's country of birth, Israel, to see the effect of start-ups in action. In their best-selling book *Start-Up Nation: The Story of Israel's Economic Miracle*, authors Dan Senor and Saul Singer document the amazing fact that Israel has more companies on the tech-oriented NASDAQ stock exchange than any country outside the United States – more than all of Europe and India combined. Senor and Singer attribute this to Israel's policies on immigration, research and development (R&D), and military service. But one factor glaringly missing is the nature of Israel; from a socio-geographic standpoint, Israel is but one long chain of urban encampments. It's a forty-five minute drive between the two largest cities of Jerusalem and Tel Aviv and less than a two-hour drive from Tel Aviv to Israel's third-largest city, Haifa. In between, a string of smaller communities dot the landscape. The urban form is ever present in Israel. And one could argue that Israel may indeed be a start-up capital, but it also relies on one of the largest institutions, the military.

This is an important qualifier on the start-up thesis because the point that is stressed in chapter 7 is that successful economic systems (whether local, regional, or national) employ enterprises of all forms (corporate and independent) and sizes (large and small). The key to their collective existence and success is the nature of the economic mission for which the enterprises are organized. Many types and sizes of enterprise are therefore useful under the right circumstances; but what is emphasized in chapter 7 is the function of cities in maintaining a diversity of economic organizations in local economic systems. This diversity is critical, since adjusting to the inevitable external changes that rock the economic environment (everything from demography to technology to globalization) is only possible when there are organizations capable of tailoring what they do to different kinds of economic activity, especially to innovation. This is why public policy at all levels (local, regional, and national) is so important, since everything from zoning laws and regulations to public infrastructure can either help foster a diversity of economic actors or can lead to a "monoculture" of corporate organizations that may fit a particular time and place (i.e., the big-box store in early twenty-first-century suburbia) but be inappropriate when circumstances (inevitably) change.

In chapter 8, we stress the importance of focusing public policy and private action on what we term "the main street agenda." Many commentators, including prominent economists, journalists, and advocates of "free markets," have stressed the importance of laissez-faire policies, to the point of arguing that all the "giants" of the economy are there because of "market forces." Such arguments greatly understate the role played by large players in thwarting competition (at least in the short-run) and by public policy in shielding large companies from competition by indirect and direct subsidization.

This emphasis of economic development policy on the "largest economic actors" downplays the importance of smaller enterprises in a modern and decidedly urbanized economy. The mistake is common both among those who focus almost exclusively on corporations as the "life-blood" of national economies and those who see the big corporation as a pariah. The effects of this mistake have been tragic, to say the least, focusing public attention and scarce public funds (through tax subsidies, credits, and most recently outright cash) on achieving growth by maintaining the largest and most mature enterprises, rather than by fostering what business historians point to as the crucial source of growth – experimentation with a wide variety of, initially at least, small enterprises.

The tendency of public policy to favour established economic players at the expense of the small and new is further discredited by the disproportionately high percentage of new jobs that are created by small, locally owned firms. Whether one interprets this finding as indicating that "smallness" per se is favourable to the growth of employment or that small start-ups often occur in fast-growing industries, it argues strongly against development strategies and urban designs that ignore, or even discourage, the formation of small, independent, local businesses. It argues equally for the framing of spending on urban amenities and city infrastructure as an investment in innovation and local job creation, both of which are fostered when cities and small businesses work and grow together.

Chapter 9, the last in Part II, gathers major recommendations and ideas that have emerged in the writing of the book and presents them in a single summary chapter with a focus on moving from what small-scale entrepreneurship is to what it can and should be. Some of the recommendations are not new and, in many cases, simply reiterate what we've heard from the streets of our major cities. As far as possible, however, we have attempted to identify ways in which the ideas can be implemented by governments, businesses, and even individual citizens.

The book's conclusion (chapter 10) and the afterword mix recollections of one of the authors who has experience in a family-run small business with some general truths about why small, locally based, and independently owned businesses have survived for so long and are still hanging on in the twenty-first century.

What We Hope to Learn

"Shopping is an economic decision" one learns in first-year economics and management courses. But it is also a social and political act with increasing ecological implications. How and where we buy (more than what we buy) determine to a great extent the impact we have on our local environment and what is to become of our city life. To try and shop locally with a fuller consciousness of the implications of doing so might seem like a burden, but in practice few things in life can afford a better return on investment.

By comparison, the supposed pleasures of buying wherever the lowest price takes you (more than likely in a windswept retail development miles from your home) are fleeting. Many people today seem perfectly content to shop in the middle of an industrial car park; it is our hope that this book will open their eyes to the benefits of redirecting part of that consumption to, at the very least, retail chains that are locally owned and operated. In the end, *Small Business and the City* is a book about the pleasures and dynamism of traditional city life based on the interaction of locally rooted businesses and their neighbourhood, the kinds of pleasures that are only deepened with local knowledge and experience.

PART I

The View from Main Street

2 The BIA Movement: Setting the Stage for Main Street Revitalization

The Birth of a Movement

On 25 February 1966, despite a typically cold Canadian afternoon, Torontonians were in a celebratory mood. The city's public transit authority had just extended the subway system eastward to Woodbine Avenue and westward to Keele Street. Only two years earlier almost to the day, on 26 February 1964, Canada's first enclosed shopping mall (Yorkdale) had opened its doors, to considerable fanfare.

These two events – a subway line extension and the opening of Canada's first climate-controlled shopping mall – inadvertently set in motion forces that would eventually create the world's first Business Improvement Area (BIA).

Prior to these modernizations most Torontonians, like most Canadians, did their shopping on main streets close to home and saved up their major purchases for visits to downtown Canadian-owned department stores such as Eaton's and Simpsons (now both sadly defunct). Yorkdale, though, was designed for both purposes, since, at the time, it was the largest shopping centre in the world and sat on the edge of the urbanized city with only farmland surrounding it. With postwar prosperity, car ownership had spread to most Torontonians, and Yorkdale, with its abundance of cheap land, had the advantage of a large free parking lot. Shoppers could now drive once a week to their new mall and stock up on all of life's material necessities, both major and minor.[1] Soon even the subway would reach Yorkdale.

Almost everyone seemed happy with this state of affairs – the exception being a small group of concerned business owners operating south of Yorkdale and above the newly built subway stations. Alex Ling, a recent arrival to Toronto, and Neil McLellan, a long-time jewellery store owner, were both part of a voluntary association of independent shops located in what has come to be known as "the birthplace" of the modern BIA movement, Bloor West Village.

Both the subway and the covered mall, it turned out, had an immediate effect on the small-scale entrepreneurs of this west-end Toronto neighbourhood. In Mr Ling's case, something akin to Ross Perot's famous "sucking sound" of jobs flowing southward to Mexico started to occur, only in Bloor West Village it was the sound of customers flowing northward to Yorkdale and of residents bypassing Ling's street in the fast-moving subway underneath.[2] Although subway cars were moving more people than the above-ground trolleys they replaced, and Yorkdale mall was attracting more customers from the nearby expanding inner suburb of Etobicoke, neither of these developments was helping those like Neil and Alex who operated businesses above ground on Bloor Street.

These two milestones in Toronto's history of civic achievement – the subway and the enclosed mall – provoked Alex and Neil to take action. Their story defines the rise of a genuinely new movement, one aimed at transforming traditional urban main street districts into revived neighbourhoods where people could once again live, work, shop, or simply relax. Considering that Toronto is the birthplace of the modern BIA concept, relatively little public attention has been paid to this uniquely Canadian invention and the history behind it. Yet despite the lack of public attention, communities across North America and around the globe have quietly adopted Canada's BIA practices (see box 2.1). Varying from landscape improvements, concerts and festivals, colourful banners, and in some cases major economic development initiatives, BIAs, at their most fruitful, have been able to transform neglected neighbourhoods into revived city areas where both local and regional needs are met.

So how exactly did this come about?

Early Examples of Private Investments in the Public Realm

The idea of private funding in the sphere of urban renewal clearly predates Bloor West Village. One of the earliest North American examples originated in San Francisco when, in an effort to rebuild and revitalize after the great earthquake of 1906, which devastated the city, business – as opposed to government – was the first to rally support for

Box 2.1: A Short Definition of the Business Improvement Area

The BIA: A Definition

The definition of the Business Improvement Area varies depending on the source and jurisdiction, but the core concept pertains to a strategy for mobilizing private funding in order to improve the environment of outdoor commercial and retail centres of activity. The tax is typically collected by a local authority but is handed over to a board run by the members of the business district, which spends the money on urban renewal projects. By the start of 2012, there were more than 1,700 Business Improvement Districts (BIDs) or Zones created in the United States and Canada alone. Toronto itself now has a total of 73 BIAs across the city, representing more than 30,500 businesses – the largest number of BIAs in a single city in North America. They generate over $24.5 million annually in funding towards street and sidewalk beautification, marketing and promotional campaigns, street festivals, clean street campaigns, and crime-prevention strategies. BIAs also act as a unified voice to address issues on behalf of their membership and neighbourhoods. The success of Toronto's BIA program can be seen in the growth in the number of BIAs in the last ten years – increasing from 42 in 2001 to 73 as of 2012. And there are new commercial areas that are expressing interest in implementing the program in their neighbourhood.

---

reconstruction. Some government officials were actually advocating relocating the city – moving it away from such a volatile and earthquake-prone fault line. Local business leaders instead established one of the first downtown associations in the world, the Downtown Association of San Francisco, to make the dream of rebuilding San Francisco a reality.[3]

Another crisis some two decades later, this one socio-economic, precipitated further development in the area of privately financed public-realm investments. In the wake of the Great Depression, business owners throughout the United States formed voluntary membership organizations in cities such as Detroit (the Business Property Owners' Association) and Chicago (the Downtown Council of Chicago) to foster commerce in the downtown core and to stem what was then known as "decentralization" – the migration of firms, retail establishments, and customers from downtown to what were then less expensive outlying suburban municipalities. Unlike the postwar suburb, a product of the spread of freeways and car ownership, these pre-war suburban centres grew as a result of expanding public street-car systems.[4]

Indeed, it is somewhat ironic that Bloor West Village, considered to-day a "prototypical central" urban neighbourhood was, at the time of its creation in the 1920s, a "prototypical Toronto suburb," which, a half-century prior to the creation of Yorkdale, was itself part of the "prob-lem" of decentralization. What differentiates Bloor West Village and the pre-Second World War suburb from its modern variants, of course, is that its street plan was still very much built in the traditional grid pat-tern found in the core of older North American cities.[5] Because cars were not yet assumed to be the primary mode of transport, pre-war planned communities were built in a compact design with a main street diverse enough to offer residents most local amenities. That is, in 1930s-style suburbs, life's necessities were still only a brisk walk or a short trolley ride away.

The Flagship Department Store: The Local Retailer's Response to the Great Depression

Much like their contemporary BIA counterparts, the members of the early-twentieth-century voluntary associations focused their attention on increasing retail sales by attracting customers and investors to their main streets using promotional mechanisms like parades, tours, and prominent window displays. These locally run organizations also func-tioned as advocates for the central business district, communicating the need for projects ranging from the construction of public squares and new parking facilities to the demolition of blighted areas.[6]

One innovation that was spurred by these efforts was the creation of the all-in-one centrally located department store. In most cities around North America, flagship department stores were either expanded or built up from scratch in this era.[7] They were the 1930s equivalent of the modern retail innovation, similar in function (but not in form) to the box-store innovations of the 1990s. The department store was de-signed to spur spending and reinvent the shopping experience. Sup-ported by the growth of car ownership in towns surrounding major city centres, the department store was designed to bring people into the city for an entire day, to eat, drink, and shop. Anyone who has watched the film A Christmas Story – the 1983 classic comedy based on the short stories of author and raconteur Jean Shepherd, who grew up in late-1930s America – can envisage the scene: countless families with their kids perched on shoulders watching the Christmas parade and Yuletide window displays of what, in real life, is the (now defunct)

Higbee & Hower Dry Goods store of Cleveland, Ohio.[8] Prior to the department store, ordering via catalogue was the most common way of purchasing non-perishable items. In Canada, anyone who has read or seen the animated cartoon of "The Hockey Sweater" by Roch Carrier knows that the story hinges on a mail-order mix-up in which a Montreal Canadiens'-obsessed young fan receives a Toronto Maple Leafs jersey instead.

The Rise (and Fall) of the Voluntary Business Association

American business leaders continued with voluntary efforts to redevelop and reposition their urban main streets and downtowns, but they all suffered the same fate. Being voluntary and with no formal payment requirements, they eventually faded away. Throughout the 1950s and till the mid-1960s, municipal and state leaders in many North American cities were simply overwhelmed by the demands of small independent business owners following the spread of interstate highways and the rise of the suburban mall. More importantly, mid-century civic leadership, unfortunately, was not yet familiar with notions of business strategy, place-making, or tourism (ideas we'll see in evidence in chapter 4). What followed was economic decline in previously successful main street shopping districts in what were once vibrant urban centres such as St Petersburg, Florida, which, not surprisingly, was one of the first to adopt a BIA model along the lines of the one developed in Toronto in the 1970s.

In America, there was another contributing factor. In the wake of the urban riots of the late 1960s, major companies rallied behind something called the National Urban Coalition (NUC) and began to support neighbourhood improvement initiatives. The NUC membership invested heavily in urban development schemes in cities where they had major plants or offices. The Ford Motor Company, for example, was involved in renovating downtown Detroit. However, it became clear that this voluntary effort was too erratic – and often unfair, in the sense that some city areas received complete overhauls while others nearby garnered no support at all.

Eventually, the efforts of major corporations proved insufficient to halt inner-city decay, and confidence in urban main streets declined. The pattern of benign neglect in traditional American city centres continued throughout the 1970s up to the early 1990s, when, in the wake of the 1992 Los Angeles riots (which had counterparts in most major cities in North America, even Toronto), efforts to revitalize urban main streets regained steam.[9]

A Closer Look at the BIA Creation Story

Toronto, like most of Canada, was not facing such crises in the late 1960s; in fact, relative to many U.S. cities, it was booming. Yet it was there and then that the pioneers of the modern Business Improvement Area got their start. This makes it doubly unusual. What is also interesting is that, when scouring through the literature on the history of the BIA or BID concept, we find that Toronto is barely featured beyond the odd sentence or, at most, paragraph. For example, in an early and influential paper on BIA development,[10] only one introductory paragraph was devoted to the role played by Toronto and Alex Ling and his colleagues.

So perhaps it is time to take a closer look at that initial moment when an idea, developed by and for main-street urban neighbourhoods, was born.

Why Bloor Street Village?

Prior to the formation of the world's first-ever BIA, Bloor West Village shopkeepers were all members of a voluntary local business association. The association was active but, as dues were collected on an ad hoc basis, there was always the problem of fee collection and free-riding. The association therefore had little power and few resources to compete with the aggressive promotion and climate-controlled cleanliness of Yorkdale. In this respect, Bloor West was following in a long line of private initiatives that were meant to improve the state of local shopping and commerce but that were unable to operate on a financially sustainable basis for very long. It was under this sense of financial and organizational adversity that Bloor Street's truly novel idea was born.

Back in mid-sixties Toronto, Alex Ling realized that he was incapable of individually advertising his store with any effect and that alone he would be unable to pressure the city to fix his local sidewalks[11] and create enough public parking spaces for visitors, as compensation for the loss of the streetcar route. In short, Alex understood that his neighbouring business owners were not his competitors but his allies in the campaign to get policies in place that would bring people back to the area to shop. Providing local residents with safe clean streets and a reason to buy locally were his overriding priorities. The only way to make this happen was for every business owner on the street to pay into a common fund designed to improve and promote the area. The inability to opt out of the payment plan would be the key to making this idea work, and the collection of dues would have to be facilitated by the city through property taxes.

The business owners of Bloor West Village therefore had a simple vision: "build and invest in a better street with sustainable local revenue" – as modern malls had with their enclosed shopping districts and obligatory marketing fees for tenants – "and local residents and nearby customers will beat a path to your store."

If only it were that easy. Much work, beyond the initial idea, was still required.

The Power of "One": Alex Ling

Although the Bloor-West Village BIA model emerged from a long history of private initiatives for revitalizing neighbourhoods and providing local amenities, the story of the world's first modern BIA cannot be properly told without talking a little more about the aforementioned gentleman, Alexander Edward Ling. Alex Ling, who was born in Hong Kong, and who had immigrated to Canada via South Africa in the 1960s, has been quoted several times over the past four decades in stories detailing the birth of the BIA movement – and with good reason: he lives and breathes small business success and the fostering of improvements to main-street life.[12]

It was Alex who managed to mobilize his fellow business owners and compel the city and province of Ontario to draft enabling legislation, passed in the provincial legislature on 17 December 1969, granting independent shop owners the right to create their own business improvement areas with the ability to impose a *mandatory levy* on all commercial and retail property owners. The levy would be collected by the city and given back to the associations to use as they deemed fit. The interesting thing to note here is that while all business owners in a specific area of the city would be able to vote for (or against) such an initiative, once a majority had voted in favour, only property owners were mandated to pay the levy. BIA coverage, though, would extend to all. As we shall see, in the case of some cities like Halifax, voting is restricted (in an era harking back to pre-war suffrage) only to property owners.

It may be hard today, some forty years later – when more than seventy other neighbourhoods in the City of Toronto and 1,500 communities worldwide contain some form of BIA – to appreciate how revolutionary this idea was. In those days, people in retail and urban planning still carried around in their heads the notion of a particular urban model of development. The model was influenced by early experience with the rapidly growing city. In an era prior to public sanitation and the spread of the internal combustion engine, cities had to be planned around a tight urban core so that people would be located near their workplaces. The resulting overcrowding, squalor, and cholera that were rife in urban centres created a sense of horror and moral outrage among the past century's greatest architects and designers.

BIA-Sponsored Traditional Urbanism versus the "City as Machine"

Le Corbusier in Europe and Frank Lloyd Wright in North America were prominent exemplars of the idea of the "city as machine," a place where rational order and separation of use would solve the problems of over-crowding and industrial waste.[13] The manifesto of the early-twentieth-century modernizers was to call for a dramatic break from the past. Le Corbusier stated quite unequivocally in *The City of Tomorrow* (1929 [2012]) that traditional city centres, with their quaint shops and small pedestrian-lined roadways, must be torn down. Simultaneously, Le Corbusier planned to abolish the city's main streets. In *The Radiant City* (1933, [1967]) he stated that traditional streets, with mixed uses and mixed modes of transport, no longer worked and were obsolete. He argued that they should be replaced by something entirely new.[14] This aspect of modern urban planning was heavily influenced by the emer-gence of the car as a mass-market item. With near-universal car owner-ship, the legitimate demands of car and citizen did not have to be constantly compromised.

The modern planner therefore recommended that the functions of a city be separated. In the postwar city, people would have footpaths all to themselves, while cars would enjoy massive dedicated roads ensur-ing that no car would ever have to slow down for the sake of a pedes-trian. There would no longer be factories, for example, in the middle of residential areas, and retail outlets would be housed in enclosed shop-ping concourses free from the vagaries of bad weather and polluted air.

Ironically, what the modernizers helped generate were the alienat-ing, isolated, and crime-infested housing estates of Chicago, New York, and Paris and their contemporary equivalents in retail form – the windswept downtown mall outlets – whose wastelands contemporary urban redevelopment has either obliterated or is in the process of retro-fitting.[15] As noted by Dr Pierre Filion and Karen Hammond, in their award-winning exhibit *The Heart of Our Cities: Ontario's Downtown Malls and Their Transformations*, much was sacrificed for the sake of these new retail operations.

> This experimental surgery [i.e., replacement of historic buildings and valuable property with shopping malls to guard against urban blight] was a near-complete failure. Far from resuscitating the city, these [modern developments] ignored the fine-grained streets and buildings of historic downtowns, leaving behind fortress-like walls, dead ends, service areas and parking structures that fractured the streetscape. Over time, even the retail performance of the malls declined, and today vacancies are common. However, these buildings have also slowly evolved new and useful functions, and despite their history, they may still hold the potential to become part of a vital downtown.[16]

In their haste to separate the uses and activities of city life, modern urban planners also lost sight of the curious symbiosis of apparently antithetical needs: work and leisure; commerce and study. A city constructed on apparently rational grounds, where different specialized facilities (the school, the house, the office, the library, and the place of worship) are separated by vast distances deprives citizens of easy and affordable access to amenities. It also eliminates one of the most joyous features of urban life, accidental discovery and surprise, and presupposes that we as citizens are always marching forth with unwavering purpose. Yet, how many times has one left the house with a single presumed objective in mind (e.g., renting a film, as we once did prior to the era of downloading) and instead stumbled upon a new coffee shop or the latest yoga studio offering free classes to new members.

As Alain de Botton in his wonderfully accessible book *The Architecture of Happiness* stealthily observes, the success of traditional main street living is predicated on this sense of individual discovery:

> The addition of shops and offices adds a degree of excitement to otherwise inert, dormitory areas. Contact, even of the most casual kind, with commercial enterprises gives us a transfusion of an energy we are not always capable of producing ourselves. Waking up isolated and confused at three in the morning, we can look out of the window and draw solace from the blinking neon signs in a storefront across the road, advertising bottled

beer or twenty-four-hour pizza, in their particular way, evoking a comforting human presence through the paranoid early hours.[17]

All of this, to paraphrase de Botton, the rational twentieth-century planner forgot.

Why Some Neighbourhoods Have "It" and Others Don't

Yet what is it about a certain neighbourhood and street that works in attracting people, while another, seemingly with the same elements, does not?

As Meric Gertler points out, this is a deceptively hard question to answer mainly because of the difficulty of understanding human needs and converting this knowledge into the unambiguous rule book of an urban plan.[18] It is easy enough to recognize when a street is lit properly and a neighbourhood easy to navigate, but it is much harder to convert this intuitive sense of a well-designed neighbourhood or shopping district into a logical enumeration of the reasons for it. Likewise, we do not experience a sense of pain when the finely drawn features of sound urban design have been ignored; instead we are forced to work harder to overcome confusion and a sense of unease.

Yet if asked why we were having problems or why we avoid a certain neighbourhood we would have trouble knowing how to elaborate which features were causing the problem and why. We might resort to statements about "bad energy" or "the wrong vibe." These terms are useful when we have difficulties articulating our displeasure but not helpful when looking to redevelop an urban area. This sense of what is wrong or right about a place is in the end traceable back to a failure of empathy for the human scale; to public zoning and private development that have forgotten to attend to the complexity of human life; and to planners, developers, and architects who were (and still are) seduced by simplistic visions of who we are as citizens and consumers.

"Rational" Separation of Use versus "Organic" Integration of Local Needs

Planning theorists and retail experts up to the early 1980s were consumed with the separation of use and their vision of the rational consumer. The enclosed mall was the future of shopping and, by extension, the main street was the past. In Ottawa an entire downtown neighbourhood of open-air shopping was enclosed to build the Rideau Centre, as was done in Toronto, to somewhat more positive aesthetic effect, with the Eaton Centre. But once assumptions of perfect human rationality are abandoned, these particular visions of the modernist planner go out the window.

Human behaviour is riddled with individual variability that frustrates attempts at prediction; but there is also very rational behaviour that is missed when the "city-as-machine" logic takes hold. The failure of planners to note the increasing congestion of wide avenues that were meant only for cars and that, not surprisingly, attracted them in very large numbers, meant that smaller-scale but more easily accessed local offerings would again become viable alternatives.

Standing Up for Traditional Main Street Living

Over forty years ago Alex Ling and his fellow Bloor West Village small store owners stood up for traditional main street living and said there should be more density of activity and more (not less) integration of use. This took guts and went very much against the grain of the times, which focused on the supposed problem of urban overcrowding and rational use of space. It therefore marks a turning point that coincided with other attempts, most notably those led by Jane Jacobs – first in New York and later in Toronto – to save traditional urban forms built prior to the 1940s.

The Toronto Association of Business Improvement Associations (TABIA), another organization Alex Ling helped found with city support and now headed by an equally pugnacious and passionate advocate of small business named John Kiru, still clings to that initial Bloor West promise. Its vision statement is that a "thriving main street is the heart of a neighbourhood, supported by the effort of the people who live and work there." In the past several years TABIA has hosted annual national and international BIA conferences and launched city-wide advertising campaigns trumpeting local living and entrepreneurs (see exhibit 2.1, inset).

The premise of these campaigns, according to Kiru, is simple. "By keeping small businesses and stores in the city healthy we keep our neighbourhoods healthy. Healthy neighbourhoods attract customers, tourists, and ultimately new residents. Support for local small business perpetuates a sustainable cycle of gentrification and growth that ultimately benefits everyone in an area."[19]

Examples of this same local ethos now abound across all great cities. Where once it was thought traditional main street shopping and living

Exhibit 2.1: One of the dozen or so posters produced by TABIA during its 2010 "Think Big*Buy Local" advertising campaign. Courtesy TABIA © 2014 *Source*: http://www.torontobia.com/index. php?option=com_content&task=view&id=113& Itemid=1

would go the way of the dodo bird, some of these same cities have, at great expense, buried urban freeways (e.g., in Boston and Madrid) in order to once again expose and revive traditional urban neighbour-hoods; and the irony of course is that what was once slated for demoli-tion is now trumpeted in tourist brochures and advertising campaigns as "the place to be" or "up and coming."

Lessons Learned from the Bloor West Village Revitalization Story

The combined efforts of individual business leaders and the BIA move-ment to maintain and revive traditional urban forms that predate the advent of the car have also preserved what we like about our cities; their streetscape. It turns out that what draws us to the traditional ur-ban village are buildings that form continuous lines around us and make us feel as safe in the open air as we would in our comfy living rooms. There is something disconcerting about a spread-out power centre that is neither free of buildings nor tightly compacted, but lit-tered with warehouse-like structures distributed around a parking lot without respect for edges or lines, a manufactured streetscape that de-nies people the pleasures of true nature or real urbanization.

When Alex Ling set up shop along his traditional urban main street, his operating assumption was that there ought to be a segment of the population that preferred a shopping experience that was local as op-posed to distant, that felt organic as opposed to manufactured, and that viewed nonconformity and smallness as advantages rather than weaknesses.

Like many of its contemporary counterparts, the Bloor West Village BIA's primary focus was on streetscape improvements and special events. This went against the accepted urban planning theories of the time. But there is theory and then there is practice.

By the end of that first operating year, 1970–71, the BIA had super-vised the installation of more than 100 planters, new benches, trash re-ceptacles, banners, light standards, newspaper dispensers, and holiday decorations. They also, over a slightly longer time period, worked with Ontario Hydro and the Toronto Hydro Electric System to remove utility poles from the street and bury the electrical services below grade. These basic streetscape elements dramatically improved the pedestrian expe-rience on Bloor Street and attracted customers back to the area almost immediately. The fact that they have been coming back ever since speaks to the universality of these main-street traditions.

By creating their BIA back in 1969, Bloor Street's local business and commercial property owners agreed to be taxed through an extra levy to pay for local improvements. Their shared revenues were then used to enhance security, provide maintenance, market and promote the area, fund cultural and social neighbourhood events, increase accessibility, and support the general economic development of the area.

Though it may seem obvious today that, by getting together, small-scale entrepreneurs could collectively punch well above their individual weight, several lessons about the Bloor West Village experience are nevertheless worth relating.

Lesson Number One: Businesses Joined Together and Formed Alliances with Local Groups

First, although Alex and his local business owners decided, in the absence of government funding or assistance, to deal with the declining state of their neighbourhood through internal mobilization, they nevertheless invited government and other groups to be part of the process of building a BIA. Instead of closing up shop and moving somewhere else, as an economist with a strict market-based tool kit would have suggested, they organized in much the same way successful social movements or political campaigns do, which is why it is fair to say that the BIA story has many of the features of a "movement" as opposed to a technocratic policy tool. They quickly formed a committee and started a long dialogue between local leaders and their fellow residents. The committee included representatives from at least twelve groups, including the local Business Men's Association, the City of Toronto Planning Board, City Council, the Department of Public Works, the Parking Authority, the City Surveyors Department, the City Real Estate Department, the City Legal Department, the Department of Streets, the Metro Roads and Traffic Department, the Department of Parks and Recreation, the Development Department, the Toronto Transit Commission, the Toronto Hydro Electric Commission, and Ontario Hydro.

Lesson Number Two: Independent Businesses Can Use Their "Collective" Voice

As mentioned above, Alex and his colleagues used their collective voice rather than the exit option in dealing with commercial adversity on their street. The story of Bloor West Village therefore highlights the advantages of political action over economic decision making, or "voice" over "exit," at least in situations where someone cannot easily move or has a stake in staying put. This is an old idea first popularized by Albert O. Hirschman,[20] but it rings true today. It turns out that, like many small-scale entrepreneurs, BIA members are more likely to be locally based, travelling (from surveys carried out by the authors and reviewed in chapter 8) half the distance on average that paid employees do to their places of work. From the start, because they were rooted in the neighbourhood, Bloor West Village business owners understood the power of collective voice.

It was this process of inclusion, dialogue, and deliberation that established the feasibility and ultimately secured the creation of the first business district with a self-imposed tax on local property owners. Absent this use of collective voice, the idea that a group of independent businesses would agree to a self-imposed tax and a self-managed fund whose collection costs would be borne by the city would have remained an illusory idea never to be realized.

Lesson Number Three: Good Ideas Can Spread Quickly

A third point worth noting is how the idea spread beyond the confines of Bloor Street West, first across the city and then across provincial and national borders. It was not long after Bloor West Village that St Petersburg, Florida, and New Orleans, Louisiana, adopted, with modifications suited to their local environments, their own business improvement districts (BID).

Why did the Bloor West Village BIA model transfer so easily and relatively quickly? With the power to tax and collect from all members of a designated commercial area, the BID/BIA model represented a more viable solution to neighbourhood decline than the voluntary associations of the past. The BIA/BID could compete with shopping centres in terms of advertising, and BIAs proved flexible enough to confront local challenges through the provision of locally tailored public services, which is why hundreds of municipal governments throughout North America have since allowed the authorization of BID organizations.

Lesson Number Four: Mandatory Payments for the Collective Provision of Public Goods Are the Key

Forty years on, the idea of businesses agreeing to tax themselves remains largely unchanged[21] though various cities differ in the methodology and implementation of BIA-type systems (see box 2.2). One of the perennial problems with the voluntary property associations was how to ensure that everyone who benefited from the system of collective provision of local services also paid in. This issue, it turns out, is what transformed the largely voluntary business associations of the past into the modern institutions they are today.

Box 2.2: A Short Definition of a Typical BIA Levy

The Mandatory BIA Levy: How Does It Work?

Every business member is charged a portion of the annual budget, based on that member's share of the BIA's total commercial realty assessment. Each year the BIA board, using input from members, prepares annual budget estimates that must be submitted to the municipal council for approval. Once the budget is approved by the municipal council, the council adds a special levy to the property tax to be paid by every owner of property designated (member) as industrial or commercial within the boundaries of the BIA. For each property, the amount of the levy will be related to its realty assessment. The exact amount of the BIA levy is determined by dividing the property's realty assessment by the total realty assessment in the BIA and multiplying by the total BIA annual budget.

For example: If a business's commercial realty assessment is $6,000 per year and the total commercial realty assessment of all businesses in the BIA is $2,000,000 and the BIA's annual budget is $100,000 then the individual business's BIA levy is:

$$\frac{\$6,000}{\$2,000,000} \times \$100,000 = \$300 \text{ per property per year.}$$

According to Hoyt and Gopal-Agge, two influential early analysts of BIA practices and their history, it was the innovation of "mandatory taxation" that fostered the legislative revolution for BIA formation and impact:

> In the mid-1960s, a small group of businessmen in Toronto, Canada, in-vented a new approach to circumvent the free-rider problem, where "free riders" were business owners in the area who benefited from the mone-tary and other contributions that were made by members of the voluntary business association, but who did not contribute to the association

themselves. Accordingly, they explored the feasibility of an autonomous, privately managed entity with the power to impose an additional tax on commercial property owners to fund local revitalization efforts. Their success in passing the requisite legislation in 1969 represents the moment when the BID model was born. Since this time, the BID model has been adopted in eight countries, while enabling legislation is under consideration in at least eight others.[22]

What is of interest to note is that this same model of compulsory payment for the provision of collective goods has been adopted in an area seemingly quite different from that of entrepreneurial success – namely, the trade union movement. Trade union members across Canada, following a series of precedent-setting decisions in the high courts, are not allowed to "opt out" of dues payments if they are being represented by a union that bargains on their behalf. This stands in contrast to the thirty-plus states in the United States that have advanced "right-to-work" laws whereby opting out is permitted. Not surprisingly, in these states union membership as a percentage of the workforce stands depressingly low. It is an odd contrast, therefore, that no "right-to-shop" provisions have emerged in the United States in relation to compulsory BID levy collection, at least so far, although, as we shall see, there are some disquieting notes emerging from the BIA movement south of the border.

Lesson Number Five: BIAs Generate Substantial Positive Spillover Effects

The Bloor West Village BIA, by helping to build a stronger community through district beautification and promotion, significantly contributed to the entire community's economic vitality and the solidification of the municipal tax base. BIAs, more generally, by encouraging neighbourhood residents to support their small-scale merchants, also play a role in generating a robust local economy that encourages economic diversification and minimizes spending/investment "leakage" from local economies.

By advocating for the consumption of local products and services, BIAs help to shorten the distance that products and services travel before reaching the customer and therefore also reduce the size of ecological footprints. By establishing vibrant shopping districts, BIA efforts to further local business interests can have a positive "spillover effect" and help to create communities where people are able and eager to work, live, and play.

Lesson Number Six: Government "Pull" and "Push" Factors Matter

A final lesson relates back to the question of how the model transferred so rapidly throughout Canada – one that hinges on public policy. Canadian governments encouraged the establishment of BIDs through direct "push" policies. In the 1970s, following the successful Bloor West experience, the Government of Ontario drafted enabling legislation for municipalities in the rest of the province and made infrastructure grants available to non-governmental authorities while ruling that only BID-type organizations were eligible for funding. The municipal governments of Ontario also directly encouraged the formation of BIAs by creating cost-sharing programs for streetscape improvements. These are the positive or push inducements created by government.

The indirect impetus, however, could be seen as a negative "pull" factor inducing BIA formation. Government has done so in two ways. First, beginning in the 1990s, governments at all levels retreated from a number of public services such as basic garbage collection and the up-keep of sidewalks and urban infrastructure. Even the maintenance of adequate neighbourhood security by police has been in question.[23] This has left a vacuum in the provision of certain basic public goods. Kelly Pike,[24] whose work covers aspects such as voluntary social responsibility codes, has termed this the public "governance deficit" (i.e., an absence of government fosters the creation of third parties aiming to meet the "social need" in question). In our case, it is local businesses, with a stake in making their local urban landscape accessible and desirable for potential customers, who have stepped in.

A second "pull" consideration comes from the model of municipal governance that was again adopted in the mid-1990s in Ontario and other provinces such as Quebec and Nova Scotia (but not British Columbia). The idea in the 1990s was to amalgamate municipal governance, which in Toronto meant abolishing, against the wishes of a majority of citizens, the former cities of metro Toronto (i.e., City of Toronto, York, North York, Scarborough, Etobicoke, and East York). The lack of a truly local voice in decision making under the megacity model is perhaps a second, though underappreciated, legacy of this period. One side-effect, of course, has been the increase in neighbourhoods demanding access to the BIA model and greater control over local investments, amenities, and social needs.

Indeed one need only look (see exhibit 2.2) at the diffusion of BIA formation since 1970 in what is now the amalgamated city of Toronto,

to see that the majority of Toronto's BIAs (52 out of 77) have been created since 1998, the year in which the old city of Toronto metropolitan
structures were abolished and amalgamation was imposed.

What Lies Beneath: Is This All There Is to Know about the Success of the BIA Model?

While most of this chapter paints a positive picture of BIA activity, we
should not leave readers with the impression that all is perfect, either
conceptually or in practice, with the BIA model. Recent work conducted at the University of Toronto,[25] backed up by empirical findings, has
pointed out that BIA benefits can be highly uneven, in that some owners benefit disproportionately more than others. Large "anchor participants," who often also own a majority of the buildings within a
designated BIA area, can use this power to skew local investments towards outcomes that serve their interests. They can also jack up rents
once increases in foot traffic follow from otherwise successful BIA activity. In other words, larger corporate owners can benefit more than
smaller entrepreneurs. And yet large anchors are at the same time crucial for the viability of the institution. This is consistent with Mancur
Olson's well-known proposition, known commonly as the "logic of collective action," which states that whenever a market failure leaves room
for a collective response, the presence of a well-organized collation of
interests that is neither too small and diffuse or too large and unwieldy
encourages collective action, and the action – even though in a sense
voluntary – has uneven benefits.

The Need for a Closer Look at "Main Street" Canada

Having provided a framework for discussion it is now time to descend
from the clouds of theory and recent history, plant our feet firmly on the
ground, and find out how things really work on Canada's main streets.
The next part of our story focuses on a more "fine-grain" assessment of
the impact of BIAs in three of Canada's major cities: Halifax, Vancouver,
and Toronto. These three urban case studies will expose the downsides
of BIA activity as well as the upsides and point to more general principles and theories of wider interest that will be examined in Part II.
Along the way, readers will also meet the many personalities and characters who inhabit our city neighbourhoods and streetscapes, bringing
life to the otherwise abstract concept of "local entrepreneurship."

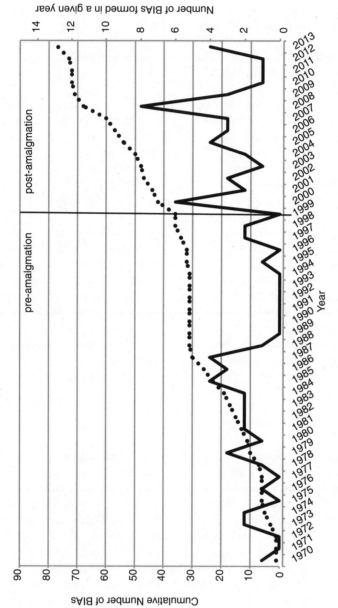

Exhibit 2.2: The Cumulative and Year-to-Year Growth of BIAs in the City of Toronto, 1970–2013. *Source:* Authors calculation from TABIA (2012) website: http://toronto-bia.com/index.php?option=com_content&task=view&id=43&Itemid=86

3 The View from Main Street Halifax: The Challenge of Being *the* Big Fish in a Small Pond[1]

In our introduction we outlined how a combination of curiosity, intuition, and observation led us to explore the topic of small business and its role in urban society. We laid out in general terms our argument that small business is a critical driver of cities' economic fortunes, as well as a formative influence on the social and psychological identity residents and visitors ascribe to a community. The preceding chapter described the origins and explained the rationale behind Business Improvement Associations, which are designed to give individual small-enterprise operators a collective voice with which to articulate their needs. It is now time to look more closely at how things really work on the main streets of Canada's major cities.

There are several reasons for beginning this exploration of on-the-ground BIA activity in Halifax, a city serves as both a unique case study in its own right and a gateway into the subsequent chapters on Vancouver and Toronto. One reason is size. Halifax is by far the smallest of the three cities we examine, so the actions of each individual business, BIA, municipal council, and even resident have a proportionally larger effect on the city as a whole. Another is history. Halifax is an old and proud city, with a distinctive heritage that is alternately a boon and the bane of its existence. History, in turn, leads us to attitude, which is perhaps the most fascinating reason to begin our Main Street tour here. That strong connection to the past, combined with an ingrained scepticism about new ideas – especially imported ones – has left Halifax languishing behind many of Canada's other urban centres in terms of a supportive approach to small business.

Will the Real Halifax Please Stand Up?

With a population of just under 400,000, Halifax is the biggest Canadian metropolitan area[2] east of Quebec but is still only the thirteenth largest nationally. For citizens and big corporations in massive urban centres like Toronto, Montreal, and Vancouver, Halifax is an afterthought, a nice place to visit and maybe even establish a small outpost, but hardly essential. On the other hand, Halifax is the unquestioned business centre of Atlantic Canada, a place where small businesses, at least in theory, should flourish. Along with the tourists who flock to the city for ocean-front adventure and the fairly substantial local population, the benefits of doing business here include a proudly small-town mentality, one where workers duck out early on sunny Fridays to meander downtown streets filled not with enormous skyscrapers but with aging brick facades and quaint, centuries-old buildings that date back to the city's founding in 1749. The small-town feel is also reinforced by the people: in no other major city, it seems, is one more likely to run into friends and acquaintances on a random stroll.

And yet, despite the fierce pride of its citizens, its personable charm, and its insistence on maintaining architectural and cultural links to the past in the face of modernity, Halifax seems something less than what it could and should be. Or, to put it more generously, it is a place that feels perpetually on the verge of some critical upward shift, some fortunate combination of municipal planning and private-sector innovation that can help it unlock its full potential. In some ways, pride has led to complacency, charm has masked the need for creativity, and history keeps trying to chop the legs out from under the future.

The Challenges of Being a Post-Amalgamated City

Positive change in Halifax will require some radical shifts in thinking by local and provincial politicians and business owners. In a municipality where the biggest employer is government and the most robust development is taking place on the fringes of the city, creating sprawling business parks to host big-box stores, small business owners in downtown core neighbourhoods seem to be a secondary priority.

Mind you, "downtown Halifax" is a somewhat nebulous concept. In 1996 (around the same time that the province of Ontario forcibly amalgamated Toronto's five metropolitan cities; see chapter 5), four separate municipalities amalgamated to form the Halifax Regional

Municipality (HRM, see exhibit 3.1). Communities ranging from the tony suburb of Bedford to the hard-knock Spryfield neighbourhood to the overlooked sister downtown in Dartmouth were brought together under a single municipal government responsible for an area encompassing 5,577 square kilometres and hundreds of competing interests and priorities, which was branded simply as "Halifax" in early 2014.

Local Voices Speak Up

Later in this chapter we will hear from members of Halifax's small business community about the challenges they face, in terms of both financial survival and the establishment of neighbourhood identities. It is these entrepreneurs whose businesses exemplify the spirit of the city, who serve as conduits for information and living connections to the past, and who define the neighbourhoods they inhabit and turn them into destinations for local citizens and tourists. No one, after all, comes to Nova Scotia or any faraway destination to shop at a Wal-Mart in suburban Dartmouth. The downtown core is the attraction, and the small, locally owned businesses that set up there make it so. Yet they are sometimes stymied by internal bickering, a suburban-minded municipal government, and a seemingly entrenched resistance to change.

One such entrepreneur with a heavy dose of civic pride is Suzanne Saul, co-owner of Attica, a modern furniture store housed in a renovated old building on Barrington Street. Barrington is a narrow street packed with heritage buildings, small businesses, and, at least during the day, bustling foot traffic. It sits just a few blocks up from the Halifax Harbour and a few blocks down from Argyle Street, which is bar-and-restaurant central, and which abuts the main shopping artery, Spring Garden Road. Saul's store is located in what most outside observers would logically conclude is Halifax's downtown. But Saul remembers aiming a question about capital reinvestment in the area at former Mayor Peter Kelly during a political debate and getting a different response.

"He told me he didn't have one downtown to worry about in Halifax, he had six downtowns," says Saul, her head shaking with disbelief.

Kelly's likening of "downtown" Spryfield to Halifax's traditional downtown may have been evidence of a warped perspective, but for the purposes of this chapter, we'll take a position somewhere between Kelly's and Saul's. After examining the Barrington Street and Spring Garden axis that forms the backbone of the city's urban core, we'll also take a look at Halifax's North End, a community that includes the

run-down – though culturally relevant – Gottingen Street and Agricola
Street, as well as the gentrified Hydrostone district. Finally, we'll ferry
across the harbour for a glance at downtown Dartmouth, an area that,
like the North End, has cried out for a major revitalization for at least a
quarter-century.

Structure of the Chapter

On this journey through the city, we'll encounter the distinct challenges
small businesses face in each neighbourhood and what owners are doing, individually and collectively, to tackle them. We'll bear witness to
the birth of a Business Improvement Association in one part of town
and evaluate the work of long-established BIAs in other neighbourhoods. We'll examine cases in which small businesses reach out to the
community to address socio-economic problems in their surrounding
area, and we shall offer a glimpse into the possible future of small business in Halifax.

So we begin our street-level observations here in Halifax because it is
a work in progress, a relatively clean slate onto which a burgeoning
small business community is attempting to imprint itself. It is the proverbial "before" picture, a city where the small business owners who
have the creativity and drive to effect positive change have consistently
faced obstacles from government, residents, and even other entrepreneurs. We begin here because the very absence of policy that provides
muscular support for small business and makes it the engine of economic and social growth makes the case that such policy is necessary.
Finally, we begin here because although Halifax is not yet what it can
be, in its uncertain struggle to fulfil its vast potential it offers lessons
for urban centres across the country.

A Tough Place to Do Business

"I find Nova Scotia in general to be one of the toughest places [to do
business]," says Mike Hachey, the owner of Egg Films. It's an opinion
shared by many of his fellow small business owners in Halifax, but one
he's especially qualified to give.

Hachey is no corporate magnate. After working for several ad agencies and production houses as an editor, he founded Egg Films and has
established it as one of the top commercial production shops in
Atlantic Canada. He's got twenty employees, not including the small

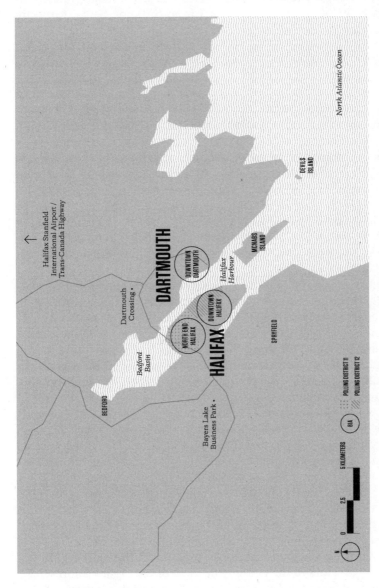

Exhibit 3.1: Halifax, post-1996 amalgamation, which includes all four of the old cities of what was once known as Metro Halifax. The areas highlighted include some of the neighbourhoods profiled in this chapter.

staff complement at Egg's sister company, post-production house Hatch Post. The firms are spread out over three floors of a heritage building on Barrington Street, a few doors down from Suzanne Saul's furniture store, Attica.

A youthful fortysomething, Hachey, in his designer jeans and crisp-yet-casual button-down shirt, comes across as the kind of businessman any city should covet. His business is based on the twin pillars of the modern economy – creativity and computers – and his offices teem with young, culturally attuned types. He and his staff work and spend their lunch money in downtown Halifax and are committed to growing the company here.

"There's nothing like being downtown, where on your lunch break you can just jet down to the waterfront. I mean, this is why we live on the East Coast," Hachey says. "Otherwise we could do it anywhere else and probably do a lot better. It's a lifestyle choice that you make for staying in Atlantic Canada with a production house. You make that decision and you know you're constantly going to be hitting ceilings unless you're able to expand – and some companies can – out of this region and still do the work here."

The lifestyle factor has kept Hachey in Halifax – mostly. He also has a satellite office in Moncton, and his experiences in New Brunswick have been illustrative of how the two provinces cater to small business. His Moncton shop was welcomed with provincial grant money and a party thrown by the city. In his Halifax home, he feels as if he's hardly on the radar. "There are no incentives to having your business in downtown Halifax," he says. "The province doesn't offer much, and certainly in the downtown Halifax doesn't do much, either."

Hachey isn't the only small business owner in Nova Scotia who feels this way. The Canadian Federation of Independent Business (CFIB) conducts monthly surveys to assess the attitudes and expectations of its members, 95 per cent of which are businesses with twenty or fewer employees. According to the CFIB's March 2014 Business Barometer, Nova Scotia posted an index score of 57.9 (an index of 50 translates to an equal balance between positive and negative expectations), the third-lowest mark in the country and only slightly higher than New Brunswick (56.9) and Prince Edward Island (57.6). The national average was 64.1.

The CFIB Business Barometer also pinpointed the most significant contributing factors to the pessimistic view of the organization's 5,200 Nova Scotian members. On the cost side, 63 per cent of survey respondents expressed concern about rising fuel and energy costs, while 52 per cent pointed to costs associated with taxes and regulation. A shortage of domestic demand (42 per cent) and skilled labour (25 per cent) were also cited as inhibitors to growth.

These results aren't indicative of a post-recession hangover. Nor are they evidence of what Prime Minister Stephen Harper once referred to as Maritimers' "culture of defeat." According to Leanne Hachey (no relation to Mike), Nova Scotian businesses have been singing the same tune for at least the ten years she's served as executive director of CFIB's Atlantic chapter.[3] "Business owners in Nova Scotia, for very good reasons, are less optimistic about the future of their businesses, the future of the economy, and the future for young people than most business owners across the country," she says. "That is worrisome."

The Role of Government: It Starts with the Province

Hachey describes a "complex web" of factors that weigh down small businesses in the province. As she speaks, however, it's clear that a few strands of this web are far more important than others. Issue number one for her members is taxes, primarily those that are levied at the provincial level and that put Nova Scotia businesses at a competitive disadvantage. "Municipally, there are some variations within Nova Scotia, but the real difference is at the provincial level," Hachey says.

"Let me go through our laundry list."

Hachey proceeds to unload the dirty laundry: the second-highest workers' compensation premiums in Canada. The highest HST in the country at 15 per cent, which combines with one of the nation's highest gas taxes to compound the dent in Nova Scotians' wallets. There's also the national-low threshold for eligibility for the small business tax rate and the national-high general corporate tax rate. The fact that Nova Scotia does not, like most provinces, index its personal income tax system to inflation, means that increases in income are more likely to spill over into a higher tax bracket. This "bracket creep" is also reinforced by the existence of five personal income tax brackets in the province, as opposed to the usual three or four. Individuals and businesses that live here are more likely to have more of their income and expenditures taxed at a higher rate, a double-whammy for business owners in that it affects both them and their customers.

"A business wouldn't flee Nova Scotia only because the tax system sucks, but it certainly isn't a draw to businesses coming here," Hachey says. "There's not as much money to spend here in Nova Scotia."

The Role of Municipal Government

To say that taxation at the provincial level is a serious obstacle for small business owners doesn't absolve the municipal government of HRM, either. In the past twenty-five years, dozens of businesses have fled to the more friendly tax environment of the suburban business parks, hollowing out much of the downtown core. This effect is particularly noticeable on Barrington Street, Gottingen Street in Halifax's North End, and Portland Street in downtown Dartmouth, where numerous buildings sit in various states of vacancy and disrepair.

Hachey notes that it makes sense for many businesses to pay the lower Suburban Commercial Rate rather than the Urban Commercial Rate downtown operators are hit with. This is especially true of businesses like big-box stores and cubicle-culture offices, businesses that need vast parking lots far more than they need a connection with a local community. Yet to Hachey and her local CFIB members, there's no logic in the city's taxing its downtown business inhabitants so harshly.

"We have economies of scale down here. There's a lot more people and more businesses packed into a smaller area, and you would think that would mean it costs less to provide services to us," Hachey says. "So why isn't that reflected in the tax rate?

"We've long said that the tax system at the municipal level is driving people out to the suburban areas. If a business can set up a few kilometres away and pay thousands of dollars less in taxes every year, why wouldn't they?"

Business owners in downtown Halifax might grumble less about taxes if they felt they were getting their money's worth. By and large, though, the feeling is that the municipal government prefers to use the money collected from Halifax's withering downtown to invest in outlying suburban areas. "They look at the downtown as a source for revenue – we're the biggest tax generator in Atlantic Canada – yet that money does not stay downtown," says Attica's Suzanne Saul. "They don't understand the uniqueness of the downtown and how important it is to have a strong downtown core."

Saul's complaint is backed up by a 2012 report by the Canadian Urban Institute, which found that Halifax had invested only $34 million in its downtown since 2000. By contrast, similarly sized London, Ontario, benefited from $174 million in municipal investment during roughly the same time period (1998–2011).

Small Business and the Regulatory Burden

It's this lack of support that leads small business owners like Mimi Fautley, one of the three founders of Barrington Street knitting store The Loop, to conclude, "The city needs to get its shit together."

Or at least clean some of it from the path of small business owners. Leanne Hachey of CFIB Atlantic lists bureaucratic red tape as another of her membership's most frequent gripes. In her mind, Halifax isn't the most difficult place to be in terms of navigating by-laws, regulations, and paperwork, but it's still tougher than it needs to be. Her members have to be on the alert for unusual and punitive by-laws, such as the one proposed several years ago that would have, had it passed, put small businesses on the hook for removing graffiti from their own buildings – and a stiff fine if they failed to comply within ten days.

Then there is the paperwork. Hachey says her Nova Scotia members collectively used to spend 615,000 hours per year on filling out forms – for the provincial government alone. In recent years, Nova Scotia's political leaders committed to reducing that amount, knocking about 123,000 hours off the total. Hachey believes the most valuable element of this outcome was to raise awareness in government circles that businesses must grind away at paperwork for municipal, provincial, and federal authorities, and that this burden is cumulative.

"It was a victory in terms of the reduction, but the real victory was getting (the government) to measure it. To get them to look at it collectively, rather than by department, which is how government typically looks at it," Hachey says. "You may not think the burden your department is imposing is that big, but you don't work in isolation. Business owners have to do it all for everybody.

"If you're a large business, you probably have a department of regulatory affairs, because regulatory affairs really is [sic] a full-time job for at least one person. Small businesses don't have those resources, so the burden falls solely on the business owners. It becomes a productivity issue that makes it very difficult for small businesses to succeed."

The Barrington Street Corridor and the Challenge of Downtown Revival

For small business owners on the Barrington Street corridor of Halifax, dealing with the regulations relating to the area's designation as a

Heritage District can be a full-time job within that regulatory full-time job they already don't have time for. Christian Rankin, co-owner of Obladee, a wine bar that opened on Barrington Street late in 2010, got caught in the teeth of these technicalities, and it almost chewed up his business before it started.

Rankin's bar occupies a ground-floor corner spot in a ninety-five-year-old building previously designated for retail use. Opening Obladee required a change in the unit's usage designation. As a "restaurant," Obladee was obligated to have a second exit, an option that was not physically possible given its small size and layout. Rankin and his fellow owners delayed Obladee's opening by two months, hiring an architect and working with officials from the city and the Downtown Halifax Business Commission to find a compromise. Eventually, the city accepted the installation of additional fire extinguishers and a large window that could be easily pushed out onto the street in the event of fire.

"Hiring an architect, paying rent during those two months – it doesn't take long to eat up an amount of money that could be invested in the business," says Rankin. "But we did find people who were willing to cooperate, and we may have made some progress for people who come after us."

Those rooting for Halifax's downtown hope that's the case. Obladee appeals to the kind of young, affluent population that can make a neighbourhood trendy. For a street that, for the most part, goes dark and quiet at night, it's a potentially transformative addition, one that the city's regulators almost snuffed out.

Rankin understands the need for regulation and has as much vested interest as anyone in ensuring his bar is safe. He'd just like to see a little more flexibility. "There is, in my view, an incentive for the city and the province and the business community for these projects to go ahead," he says.

But the city has historically had trouble seeing that incentive, or at least acting on it. On Barrington Street, the desire to protect Halifax's unique architectural history has competed with the desire of entrepreneurs to breathe modern life into the downtown core, resulting in a frustrating stalemate. Many storefronts have been boarded up for years, even decades, as developers sat on crumbling properties and waited to hear what they could do with them. They have waited a long time.

"One of the most positive factors for landlords is a clear set of rules and guidelines," says Eric Crowell, director of the St Mary's University Business Development Centre and the author of How to Grow a Business.

"It doesn't really matter what they are, as long as they're clear. If the city says they don't want any buildings higher than three storeys, fine. If they say it's a free-for-all and thirty- or forty-storey buildings can come in here and block the viewplanes, fine. Just be clear. Once the rules are clear, it takes a huge amount of risk away from the developer's perspective."

A Modest Proposal for Reform

In 2009 the city approved a twenty-five-year plan dubbed HRM By Design, and also officially designated Barrington Street as a Heritage District. In theory, at least, this plan clarifies some of the limitations and allowances with respect to the height and cosmetic nature of buildings on Barrington Street and elsewhere in the city. In practice, though, restrictions in the design plan – particularly with respect to the height of buildings – have already been overridden by council in the case of several proposed developments.

Scott Colwell, who's watched Barrington Street fade over the twenty-five years he's operated his cafe and catering business (Certainly Cinnamon), would like to see more development, tall or small. Specifically, he believes Barrington Street needs more residents as well as more homes for entrepreneurs. "We need more high-density housing down here," says Colwell. "We need people [living] in these office towers that have been empty for twenty or thirty years." And there is evidence to suggest that such projects are at least partially supported by the local populace. A 2010 economic analysis by the Greater Halifax Partnership, a public-private organization proposing more robust urban growth in Halifax and neighbouring Dartmouth, found that about half of residents surveyed felt commercial and residential development should be happening at a quicker pace downtown.

The Greater Halifax Partnership has called for a $50 million infrastructure investment in downtown Halifax and has also created a five-year strategic plan with the goal of increasing both private investment and population in the city. Colwell says having more people living in the downtown area not only will be good for businesses like his, but will make the neighbourhood a safer, more attractive place to go for shopping, eating, and walking – Jane Jacobs's "feet on the ground and eyes on the street" notion. A safer, more vibrant neighbourhood could also lure more young adults, which in turn would address the troubling demographic trends faced by businesses in the city and the province in general.

"You have an ageing population, so there's increased demand for social services like health care, and at the same time you're seeing a shrinking of the group that pays for this stuff, the people working and paying income taxes," says Leanne Hachey of CFIB Atlantic.

We're back to taxes again, but as Hachey and Halifax's local business owners note, high taxes aren't the only thing that makes it difficult for entrepreneurs to succeed here. There's also a slow-moving local bureaucracy that has largely ignored the city's downtown neighbourhoods for decades in favour of suburban expansion – a prevailing culture that, evolving as it has on an island disconnected from the rest of the country, is sceptical of importing innovation from other cities.

For all these struggles, though, Halifax remains a place with enormous potential. The same sense of history that has often impeded progress is also one of the city's primary tourist draws. The same architecture that is falling apart can be, in the hands of the right people, restored in a way that maintains the downtown's distinctive character. The same collective pessimism that business owners have demonstrated about the future is also a window into how easily collective thinking comes to Haligonians. When small businesses in the city band together, they can be – and have been – a force for social and economic change.

Turning individual small business voices into a chorus is a fundamental principle of business improvement districts. The issues that face the small business community in Halifax make it the ideal city in which to test the BIA concept, and in fact there are eight BIAs already operating in Halifax, the most recent of which was born, in complicated and contentious fashion, in 2011.

Capitalizing on the Halifax Potential: The "Complicated" Birth of the North End BIA

The crowd gathers in a large classroom at the Bloomfield Centre, a community centre located on Agricola Street in Halifax's North End. The attendees are a motley crew, with stuffed-shirt city politicians circulating alongside blue-collar small business operators and commercial property owners in expensive suits. Music bleeds through the walls from the next classroom over, where a group of senior citizens are being put through their paces in a line-dancing class. In this room, however, there is more serious business on the agenda. Representatives from the business community and municipal government have convened an information meeting about the proposed establishment of a Business

Improvement Association for the North End area. In just over two weeks, property owners in the area must vote on whether to create such an association. They're here, like the business owners who work out of their buildings, to get some answers.

Presentations are made to the hundred or so people seated in plastic chairs. Scott Sheffield, community developer for the city, explains the mechanics of how the city would establish a BIA if voters called for one. His city colleague, manager of economic development Jim Donovan, outlines his personal commitment to small business, a claim that some in the audience would no doubt question, and gives his endorsement to the BIA concept. "Local business clusters are an integral part of community development and how communities present themselves," he says.

The Example of the Spring Garden Area Business Association

Presenters from other areas of the city have also been called in to make the case for a North End BIA. Kurt Bulger, for example, owns a souvenir shop on Spring Garden Road called Jennifer's of Nova Scotia. Standing up in front of the crowd, he apologizes for not being an accomplished public speaker, then proceeds to deliver a strong and articulate endorsement of the Spring Garden Area Business Association (SGABA), the BIA he's been interacting with for twenty-five years.

"Without the business association I'm not sure we would have had the ability to see the trends coming with Bayers Lake, Dartmouth Crossing, and the other power centres," he says, alluding to suburban retail parks. "Many businesses on Spring Garden have changed who they are or what they sell, or have gone more upscale or downscale. But they had the time to make those changes. The association also allows a collective marketing voice to rise above the chatter in the advertising world. This, as you may know, is a tactic used by every mall."

Bulger and his Spring Garden landlord, Mike Veres, go on to talk about the contributions the SGABA has made to the community by supporting social services and neighbourhood beautification efforts. Their message is unequivocal – their local BIA is one of the key reasons Spring Garden Road has maintained its status as a prime shopping district in the face of Halifax's mall sprawl.

In speaking at this meeting, Bulger and Veres are not merely standing up for the BIA concept. They're standing up for a man, a dapper, rosy-cheeked bundle of energy who, if he were not so tall, could be fairly described as elflike They're standing up for Bernard Smith, who worked diligently through the early months of 2011 to consolidate support for a North End BIA.

Few could be more qualified than Smith to explain and advocate for the concept of collectivizing a local business community. After spending twenty-three years as treasurer for the city of Halifax, Smith led the SGABA for six years, instituting several marketing and community outreach programs (some of which we'll examine closely later in this chapter) on behalf of his members. Those who have worked with him in the Spring Garden Area, as well as those who've come to know him through his tireless efforts in the North End, speak reverently of him.

Although he's disarmingly charming and does not come across as arrogant or conceited, Smith doesn't suffer from any false modesty. He's proud of what he accomplished in the Spring Garden area, where national brands like Le Chateau and high-end locally owned stores such as Mills share the main street with pubs and restaurants and where independently owned boutiques line the side streets. Over coffee at Alteregos, a Gottingen Street cafe that doubles as a hostel (called Backpackers), Smith says the key to enabling Spring Garden to hold its own against the suburban big-box stores was the neighbourhood's distinctive character.

"We had to be very careful to make ourselves different from malls and big-box retail," Smith says. "We decided we had to focus on quality. We had to give much better customer service – we couldn't compete on price, but by gosh we could compete on customer service.

"We wanted to make shopping an enjoyable experience."

No Two Neighbourhoods Are Exactly Alike

The North End area where Smith wants to establish a BIA – and become its executive director – does not have the same natural advantages as the Spring Garden neighbourhood. In the Gottingen Street and Agricola Street corridors, particularly, crime rates are high and foot traffic is low. Graffiti and broken windows dot a streetscape littered with run-down buildings and empty lots. Gottingen could once lay claim, in the middle of the last century, to being Halifax's main downtown street, but the area has been in decline for several decades. And yet, Smith sees potential for a North End rebound, powered by a BIA.

"It's absolutely glaringly obvious," he says, his face brightening under his trademark fedora. "This is the new growth centre of the city. It's the place where real estate is still relatively cheap and where communication and transportation are good."

Smith goes on to outline his vision of the North End as a hub for artists and tech companies, a place where like-minded business people can congregate and establish a clear neighbourhood identity. He has no doubt that the area's reputation for danger and darkness can be repaired. "There's a perception issue, but there was a perception issue about Spring Garden, too, and we dealt with that.

"I believe in the product," Smith says of the BIA concept. "It's easier to sell things when you're convinced you're right." But Smith is not the first person who has tried to convince North Enders of the value of a BIA. Michelle Strum, owner of Alteregos and a prime ally of Smith's in the current fight to establish a BIA, recalls trying to foster a more collective mentality in the years immediately following the launch of her business in 2001.

"There was a little initiative happening on Gottingen, a little initiative happening on Agricola, a little initiative happening in the Hydrostone. We thought that if we united the three we'd have much more volunteer power and more dollars to work with," Strum says.

Like Strum, Fred Connors, proprietor of Fred Salon and Whet Cafe on Agricola Street – and a 2012 mayoral candidate – tried to rally area businesses into a collective association after opening his business in 2004. He and Strum connected and did much the same thing that Smith has been doing, working for several months to bring ad hoc associations in the Gottingen, Agricola, and Hydrostone neighbourhoods together into a North End BIA. So encouraged were they by the response among business operators and city officials, one of whom told Connors that his efforts were "a textbook example of how to launch a BIA," that they raised the money to send ballots out to commercial property owners, confident that they would vote in favour of an association.

Instead, the BIA's bid was crushed.

Landlord versus Tenant: Getting Everyone on Side

"The people who tend to own businesses in the North End, who want an association, are not the same people that own the properties, and [unlike in other cities like Toronto] the ballot [only] goes out to the property owners, not the business owners who rent the commercial space," says Connors. "And the property owners see levies, they don't see benefits. Even though the levy should be passed on to business owners in the form of a rent increase, they just see more administration and more taxation."

Of the 485 ballots Connors, Strum, and their backers sent out, only 100 were returned. Eighty-seven respondents voted against the establishment of a BIA. "It was hugely disappointing because of all the hours we spent engaging the community to promote all of the benefits associated with a BIA," says Connors. "But we weren't really reaching the people we needed to reach."

At the Bloomfield Centre meeting, Smith, Strum, and several other presenters make a last-ditch appeal to reach the right people. The degree to which they are successful is difficult to calculate. A handful of property owners raise sceptical questions, wondering aloud why a BIA is required to deal with issues such as graffiti, community safety, and beautification – tasks they feel are the responsibility of city departments to perform with the tax revenue they already collect. They've yet to be sold on the idea of paying BIA levies, or on the idea that the work done with this money could be considered an investment in the community – an investment that could eventually raise their property values. Their short-term bottom line is a greater priority than building up the downtrodden neighbourhood.

At the meeting, other questions come in from property owners and business operators alike. The diversity of the North End, which has been touted by the meeting's presenters as an advantage, has some attendees wondering why Gottingen, Agricola, and Hydrostone should be lumped together. Those located in the more upscale Hydrostone area are concerned about the possibility that the new BIA, funded in part by their levies, would be more focused on revitalizing the Gottingen and Agricola areas. There isn't even unanimous agreement on what, exactly, constitutes the "North End." Before leaving for another meeting, city councillor Jerry Blumenthal stands up from within the crowd and claims that the North End's southern border is North Street, meaning the area cannot possibly include Gottingen and Agricola.

Smith, Strum, and the other BIA advocates remain calm in the face of the questions. They repeatedly assure prospective members that the levy amounts and priorities of any BIA are not yet set in stone and will be shaped by the membership. As the meeting draws to a close, Strum positions the BIA vote as a stark choice between an unsatisfactory status quo and a potentially brighter future. "The option is what we were doing before, which was working with no money and a really small volunteer voice, or coming together with a united voice and a united volunteer force working on the same issues and having more money to work on them with," Strum says.

The attendees file out of the room, bringing their scepticism and optimism with them. Two weeks before the vote – one that will, according to the city, represent the North End's last chance to establish a BIA for at least two years – it's unclear which future the neighbourhood will choose.

Downtown Halifax: The Challenge(s) of Running the Largest BIA in the City

As seen in the case of the North End, giving birth to a new institution can be hard and fraught with risk. At the other end, setting a BIA on its feet and getting it to move forward also presents its share of challenges. Nowhere is this more evident than in the case of the Downtown Halifax Business Commission (DHBC). With more than 1,800 members and a budget of almost $850,000 for 2010–11, it is the largest Business Improvement Association in Halifax. Its geographical borders are Brunswick Street to the west and the harbourfront area to the east, with the Cogswell Interchange and the southern endpoint of Barrington Street framing the area from the north and south, respectively. It was officially established as a BIA in 1987, replacing the informal volunteer associations that had operated in the area for decades. It is a massive entity run by executive director Paul Mackinnon, a soft-spoken, unassuming man who has been in the BIA business for most of his professional life, first with the Spring Garden Area BIA and, for more than a decade, with the DHBC.

With his membership spread out over such a broad geographical area and comprising both major corporations and small mom-and-pop shops, Mackinnon must deal with a wide range of priorities, complaints, and initiatives. The DHBC's annual to-do list includes collective marketing efforts – such as a 2010 campaign that invited visitors to post social media videos about how to enjoy a day downtown with a $100 budget – as well as street-cleaning initiatives and event planning. Much of this work is handled by volunteer committees, including a dedicated marketing group. Mackinnon himself is largely focused on the other aspect of the DHBC's mandate – advocacy. Acting as a policy voice and liaison with government has, says Mackinnon, become an increasingly vital part of the BIAs' agenda since the city amalgamated.

"The general feeling is that the power disappeared from the downtown, so there's a need for someone to speak up around things like infrastructure and investment," Mackinnon says. "We've had success being heard. Whether there's been a turnaround or not is a different thing."

Victory and Defeat

Indeed, the DHBC's track record includes both satisfying victories and some frustrating defeats. The commission was a strong supporter of the HRM By Design plan that passed in 2009 and gave developers a better sense of what they could build in the area. It has conducted research comparing government investment in downtown Halifax to that in other urban centres. At a more grass-roots level, the DHBC successfully acted as a broker between city inspectors and Christian Rankin's Barrington Street wine bar Obladee, helping both parties come to an agreement about the second exit required by the fire code. On the issue of parking – the lack of which is a chronic complaint about the downtown of this car-oriented city – the commission has been able to reverse at least one nonsensical city policy, the one that, until recently, slapped a $25 ticket on citizens who parked at broken metres.

But dealing with strange bits of municipal bureaucracy is an ongoing job. Mackinnon recalls the city fumbling a well-intentioned attempt to remove snow from the downtown area to make the streets accessible for the 2011 Canada Games, which were held in Nova Scotia. On a Thursday night at suppertime, when restaurants in the neighbourhood were doing peak business, city workers swooped in and demanded that patrons remove their cars from the streets or risk being ticketed and towed. Most customers simply went to their cars and kept going, emptying out the bars and restaurants on what should have been a profitable evening.

"Removing the snow was a great idea, but three a.m. is the time to do it," Mackinnon sighs. "To come and do it at six o'clock on a Thursday night, it just makes no logical sense."

A Contrast in Visions

Illogic is a recurring theme for a municipal government that pays occasional lip service to revitalizing downtown neighbourhoods but is often clueless about what these areas need. When Attica, the high-end furniture store, set up shop on narrow Barrington Street, the DHBC appealed to the city to make the area in front of the store a loading zone – a necessity for a business based on large items going in and out the door. "Basically, the response was, 'A furniture store shouldn't be downtown. Why don't they go to Bayers Lake?'

"Obviously there was no sense that revitalizing Barrington Street with actual stores was a good idea." Mackinnon, though, believes it's a good idea to have a varied mix of businesses downtown, so he continues to fight on multiple fronts. But he and the DHBC are underdogs, and their mixed results over the years have led several of their members to question their effectiveness. Scott Colwell, proprietor of Certainly Cinnamon, says that after two years as a DHBC board member, he became disillusioned with the ratio of talk to action.

"I went to meetings twice a week for two years, and it was a colossal waste of my time," Colwell says. "I think Paul does as good a job as he can. The guy's a great guy and he goes to bat for us year after year, but his hands are tied."

These tied hands, according to Colwell, are a result of the fact that few downtown proprietors actually live in the area, meaning they do not get to vote for the neighbourhood's government representatives. Those representatives can then safely ignore downtown business needs while collecting tax revenue. Nevertheless, Joanne Macrae, owner of The Hub, a small business that acts as a community office space for a variety of professionals, would like to see the DHBC do a better job of representing independent owners like her. She takes issue with what she perceives to be the commission's emphasis on its larger members.

"People feel like the DHBC doesn't meet the needs of the small, independent retailer or the small business, really," says Macrae. "It's like they're more focused on the bigger tenants, the bigger projects, the bigger developers."

A Closer Look at Spring Garden

An organization as large as the DHBC is bound to disappoint at least some of its members, of course. By comparison, Nancy Tissington, executive director of the Spring Garden Area Business Association, has a much more tightly defined job description. The SGABA, which operates as a separate entity despite the fact that some of its membership resides within the DHBC's geography, represents a far more homogeneous group of businesses. And although the association lends its voice, along with Halifax's other BIAs, to advocacy issues, it's far closer to the street – as is Tissington, who took over from Bernard Smith in the fall of 2010 after working as a municipal liaison with BIAs across the city. Having seen things from the other side, she is pleased to have escaped government bureaucracy. "We're a lot more nimble, so the things I want to do in the community I feel like I can do a little faster than in municipal government."

With her background in marketing, much of what Tissington wants to do centres on collective promotion of the area's retailers. She has encouraged members to become active in social media, both with customers and with each other. She has also brought in a consulting firm to figure out how to institute more cross-promotions between her members. According to Tissington, her approach involves looking at the Spring Garden area from the viewpoint of a customer. From a market positioning point of view, she feels the neighbourhood's independent owners are its biggest advantage.

"Getting that unique find and knowing you're supporting local, that was a big piece for me," she says. "And I think there are many people out there who feel the same way."

It can't all be promotion, of course, even for the marketing expert. Tissington has inherited many age-old issues from Bernard Smith, including the ongoing battle to keep the area clean and safe. The SGABA works closely with a community constable and also employs its own private security staff to act as a deterrent to vandalism and violence. However, she acknowledges that conspicuous displays of security can actually have the effect of deterring visitors. "That's some of the reporting I'm trying to get right now – what is the perception?" Tissington says. "If there's a perception that there's too much security, people wonder what the heck is going on down here."

Ask suburbanites about their perceptions of Spring Garden Road and they'll most likely put the prevalence of panhandlers at the top of the list. Not surprisingly, the downtown's primary retail strip is lined with struggling folks hoping to collect "spare change" from shoppers. Regardless of whether visitors to the area regard spare-changers with contempt or pity, the presence of panhandlers understandably diminishes the experience of coming to the downtown.

"My daughter, when she comes down here, it bothers her, because she wants to give," says Tissington, referring to the natural desire to help people in need. "Part of it, too, is what we do about visitors and people who have the perception that it doesn't feel safe. People don't like to be approached, and it can feel aggressive."

To a great many businesses and residents, it may have been tempting to treat panhandling as a policing issue. But as Tissington notes, businesses in the Spring Garden area have a social conscience, which is why they supported the SGABA in the creation of a program that takes a more constructive and innovative approach to the problem. The brainchild of Bernard Smith, that program is called The Navigator, and it is the most striking example of the positive role small business has played in the community.

BIAs and Local Social Policy Innovation: The Case of "Navigator"

Sitting across from E.J. Davis in Steve-O-Reno's, an independently owned coffee shop in downtown Halifax, it is difficult to imagine someone less likely to confront some of the area's most street-hardened residents. He is slim and compact, his youthful face framed by a dark beard, his eyes darting energetically behind thick, black-rimmed glasses. He looks like an artist or a musician or an up-and-coming advertising executive, someone more likely to be discussing issues like homelessness from a safe, abstract perch than pounding the pavement in search of solutions. As the head of the Navigator program, however, solving problems while putting miles on his sneakers is what Davis does every day.

Davis is a social worker by trade, and the latest administrator of the Navigator program, launched four years ago by former Spring Garden Area Business Association executive director Bernard Smith. Davis's role requires him to personally reach out to members of the downtown area's street-involved community and help them reach a more productive phase in their lives. Sometimes this means connecting people with mental health and addiction services. Often it means dealing with the numerous barriers to employment faced by people without a fixed address – on a given day, Davis may procure an identification card for one person, a pair of construction work boots for another, and a place to stay for another. Eight months into his tenure on the job, he estimates he has formed relationships with about 250 people, including roughly eighty panhandlers.

It is challenging work, to be sure – during our half-hour conversation, Davis takes a phone call about a fistfight between two Spring Garden regulars. The people who have elected to take advantage of Davis's services face an uphill climb to rebuilding their lives. Others are so entrenched in addiction and mental health issues that they do not even ask.

"It's really an attempt to build a network around folks, so that if something falls apart or there's a moment where they're like, 'Okay, something needs to change for me,' the network is there and ready to go," says Davis.

Davis is the only employee in Navigator, a program that, according to Nancy Tissington, executive director of the SGABA, costs about $100,000 per year to operate. The municipal government has, over the years, matched funds from the SGABA and the Downtown Halifax Business Commission, and the provincial government has for two years contributed money through its Justice Department. Though his salary comes from a variety of sources, and his job requires liaising with publicly run community agencies, Davis is an employee of the SGABA and the DHBC. And the Navigator program is a product of the local business community, channelled through its two BIA organizations.

"Every businessperson who puts money into this program recognizes that these people are struggling with something," says Davis. "Businesses have more frustration with the fact that they pay taxes for the government to care for these folks, and they don't see that happening. The fact that my position was created comes out of that frustration, from seeing the same people on the street every day panhandling."

Davis says his lone wolf status means he doesn't have to hack through the same bureaucratic thicket that his colleagues in community mental health do. As an example, he points to the barriers faced by a person on income assistance who has been offered a construction job – a potential first step to a life off the street – and tries to jump through government hoops.

"If the employer says that person needs work boots, that person needs to make an appointment with an employment counsellor, which could be a three to six-month wait. And maybe they'll get money for boots, but they'll have to go out and get [price] quotes from three different places and bring their counsellor those quotes.

"By then they've lost their job."

In a similar vein, Davis recounts the story of a street-involved person who received an employment placement at the SPCA but was caught stealing – and eating – dog food because the organization, like most employers, withheld pay until he proved himself reliable. "Anyone you work for will usually hold your pay for three weeks to make sure you show up," says Davis. "If you're in a shelter or sleeping on a friend's couch, that's a long time to be working twelve-hour days with no money." Stepping into this void, the Navigator program provides money for new employees until their first paycheque.

While a certain percentage of street-involved people simply aren't ready or willing to take advantage of the Navigator program, Davis says the program has helped change the environment on Spring Garden Road. "Four or five years ago there were a lot more youth hanging around on the street, and it was definitely a bigger issue," he says.

Back then, it was Bernard Smith who realized that helping struggling people better their circumstances was a more productive approach to panhandling than asking police to shoo "undesirables" off the street. In the early days, Smith did it himself, in part by locating local businesses willing to offer part-time work to street-involved Spring Gardeners. "I'd looked at what the aggressive, confrontational approach did. It didn't do anything. It caused bad press and no positives, and I like good press and lots of positives," says Smith. "It was a business decision."

And businesses in downtown Halifax have largely bought in. A week prior to our conversation, Davis sent out a call to the local business community via Twitter for used cell phones, so he could set them up for street-involved clients who needed a place for employers to reach them. Within three days, he had eight phones in hand, leading to new employment opportunities for two of his outreach clients.

Local Business, Social Conscience, and the City's North End

Impressive as it is, the Navigator program is just one example of how small business contributes to the welfare of communities in Halifax. Over in the North End, Michelle Strum has long operated her cafe, Alteregos, and traveller's hostel, Backpackers, with an eye to serving the needs of the neighbourhood as well as her customers. To Strum, the choice between social and business imperatives is a false one. "We believe every decision we make from a business standpoint should be beneficial to us and beneficial to the neighbourhood," Strum says. "That helps create strong neighbourhoods and dollars that are made in the community and stay in the community."

One of the ways Strum keeps dollars in the community surrounding Gottingen Street is through her hiring practices. The North End has one of the city's highest rates of unemployment, with many residents restricted from opportunities by lack of education, training, and experience. Unlike most customer-service businesses, Strum's Alteregos and Backpackers are willing to put their faith in people who have the necessary personality traits for success. "We have actively gone out to see what kinds of opportunities people are looking for and we've tried to put a real focus on hiring locally. Even if we can't find someone who has the experience, we will mentor someone into a position so we can have a great impact in our community," Strum says. "The impact has not only been great in the neighbourhood, but from a business stand-point we have about a three-year retention rate for employees. In cafe and accommodation, you'd typically have people kick around in the job for about six months, so in terms of saving dollars for the business and being a good business decision, it works." This is a classic example of how small-scale, locally based, and independently owned businesses are the primary drivers of neighbourhood job creation.

Strum's mission to provide gainful employment in an economically depressed neighbourhood made her a leading contender to win the em-ployment category in the 2011 Small Business, Big Impact Challenge, a joint venture between Scotiabank and the Atlantic chapter of the Canadian Federation of Independent Business.

Not Just Dollars but Sense

Fred Connors, proprietor of Fred Salon and Whet Cafe on Agricola, shares Strum's commitment to the North End community. Both have advocated strenuously for the establishment of a neighbourhood BIA, but neither has let the lack of such an organization stop them from roll-ing out their own initiatives.

In Connors's case, those initiatives include breakfast and mentoring programs for inner-city youth, as well as frequent fundraising events for non-profit groups like Adsum, an organization dedicated to helping women and children who are homeless or at risk of being so. Fred Salon, which includes gallery space, is an ideal location for art and music-based fundraisers, and Connors believes that engaging the community in this way has paid business dividends.

"I realized that this was a much more positive way to advertise our values as a business than traditional advertising ever could be," he says.

Connors admits that the bottom-line benefits are more intuitive than concrete, but he's a believer nonetheless – especially considering that his upscale shop is located in one of the city's hard-luck areas. "I can't look at my investments in community groups in terms of dollars. If I'm working with a community group and we've fundraised $13,000 for them to mentor youth away from violence through the arts, am I going to get that $13,000 back? Am I going to see $13,000 in increased reve-nues as a result of that initiative? No. But will I see less disenfranchised youth on the street beating people up? Absolutely. And as we see less violent youth in neighbourhoods, do we tend to see more families and more pedestrians and more moms in strollers? Absolutely."

Connors doesn't think his long view of the relationship between his business and the surrounding community is especially radical. "I want people to be supported so they can continue to be our customers and feel like they belong in this neighbourhood. The more people who feel they belong here, the longer I'm going to be able to be here.

"It just makes sense to me."

The Hub: A Case Study in Doing Well by Doing Good

In Halifax, small businesses have played a key role in helping not only society's less fortunate, but also each other. Nowhere is this more evident than at The Hub, the aforementioned independently operated Halifax node of an international network whose locations give professionals a place to work, interact, and dream. Headed by Joanne Macrae and located on Barrington Street, The Hub, which opened in 2009, is an open-concept office space complete with computer terminals, boardrooms, and a functional kitchen. Hub members, who pay $125 for every thirty hours they use the space, can come here to work on side projects outside of traditional work hours, hold professional meetings, or build their own business from the ground up.[4]

The idea, says Macrae, is to put different brains from the local community together in unlikely combinations and see what they come up with. "What we wanted to do was get as diverse a group as possible within the same space," she says. "What happens when a lawyer's sitting next to a graphic designer who's sitting next to a software developer who's sitting next to someone from a small non-profit?"

Occasionally, the answer is magic. Macrae cites the example of Mindsea, a mobile application development company created by three professionals who met at The Hub and came up with the idea for a phone app that told users when transit vehicles were due to arrive at their stop. Chipping away at the idea during Hub sessions and using The Hub as a business address, the Mindsea partners eventually developed a successful product – so successful that, by December of 2010, they were forced to relocate. Their "graduation" was, to Macrae, a bittersweet moment.

"We're not a space built for six employees working eight-thirty to five from Monday to Friday, and that's what [Mindsea] grew to," says Macrae. "We don't have a way for people to scale up to that level within here, even though we'd like to be able to keep people in the family." Macrae is so dedicated to her family that, despite her reservations about the efficacy of the Downtown Halifax Business Commission, she serves on its board. Outside of that, she has also canvassed area businesses tirelessly, introducing entrepreneurs to their neighbours and inviting them to the Hub for brainstorming sessions.

Individual Entrepreneurship and Social Connection

"In a meeting one night, there were two women sitting there, and one said to the other, 'Do you let people with food into your store?' " Macrae laughs. "It was just so basic, but sometimes being involved in your own business is very isolating."

Other times, however, being a business owner creates a reason to reach out, rather than withdraw, from one's community. Mimi Fautley, co-owner of The Loop, a knitting store on Barrington Street, considers her shop a hub of information for a niche market of wool-pullers. She's in the business of selling products, of course, but gets just as much satisfaction from the workshops The Loop runs.

"From a business perspective that aspect has been great, because we've been growing our market by teaching people how to do the thing we sell the stuff for," says Fautley. "It also gives us a chance to interact on a social level and connect people to each other in the classes. It adds a really rich dimension to a retail business that, at the heart, is about buying and selling things."

Fautley believes it's as important to maintain a connection with fellow business owners as it is with customers. She mentions the craft shop Deserres, located across the street, as well as two similar stores in the area, and says the relationships between the proprietors is strong enough that one store will refer customers to another. "It's very much a neighbourhood. I know my neighbours here as well as I know the neighbours on my street" (at her home in the North End).

Like so many of her fellow small business owners, Fautley has her frustrations with the city and with the slow pace of change in a neighbourhood that sorely needs and deserves it. Yet she remains committed to Barrington Street, committed to the Halifax downtown, committed to the idea that, on everything from socio-economic issues to giving other entrepreneurs a helping hand, the small business community holds the keys to the future.

"All the positive changes we've seen on Barrington since we've been here are a result of small businesses," she says.

After decades of waiting, change could finally be in store.

The Move to Create the City's First North End BIA: Election Night

On 6 May 2011, voting on the establishment of a new business improvement district in Halifax's North End was completed. The vote
resulted in the creation of the city's eighth BIA, dubbed the North End
Business Association (NEBA). But the birth carried with it some bit-
terness, as the Hydrostone district, a patch of upscale stores, opted
out of the group. Apparently, property owners in the area saw no advantage to forming an association that would require them to share
their brand with their more rugged neighbours on Gottingen-Agricola.
"It was a bit of a downer," admitted Bernard Smith, who led the
charge for the creation of NEBA. Nevertheless, after years of painstak-
ing effort by the likes of Smith, Michelle Strum, and Fred Connors,
two struggling neighbourhoods in the North End were finally united.
Work could be done – the formalization of budgets, priorities, and
subcommittees – and small businesses in the area could move forward with a *collective voice*.

What that voice says will be both similar to and different from the
vocalizations of Halifax's other BIAs. The North End, with its com-
paratively cheap rents, unkempt buildings, and reputation for crime,
has the potential to become a playground for artists and start-up companies. A more cynical point of view, however, would be that it has
enormous potential to be whitewashed by gentrification. Prior to the
successful BIA vote, Strum explained that she wanted to see the area's
fortunes improve while continuing to support its current residents.

"Everyone wants clean, safe, vibrant communities, and that's our
biggest reason for doing this," says Strum of why she's worked so hard
to support the BIA. "This whole area has more residents than businesses, and it's much more of a work-live community."

The fledgling NEBA had a busy first year of existence. It organized
neighbourhood clean-ups and outreach initiatives. It staked out a public position to limit rising commercial property assessments, which
Smith believes may be the result of assessors anticipating the windfall
from the massive shipbuilding contract awarded to Halifax by the federal government in 2011. NEBA has also voiced its concerns over proposed bicycle lanes that could limit parking spots the organization
believes are essential for business, arguing that bike lanes should go on
smaller streets rather than major arteries. Regardless of outcomes,
NEBA has inserted itself into the conversation about the future of the
North End.

"Having advocacy, having a voice, there's always something useful about it," says Smith. "Suddenly now, business has a voice."

Smith says that the wobbly beginning of the North End BIA had him dreading the group's first Annual General Meeting. But he was pleasantly surprised. "Everyone was enthusiastic. Even the people I knew that voted against it were [now] supporting it."[5]

The new BIA has shown individual businesses in the North End that there is strength in numbers. And there's some evidence to suggest that municipal government, so long a whipping post for small business owners and BIA leaders, is coming to recognize that strength. Jim Donovan, the city's manager of economic development, appeared at the information session for prospective North End BIA members and pledged his support for small business. A false veneer of sincerity may be a politician's gift, but Donovan appeared to be genuine, and the passing of the five-year Economic Strategy proposed by the Greater Halifax Partnership could be a small step in changing the relationship between entrepreneurs and council from adversarial to amicable.

Rebirth in the Downtown Core: Is the Timing Right?

Over in the heart of downtown, developer Louis Reznick, whose Starfish Properties owns several buildings on Barrington Street, has begun to move forward on a handful of projects, including a renovation of the historic Roy Building. Important development is also taking place up on Spring Garden, with ground broken early in 2011 on a mixed-use residential and commercial building that promises to bring more commercial activity – and resident customers – to the downtown core. Across the harbour, developer Frances Fares has begun his massive King's Wharf project, a blend of high-rise residential and commercial buildings that could benefit small businesses by increasing both customer base and available retail space.

Paul Mackinnon, executive director of the Downtown Halifax Business Commission, says that, despite the oft-reported "death of Barrington Street," he's getting more calls from proprietors interested in opening up shop there. As more previously unusable old buildings get a cosmetic and functional makeover, there will be more space for these new occupants. Mackinnon's expectation is that most of these new arrivals in the coming years will be small businesses.

"Our focus is, how do we promote this area as one that's open to entrepreneurs? We want to make it the place where people come and try new ideas, as opposed to trying to convince a national chain to come here.

"I think we have turned the corner," Mackinnon adds. "A year ago, that was when we had our peak vacancy period. In the last year, I think six businesses have opened up in the district."

Having more quirky, independent shops figures to make downtown Halifax more appealing to non-retail businesses like Mike Hachey's Egg Films – businesses packed with urbane, affluent professionals eager to explore their surroundings. Reznick's proposed re-imagination of the Roy Building as an "e-learning centre" could be home to some of these new-economy, white-collar workplaces. "They want more digital-type companies in these buildings," says Hachey.

"You need businesses like ours that continue to go to the more independent shops," Hachey continues, noting that he and his employees once spent $55,000 in a single year at a single local pub and restaurant, the Economy Shoe Shop on Argyle Street. "That's what downtown Halifax brings, and eventually it'll be even better as Barrington continues to be developed."

BIAs and the Move of Entrepreneurs beyond
the Traditional Urban Core

Certain marketing trends also appear to favour the growth of small business communities in Halifax's less (outwardly) trendy urban areas. Nancy Tissington, executive director of the Spring Garden Area Business Association, identifies the increasing desire on the part of consumers to buy local as a trend her membership can capitalize on through joint marketing efforts. "When you come to Spring Garden, you get that local, independent, grassroots feel."

Tissington also mentions social media, which has allowed small business operators to connect with each other and with customers. The power of applications like Facebook and Twitter as direct and collective marketing – and community-building – tools is substantial, as evidenced by the way the Two If By Sea cafe in downtown Dartmouth used them to build a customer base.

The neighbourhood is one of Halifax's neglected urban areas, and cafe owners Zane Kelsall and Tara Macdonald were inundated with negative predictions about the prospects for success for their gourmet coffee and baked-goods business in such a neighbourhood. Rather than heed these warnings, however, Kelsall and Macdonald banked on the pride of Dartmouth residents and the ubiquity of Facebook and Twitter, reaching out to potential customers and building an online community in the months prior to opening in the fall of 2009.

There was a long line-up when the doors opened at Two If By Sea, and it has continued ever since. Kelsall and Macdonald, who sell t-shirts and pins emblazoned with "I (heart symbol) Dartmouth" in addition to coffee and croissants, say their belief in community and facility with social media were critical to their success. Their success has also created a small shift in the perception of the neighbourhood, often referred to as "The Dark Side" of Halifax. "One of our staff members' dads called it 'a little pocket of culture,' which I think is pretty apt," says Kelsall.

"I think the neighbourhood is really transforming, and I think our business has played a vital role in showing that it's okay to take a risk on the neighbourhood."

Is There a Common Thread?

Is there a unifying principle running through the varied stories about small business in the city of Halifax? If there is it starts with the concept of "risk." It's an essential element of – indeed, a prerequisite for – change. It's also an inherent component of small business ownership, which is why entrepreneurs are especially qualified to lead the charge in improving their local communities. Business Improvement Associations are a risky proposition, resulting as they do in the implementation of additional levies that property and business owners must trust will be applied wisely. That the North End business community voted to join the BIA movement suggests that, as bumpy as the road has been for such commissions in Halifax, the value of a unified voice outweighs the risk.

The specific actions of a BIA or an individual business are also often risky. Bernard Smith and the SGABA took a chance in developing the Navigator program, in providing outreach to needy Haligonians rather than trying to lock them up, out of sight of business owners and customers. Michelle Strum has taken risks by hiring inexperienced employees. Fred Connors has invested his time and money to support socially conscious initiatives. Zane Kelsall and Tara Macdonald took a risk on opening an unlikely business in a forgotten neighbourhood. All of these risky decisions have been rewarded with improvements to both the bottom lines of entrepreneurs and the communities they operate in.

Main Street Halifax: Charting Its Own Way Forward

We have seen in this chapter that Halifax is a challenging place for small businesses to operate, with high rates of taxation relative to services, thick government bureaucracy, a population base that has expanded out into the suburbs, and a generally conservative attitude towards new ideas among the many obstacles. Yet it is a city that has embraced the notion of the Business Improvement Association, with various BIAs producing results that have left small business owners sometimes frustrated but mostly buoyed. We have examined the way the innovative Navigator program has changed one urban neighbourhood, and heard from several individual entrepreneurs about the positive role they wish to play in the social and cultural milieus of the communities that surround them. We have seen that Halifax is a proud old city searching for a way into the future, with small business at the forefront of the struggle for viability and vitality.

The next chapters in this section of the book will take us to Vancouver and Toronto and will explore issues such as the source of community leadership (bottom-up versus top-down) and the idea of "place-making." While these notions will be discussed in more depth in subsequent pages, the examination of Halifax in this chapter is, we hope, a useful precursor, an example for readers to bear in mind as they make their journey westward – figuratively speaking – through the book. After all, Halifax exemplifies what it means for the creativity and passion of small business owners to chafe against unimaginative governance. And Halifax – despite a rich history – is a place still in need of making.

Halifax Postscript

A few things have changed in Halifax since the bulk of the reporting for this chapter was completed. The evolution is statistical and anecdotal, visible in research reports and on the city's streets, and in the interest of providing the most accurate picture possible of where Halifax currently stands, we'll briefly enumerate some of these changes here.

In terms of statistics, updated numbers from the 2011 Census and the Canadian Federation of Independent Business have been included in the chapter itself. The CFIB update shows a slightly more confident business community than existed in previous years. However, a reduction in pessimism doesn't equate to outright optimism, and Nova

Scotia still trails most of its provincial peers on the CFIB's positive-feelings metrics.

Change has also swept through government at both the municipal and provincial levels. Mike Savage, a former Member of Parliament for the federal Liberal Party, easily won a 2012 election to become mayor of Halifax. Replacing the scandal-plagued, suburb-focused Peter Kelly, Savage has shown an inclination to engage Haligonians in discussions about the kinds of communities they wish to create. He also has deep ties to political and business elites, and voters and small business owners will be interested to see how he balances his grassroots charm and his establishment pedigree. A year after Savage took office, the provincial Liberal Party swept the New Democrats out of government, winning a majority for new Premier Stephen McNeil. It is too early to draw any conclusions a few months into the Liberals' tenure, but the party will certainly have their hands on policy levers that are relevant to small business.

A tour of the Halifax streets indicates that at least a few more entrepreneurs are trying to imprint themselves on the city's culture. In recent months, several new restaurants and bars have opened, many of them sporting inventive menus and an ambience geared to a younger crowd. Such establishments have created a palpably different feeling on streets like Gottingen and Agricola. And in that community, the North End Business Association has given merchants an organized voice despite some instability in its executive ranks.

Encouraging for these fledgling businesses is an increase in the number of downtown residential developments. Residents have begun to populate new condominiums in the North End and Dartmouth, and, on Barrington Street in the heart of downtown, the historic Roy Building is set to be rebuilt as a condominium-commercial hybrid. If these projects succeed in bringing a financially stable residential base back to the city core, small businesses could benefit from both foot traffic and the fact that politicians will have a larger, more invested group of urban residents to answer to.

Not all the news is good, though. Many or most of the new businesses that have sprung up have displaced failed ventures. The Hub, the Barrington Street business incubator that seemed to offer an ideal home to flexible and ambitious members of the creative class, decided to downsize early in 2014 in the face of a funding shortfall, moving out of its offices and reducing its services. New development projects continue to be criticized for exceeding height restrictions laid out in the city's planning documents. Controversy rages over the new convention centre project that has broken ground, an initiative that supporters like Mayor Savage say will be a boon to businesses large and small – and that detractors, pointing to projections by independent auditors, claim will be a money-losing boondoggle for generations of taxpayers.

Still, Halifax has seen some promising changes, and there is no doubting the opportunity for place-making in this time of transition.

4 The View from Main Street Vancouver: A City Region with an Emerging Sense of Place[1]

On a warm day in late March, just as the sun begins to heat the sand on the shores of Harrison Lake after a long and gloomy "wet coast" winter, about 150 local government officials, politicians, bureaucrats, academics, and other progressives gather at the annual Progressive Governance Forum in Harrison Hot Springs (see exhibit 4.1) organized by the Centre for Civic Governance. The list of attendees is impressive and includes mayors and councillors from the largest municipalities in British Columbia and leading intellectuals in the field of community "place-making" and sustainability.

In attendance are speakers such as Michael Shuman, director of research and public policy at the Business Alliance for Local Living Economies (BALLE) and author of *The Small-Mart Revolution: How Local Businesses Are Beating the Global Competition*; Mark Lakeman, architect and the brains behind the revolutionary "City Repair" initiative in Portland, Oregon; Councillor Andrea Reimer from the City of Vancouver; Mayor Darrell Mussatto from the City of North Vancouver; and Mayor Derek Corrigan from the City of Burnaby, to name a few.

The 2011 forum theme is "place-making," and this is not coincidental. For decades now, architects and planners have talked about the key role that urban design plays in shaping the public realm – including everything from how we move around to how we see ourselves and our neighbours – and determining the business and economic opportunities that are available to us. At its core, place-making is about the identity of a location and the implications that identity has for the individual residents and businesses, all of which are interconnected and interact in a complex social web. This concept of place-making and its importance – particularly to small retail-based businesses in our municipal cores – is one that is just starting to be uncovered by city governments and small business.

Place-making reaffirms that the neighbourhood where you choose to locate your store, cafe, or restaurant is the most critically important decision a small-scale entrepreneur can make. Often before opening a business, the proprietor puts much thought into the development of a business plan, including consideration of the customer base, market, and business location. Yet, neighbourhoods that statistically appear quite similar somehow attract different residents, visitors, customers, and employees – all of whom are critical to the long-term viability of a business, independently of the strength of an "individual business plan." Moreover, neighbourhoods and communities are always changing and evolving, making the effect even more important over the long run.

Making Sense of the Places We Live and Work In

A few short blocks away from the forum hotel, Robert and Sonja Reyerse run a quaint bed-and-breakfast operation right in the centre of the village core in Harrison Hot Springs. Robert and Sonja are small business owners who clearly understand the importance to their business of neighbourhood-wide improvements and place-making. Between the two, they are actively involved with the local Chamber of Commerce, the local tourism destination marketing organization, and local municipal politics – Sonja is a councillor. A brief conversation with Robert or Sonja reveals their passion for the community. As small business owners they understand that the success of their enterprise is fundamentally tied to the well-being and success of the community as a whole, and that their business identity or brand is connected to the community's identity. Their work to support village renewal, beach redevelopment, business networking, and public community events and festivals within the municipality exemplifies their understanding of how critical place-making is for their business success.

Sociologists like Richard Jenkins have long argued that without social identity there is no human world.[2] The way we understand who we are as individuals and how we see others are vital social processes. Without the framework of social similarities and differences, people would be unable to relate to each other in a consistent and meaningful fashion and distinguish between business identities. Just as human identity is both individual and collective, so are business identities and community identities – they exist in the context of both singular and plural.

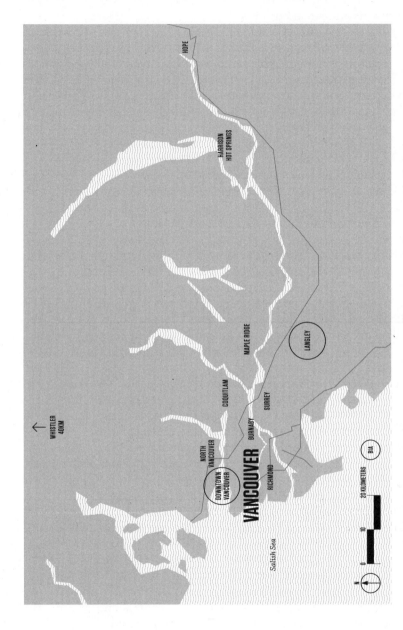

Exhibit 4.1: The Greater Vancouver metropolitan region. The areas highlighted include some of the areas and neighbourhoods profiled in this chapter.

In Jenkins's own words, "identifying ourselves or others is a matter of meaning, and meaning always involves interaction: agreement and disagreement, conversation and innovation, communication and negotiation."[3] Identities and reputations are ongoing processes that are always evolving. This understanding of identity and the processes of ongoing change at an individual human level, as well as at an individual business level and a collective community or place-making level, is critical to business success – as those in marketing and corporate branding probably understand best.

How we perceive our personal identity determines what we consume and where/how we acquire a product or a service, and this has implications for businesses and the communities in which they are located. That is why certain people prefer specific businesses and choose to live and shop in specific communities.

Of course, identity is a highly complex and multifaceted matrix, but the point is that individuals, businesses, and communities do not exist in a vacuum but continuously interact with, reinforce, and change their own and each other's identities.

This is a roundabout way of saying that place-making is at the core of business development and that small business leaders should pay attention to it and how it impacts their bottom line.

The Vancouver Region: Place-Making and Local Economic Development in Context

We started this discussion about place-making and business development in the metropolitan region of Vancouver in the small municipality of Harrison Hot Springs some ninety minutes' drive from downtown Vancouver. This was done for two reasons. First, place-making is easier to discuss in the context of a small, well-defined community such as Harrison Hot Springs. Second, Vancouver is an interesting Canadian metropolitan anomaly, harder to define as a city than as a region. Unlike other major metropolitan centres in Canada, the Vancouver region has not adopted the amalgamated megacity model that Toronto, Halifax, Ottawa, Hamilton, Winnipeg, Calgary, and Edmonton have. Instead, metropolitan Vancouver is a federated system made up of two inter-municipal regional districts: Metro Vancouver Regional District and the Fraser Valley Regional District. This, it turns out, makes a big difference.

The Metro Vancouver Regional District (formally the Greater Vancouver Regional District) – which administers some resources and services that are shared across the metropolitan area – such as community planning, water, sewage, drainage, housing, transportation, air quality, and parks – is made up of twenty-one incorporated municipalities, including the City of Vancouver, and one unincorporated area. According to the 2006 census, some 2,116,581 people call the regional district their home (of that, only 578,041 people live within the City of Vancouver). Some of the fastest-growing areas in the Vancouver metropolis are in the Fraser Valley suburbs within and beyond the eastern boundaries of Metro Vancouver, in municipalities such as Surrey, Langley, Abbotsford, Mission, and Chilliwack. In fact, it is expected that the City of Surrey will exceed the population of the City of Vancouver in less than ten years.

Just east of Metro Vancouver is the Fraser Valley Regional District with an additional population of 257,031 people, according to the 2006 census. Today, because of the growth of the Fraser Valley Regional District, its six municipalities and eight electoral areas almost seamlessly blend with the Metro Vancouver Regional District.

Collectively the two regional districts make up what could be called the Greater Vancouver metropolitan region, which stretches from the gulf waters of the Pacific Ocean to the District of Hope, some 160 kilometres from the shoreline. Although unusual, the regional district system has proven to be successful in British Columbia over the last forty years. The Vancouver metropolitan region is not only one of the fastest-growing urban areas in Canada, as measured by population growth and urban expansion,[4] it is one of the fastest-growing in North America as well. But growth like that comes with substantial environmental, social, and economic pressures. Ongoing tensions include the increasingly multicultural face of the region, as well as the growth of development on some of the best agricultural land in a province where only one-quarter of the land is suitable for any form of farming.

When it comes to the economy, there is also a growing dichotomy between the metropolitan Vancouver region and the rest of the province. Historically, the British Columbia economy has been primarily resource-based and dominated by the logging, mining, and fishing industries. For most of the province this is still the case. In contrast, southwestern British Columbia and metropolitan Vancouver are now service-oriented, with a strong reliance on personal and corporate services, including sectors such as tourism, the film industry, education, transportation, and the growing "green" sector.

From the point of view of business development and place-making, the metropolitan Vancouver region provides a range of opportunities for the small-scale entrepreneur within this complex mosaic of cities, towns, villages, and neighbourhoods, each with its own economic narrative. Within the region many municipal governments and business owners are starting to work closely together in an effort to support and grow the existing local economy, entice other businesses into their jurisdiction, and make the area more attractive to employees and residents. It might seem obvious, but without a functioning local economy, communities suffer.

Gaëtan Royer, former manager of metropolitan planning, environment, and parks for Metro Vancouver, has been a vocal advocate of municipal financial restructuring. For Royer, municipalities derive minimal direct benefit from local economic development initiatives, which is why he's not convinced that municipalities should actively try to promote local economic development.[5] Royer points out that the benefits of lower unemployment flow to the federal and provincial governments, as they collect income tax. Higher business activity and sales benefit both the federal and provincial governments, as they also collect sales tax – in British Columbia's case, federal Goods and Services Tax (GST) and Provincial Sales Tax (PST). However, traditional economic development has little impact on the largest source of municipal revenues, property tax. As a result, in the current context, Royer argues that municipalities have few incentives to develop and grow local economies. They do it because they have a holistic view of their communities and because municipalities realize that it's simply the right thing to do. And, perhaps more importantly, they do it because it's crucial for place-making and because secondhand stores, pawn shops, and run-down commercial streetscapes don't create vibrant street life.

Forward-thinking municipalities realize that the right mix of attractive commercial and residential development does eventually lead to higher municipal revenues through greater property assessments and property tax. It is here that Royer makes an especially prescient point: municipal access to sales tax revenues would properly incentivize economic development for local governments and would probably benefit all levels of government as a result – particularly given the extreme service downloading from senior levels of government that has occurred over the last decade. Despite the challenges for municipalities, local economic development is in fashion within the metropolitan Vancouver region, and it has become highly popular to talk about the local economy. But what constitutes a successful economic development plan or determines the success of one particular city over another?

Macro-economic factors such as globalization and shifting markets are often the main culprits pointed to when explaining why some local economies do better than others. However, research into local economies shows that global shifts alone fail to explain the divergent economic realities faced by communities, particularly at the regional level. This is because local economies are also affected by factors such as population dynamics, local identities, and cultural and natural environments.[6] Naturally, how a community responds to global and local changes and whether that response is effective is conditioned by a number of internal variables.[7] A community's local leadership, history, institutions, and internal and external networks can all affect its capacity to respond to change. According to Dutch author Ida Terluin, these local responses "depend to a large degree on the structural and institutional make-up of a community, its history, the local leadership, and how the effects of restructuring are interpreted: as a threat or as an opportunity."[8]

Although it has become common in British Columbia to talk about the "local economy," it's not always clear what is meant by this term. To help clarify the meaning of the term we have to break it down into its two constituent concepts: "local" and "economy." Let's begin with the idea of what's local.

What Exactly Do We Mean by "Local Economy"?

Of late it seems that everyone is talking about what's local: local food, local businesses, local services –the list goes on. Some people like to think of "local" in terms of bioregionalism, or naturally defined regions such as watersheds, soil, or terrain type. The truth is that perceptions of localness vary, especially when we are talking about different commodities. Local energy might mean energy that is developed within the province, whereas local food often means food cultivated in the region. As discussed in chapter 1 (see exhibit 1.2), the local scale speaks to our understanding of community and place, and it also speaks to place-making and our connection to our community. Although distance must enter into our strategic vision, the idea of local tends to reflect our ideas about community and the shared benefits we reap when we work on building our communities.

The word "economy" is perhaps more straightforward and refers to the processes of the production, consumption, exchange, and distribution of goods and services. Generally we speak of the "global economy" or the "national economy," though recently the idea of the "regional economy" or the "local economy" or the "community economy" has become popular. Thinking about our economies at the local level means focusing on how goods and services are produced, consumed, exchanged, and distributed in the places where we live and/or work. The focus is on how neighbourhoods, cities, or regional districts evolve and how these systems might be improved. How is wealth created within the local economy? How and why does it leave the community? Are local economic systems serving our collective interests? How can we strengthen our local economies?

These are just some of the questions that communities within the metropolitan Vancouver region as a whole are attempting to understand.

Local Vending Regulation: A Case Study in Real Local Economic Development

In the City of Vancouver a new policy to encourage street vending as a means of bringing the community together is a good example of local economic development in the truest sense. The newly allowed sidewalk mobile kiosks provide great food options while at the same time facilitating opportunities for social interaction. The street vending municipal policy is well-balanced, and the process of awarding permits is based on a score card that takes into account factors such as food safety; innovation in menu; nutritional content; use of local, organic, and fair trade foods; as well as vending location and waste-reduction strategies. To encourage street vending, the city implemented an active media campaign, including the use of some social media techniques such as the Street Food Vancouver app software program designed for both iPhone and iPad that allows users to learn about street food vendors around town in an interactive way.

While the vending story is a classic case of promoting urban self-sufficiency through smart municipal regulations, the metropolitan Vancouver economy functions within broader national and provincial economies. While some people might espouse the goal of self-sufficiency above all else when discussing the local economy, the fact is that, for now, local economies in metropolitan Vancouver rely on relationships with external markets. The trick, however, is to learn how to keep more money within the local economy while at the same time maintaining foreign export and tourist links, thereby moving towards true self-sufficiency. A focus on local economies is not about protectionism but rather about creating and sustaining vibrant communities that we all want to live, work, and play in, and travel to, regardless of how well (or how poorly) the macro-economic or global economy is doing. This is the point that many in the provincial business community have not fully comprehended and supported.

For British Columbia, a province endowed with abundant natural resources, the staple economy has shaped the province. All across British Columbia, towns and regions grew out of the foreign appetite for resources, and this induced the development of a resource-based economy. The problem with the staple model is that communities can become overly dependent on external demand for the resources they extract and export. Things may be going fine when there is sufficient demand, but when global growth falters, the effects on local communities can be devastating. As such, this model of development does not foster economic resilience, nor is it very sustainable.

However, some communities without abundant natural resources may have certain locally produced goods or provide specific services that others cannot offer as efficiently. Usually, economic specialization grows out of community-specific features such as geography, climate, access to markets, availability of labour skills, and other factors.[9]

By exporting products and services and engaging in what is known as primary economic activities, urban communities earn income that can then be used for local spending on products and services intended for local consumption or for reinvestment in human, social, physical, and ecological capital. Thus, metropolitan Vancouver's external revenues from exports and local sources, such as retirement savings and social assistance, allow for the establishment of services intended for local consumption – what are known as secondary economic activities, such as day care, restaurants, and construction. These are the main principles of the traditional local economic development model. The question is, can we do better?

Local Government and Small Business: From Adversity to Partnership

Back in Harrison Hot Springs at the Progressive Governance Forum, the discussion has turned to new efforts to strengthen local economies and to ways in which the local businesses can also help achieve community sustainability goals. Indeed, the goals of moving towards environmental, social, and economic sustainability compel us to consider how our economic system works and the roles played by various actors in that process. Do our economic activities help or hinder our ability to protect the environment and quality of life? Do our economic activities build on our strengths as a community? These are some of the questions that are now being discussed at the regional level. Of course, these are high-level questions that are not easily answered. In fact, we are now only beginning to scratch the surface of the complex and multifaceted topic that we call sustainability.

We now know that supporting and growing the local economy can also indirectly bolster sustainability goals and aid in the establishment of more "complete" communities, in the sense of providing for most of the amenities required of a local population. A healthier local economy leads to a broader and larger tax base for local governments, and greater tax revenue means more funds for local governments to carry out other initiatives, initiatives that can further support economic and social development.

Local governments and businesses in metropolitan Vancouver are starting to understand that their goals are indeed aligned. For too long the business community and local governments have had an adversarial relationship. A case in point is the recent initiative in the City of Vancouver to develop separated bike lanes on Dunsmuir Viaduct, Dunsmuir Street, Hornby Street, and Burrard Bridge to allow easier access for cyclists into the downtown core. The initiative first met with strong opposition from the business community. The concerns over loss of on-street parking space and vehicle lanes resulted in a strong push-back against the city's policy to diversify modes of transportation and move away from single-occupancy vehicles. The city's current plan to become the greenest jurisdiction in North America was in jeopardy as a result of a lobby – spearheaded by downtown businesses that could not see how their interests would be served by these new transportation priorities and policies.

The debate over transportation and access to downtown is not new, however. The City of Vancouver is one of the few major cities in North America without freeways. In the early 1970s, the city and its residents killed the plans to connect the downtown core with the inner-ring suburbs with an American-style system of freeway networks in favour of public transit and alternative transportation solutions. Today, this absence of a freeway network into the downtown largely shapes Vancouver's identity and image. It is also one of the major reasons for Vancouver's high quality-of-life ratings.

Today the cold, adversarial relationship between local governments and the business community is starting to slowly warm up. More and more businesses are realizing that basic municipal issues such as land-use planning, transportation, and recreation services do have implications for their financial bottom line. Moreover, businesses are starting to see that sustainable municipal services are important to their long-term viability. Those business leaders who see the big picture understand that low taxes are not always in their best interest – while value for money and essential services are. This realization is leading to a new local development model that is increasingly concerned about local issues and place-making.

Giving Local Government the Right Policy "Tools"

Local government is the level of government that is closest to the people. Local government officials often have an intimate understanding of the issues affecting their communities. They see at first hand how an external factor affects the well-being of residents, whether that factor is a booming housing market, high unemployment, or cuts to social services. Business leaders are also starting to connect these dots. For example, the green image of metropolitan Vancouver is attracting both the creative-services workforce and clean technology business firms, companies such as Vancouver-based Nexterra Energy Corporation, Burnaby-based Lignol Energy Corporation, and the Surrey-based Endurance Wind Power.

Unfortunately, Canada's political structures fail to recognize that local governments are those best positioned to find solutions to the challenges communities face. In the case of local economies, senior levels of government often make the most important decisions, whether they concern a trade agreement, deregulation, or infrastructure. Although communities feel the impacts of these decisions, local governments very rarely have a meaningful say in their design. To make matters even more difficult, as previously discussed, local governments are forced to rely on property taxes to generate most of the revenue needed to fund the services and infrastructure that support urban economic activity, since, despite all the service downloading from senior levels of government, local governments today only receive about eight cents of every tax dollar raised in Canada.[10]

Indeed, current government arrangements largely impede the ability of metropolitan Vancouver communities and other Canadian cities to respond effectively to economic challenges. Those within the business community should be concerned about this; they need to become active advocates for a governance structure that would support local accountability and economic sustainability with a double devolution – a shift in resources and responsibilities away from the federal government to provincial and territorial governments and from provincial and territorial governments to local governments. Until this devolution occurs, however, communities will have to find ways to support their local economies with the tools and instruments they have at their disposal. In this respect, local governments in metropolitan Vancouver have shown that, despite the constraints they face, they are able to make a positive difference. It turns out that if they act creatively, local governments do have a number of tools and instruments they can use to support local economic development.

Researcher Michael Jacobs identifies four categories of tools and instruments available to local governments: regulations, voluntary instruments, expenditures, and financial incentives.[11] The first two categories of policy tools (regulations and voluntary instruments) do not necessarily require extensive monetary support. However, the latter two (expenditures and financial incentives) can be costly for local governments and the community residents they represent. All these instruments can be used in conjunction with one another, but doing so requires a mix of vision, creativity, outside-the-box thinking, determination, and perseverance on the part of local leaders. For businesses, understanding that local governments have tools and instruments to influence local development is critical, as these tools can help improve the economic landscape within the community and provide business opportunities.

Getting Local Economic Development Offices Involved

To address the challenge of local economic development, local governments in metropolitan Vancouver commonly establish an economic development office. This is done voluntarily and often without provincial funding. Sometimes these organizations operate at arm's length from the local government and have their own staff and mandate. Economic development offices can undertake any number of initiatives, from engaging the community in long-term visioning, to providing coaching services, to establishing a community corporation. There really are very few limits on what community economic development offices can do, as long as actions are legal and aim to benefit the community as a whole. Most often they are responsible for business data research and collection, the development of business synergies, and the establishing of municipal policies and plans that are favourable to, or at least cognizant of, business interests and business marketing and promotions. These municipal economic development offices often work closely with local Chambers of Commerce and other local business interest groups such as Business Improvement Areas.

This is the case in communities like the City of Vancouver, the District of Mission, the City of Langley, and the City of New Westminster, among others. The structure, size, budget, and scope of work of these municipal agencies often vary. However, on a regional scale there are multiple local economic development offices that work to promote investment and business growth.

The popularity of municipal economic development offices speaks to the importance most municipalities within metropolitan Vancouver now assign to local business and economic development. While this may sound like an obvious no-brainer for cities, one must remember that this is not a traditional municipal service and there is little in the way of direct taxation and fiscal benefit for municipalities that encourage local economic growth. Most municipalities, however, see economic development as a prerequisite for creating sustainable communities and place-making.

There are also progressive regional economic development initiatives within metropolitan Vancouver, such as the Experience the Fraser Project. This initiative is designed to celebrate the Fraser River's cultural, recreational, and economic opportunities and to showcase and promote the lower Fraser River corridor as a tourism jewel. In 2009, the provincial government allocated $2 million towards the development of the concept plan for a 300-kilometre-long multi-use trail that would connect amenities in the District of Hope, the Strait of Georgia, and all the communities in between. As part of the initiative, two demonstration projects along the river took place in Historic Fort Langley and the District of Mission. The goal of this initiative is to improve the regional mobility infrastructure along the river, to build tourism capacity and infrastructure, and to grow respect for the Mighty Fraser among the waterfront communities. This initiative also presents fantastic eco-tourism opportunities.

To date the Experience the Fraser initiative has been met with great enthusiasm and support from all parties, although long-term financial support for it, especially from the provincial government, is uncertain. For such a project to be successful, long-term funding support is required from senior levels of government.

Community Economic Development Plans: The Next Step in Private-Public Partnership

Although some municipal economic development offices still see economic development in traditional terms, where any growth and jobs are welcomed, more and more municipal economic development in metropolitan Vancouver is focused on the principles of the community economic development (CED) movement.[12]

The CED does not prescribe a set of rules for how communities should proceed; rather, its focus is on facilitating a continuous, grassroots improvement process that aims to create a more resilient local economy. The Centre for Sustainable Community Development at Simon Fraser University, one of the B.C. region's local pioneers of this approach to development, offers this definition of CED:

> A process by which communities can initiate and generate their own solutions to their common economic problems, and thereby build long-term community capacity and foster the integration of economic, social, and environmental objectives.[13]

While CED focuses on the economic fortunes of a community, it also looks at qualitative aspects such as quality of life and social equality. CED emphasizes the community and the importance of place-making. As a process, CED focuses on ongoing, community-based strategic planning. For communities and businesses looking to take control of their local economies, CED offers eight basic principles that may help guide their efforts: (i) collective action, (ii) community building, (iii) localization, (iv) local participation, (v) efforts to reduce environmental impacts, (vi) asset-based development, (vii) campaigns that reinforce policy capacity building, and (viii) efforts that support networks and interactions within and between localities and their people.[14]

Although still relatively new, these CED principles are becoming the norm rather than the fringe within the economic development community in metropolitan Vancouver. It is not uncommon today within the region to see the CED principles form the core of local economic development plans and strategies. One key area of interest for municipal economic development offices that happens also to correlate well with CED principles is downtown and main street revitalization – a focus that also highlights another important "modern" urban development tool seen in our opening chapter and in the case of Halifax's efforts to revitalize its main streets, the Business Improvement Area.

BIAs and Revitalizing Main Street Districts

Beginning in the 1950s, with the advent of hyper car culture and the explosive growth of the suburbs, the downtowns of many metropolitan

Vancouver municipalities witnessed a steady decline in business as people moved out into the newly developed municipal peripheries. Suburbanization gave birth to multiple strip malls and, later, shopping malls and further contributed to the decline of the downtown and main streets. However, the late 1980s saw a gradual resurgence of downtowns and main streets in British Columbia with the creation of Business Improvement Areas (BIAs) and various other popular and successful urban revitalization initiatives.

BIAs, as we know from chapter 2, originated in Toronto, Ontario, in 1969. In 1988 British Columbia became the eighth province in Canada to introduce legislation allowing local governments to form BIAs. In 1989, Salmon Arm was the first B.C. community to establish a BIA. Later that year, Vancouver followed, with two BIAs in the neighbourhoods of Gastown and Mount Pleasant. Today, the BIA model has successfully expanded to various parts of British Columbia and, indeed, the world. There are BIA-like structures in the United States, the United Kingdom, South Africa, Holland, and Japan.

BIAs and Local Governance

Despite the now almost universal ubiquity of BIAs, most residents of or visitors to cities have probably never heard of them and are unaware of their purpose; yet most of us have lived in or visited areas and districts that they oversee. Certainly, BIAs and their popularity as economic development tools within metropolitan Vancouver raise important practical and theoretical questions about governance, the use of public space, public policy, municipal service delivery, and economic development. It appears that, over the last twenty years, BIAs have become synonymous with downtown and main street renewal in British Columbia. In fact, it would not be a stretch to conclude that, in some communities at least, BIAs have become another de facto level of government. Certainly, today, the BIA is a fundamental part of the governance structure of many communities in the region.

The success of the BIA concept speaks for itself. Today, when people think of the most vibrant, exciting, and happening areas of metropolitan Vancouver they would most likely hit on places under a BIA jurisdiction – areas such as Gastown, Robson Street, Cambie Street, Downtown Vancouver, Chinatown, Yaletown, Commercial Drive, and many others. These BIAs, and others in British Columbia, are member-led organizations that work to assist local business people and property owners in upgrading and promoting their businesses, shopping districts, and the overall vitality of their neighbourhoods. By focusing on place-making, they encourage trade, commerce, and socio-economic activity.

BIAs in British Columbia are created by local governments, usually upon the request of the local business community. They raise funds through mandatory membership levies based on assessed property values that are used to manage and enhance the business area. Individual BIAs in British Columbia determine their own funding arrangement in their by-laws. The by-laws and BIA structures are reviewed on a regular basis by the membership, often at the BIA annual general meeting when the board of directors is elected. With input from the membership and assistance from the BIA staff, it is the responsibility of the board of directors to oversee the operations of these organizations.

BIAs and Local Advocacy

As we saw in Halifax, BIAs in the Vancouver region have also played an important advocacy role, speaking out and raising awareness about issues that are important to the membership. By provincial regulation BIAs are required to be open and transparent organizations, particularly when it comes to finances. Every BIA in British Columbia is created with a predetermined mandate, time limit, and expiration date, or "sunset clause." A BIA's mandate can last for as long as twenty years, but is more commonly between five and seven years. As a result of the "term limited" nature of BIAs, boards and staff are tasked with undertaking a process to renew and, with membership support, effectively re-establish the mandate of the BIA for each subsequent term. As well, the host municipalities require the BIAs to provide annual financial statements for accountability purposes.

According to Business Improvement Areas of British Columbia (BIABC), the umbrella organization that represents all BIAs in the province, there are currently about fifty BIAs in British Columbia, of which about thirty-three are located in metropolitan Vancouver (the second-largest number after Toronto).

From the community's perspective, a BIA offers many advantages. As self-help organizations, they provide services to the community at little or no cost to local residents. For example, many BIAs within the region provide benches, flowers, banners, security, greater accessibility initiatives, marketing programs, festivals, and many other services that benefit the community as a whole. Of course, the businesses do this to create a climate conducive to shopping and to compete with the polished environments of regional shopping malls, but BIAs can also support localization and local economies. As seen in chapter 2, BIAs often focus on local business retention and promotion as well as the overall economic health of the shopping district by promoting "buy local" campaigns and marketing properties that are available for redevelopment.

BIAs and the Turning of the Suburban Mall Concept on Its Head

Interestingly, although the BIAs started out as initiatives to help main street and downtown businesses to compete with major shopping malls through place-making, today, forward-thinking retail space developers and mall operators, such as Shape Properties Corporation in Vancouver, are applying lessons learned from successful main street redevelopment to revitalize old covered shopping malls and design new shopping centres that are greener, pedestrian oriented, and connected to community.

Shopping malls such as the new Highstreet in Abbotsford are blurring the lines between main street and shopping centre experiences by injecting flavours of place-making and community into suburban mall developments, while in the process reshaping suburbs and further redefining the traditional town square. This type of innovation in shopping mall design will keep shopping malls relevant and competitive but will also pose a competitive threat to downtown and traditional shopping districts. If shopping malls are able to establish a unique sense of place and create more human-scale experiences while blurring the line between organic and created culture, the downtown and local shopping districts will lose a key competitive advantage – as destinations that offer a uniquely authentic, individualized, culturally familiar experience on a human scale.

The Importance of Understanding BIAs on Their Own Terms and in Their Own Local Culture

That BIAs do not fit neatly into any previously established categories or boxes is by now probably quite obvious. As local business advocacy groups, BIAs are probably most closely comparable to the local chambers of commerce mentioned earlier; and yet BIAs are much different and more complex, in that their membership levy is mandatory and because they deliver many public "goods" to both members and the community at large. The BIA mandates, structures, priorities, accountability measures, and activities probably more closely resemble those of local governments or trade unions. In fact, BIAs in the metropolitan

Vancouver area are struggling with many of the same issues as local governments and traditional unions, issues such as service downloading, member apathy, funding for services and initiatives, social issues (homelessness, crime, security), land-use issues such as neighbourhood aesthetics, and promotion and marketing of the jurisdiction.

A final word of caution should therefore be sounded before we end our discussion of the broader B.C. BIA movement. Though there is value in trying to understand BIAs as a movement on their own, one should always remember that BIAs exist in particular environments that determine their opportunity structures. A more complete picture of the BIA and its impact on a locality can only be achieved if one includes local host community conditions (such as infrastructure evaluations, service-provision levels, and so on) as well as more macro provincial, national, and international environmental factors (such as the economic system and trends, prevailing ideological beliefs, the political system, and constitutional factors, among others). For example, a preliminary finding related to the BIAs in the region is that the number of members affects the amount of funds and political powers available to a BIA and, in turn, the level of services to its members and the community and the efficiency and transparency with which they are delivered. Moreover, determining the perfect or optimal BIA membership size is difficult without a comprehensive understanding of the environmental conditions in which BIAs operate.

The existence of BIAs is often explained and justified by the need to deliver services that are not provided by the public sector or that are not delivered by the public sector efficiently. To prove this or the contrary, and to achieve a deeper understanding of BIAs as an economic tool, a mixture of quantitative and qualitative analysis of BIA environmental conditions is required, and to date there has been very little research in this area. What is interesting is that the BIA movement is helping to draw some fundamentally important connections between place-making and economic development.

Before we conclude, let us briefly examine three case studies of BIAs in metropolitan Vancouver that are doing just that.

Vancouver BIAs: Three Cases of Place-Making in Action

Downtown Langley

The Downtown Langley Merchants Association (DLMA) focuses its efforts on attracting new customers to the area, improving accessibility to the district, and branding. This vibrant shopping district association represents some 600 unique shops. The DLMA works cooperatively with many community groups and the City of Langley to promote and enhance the area and is one of the groups that were consulted in the development of the Downtown Langley Master Plan.

But the DLMA does more than advocate. It promotes a strong community identity and gives back to the local community by putting on annual community events such as the Magic of Christmas Parade. The DLMA is a strong economic development and community building agent because the organization focuses on improving the experience of visitors, residents, and the business community.

By focusing on developing the downtown of Langley as a unique and a desirable place to experience, the DLMA has been able to develop a "product" that is easier to market and promote for both shopping and redevelopment purposes. And in the process they have also developed a more committed clientele that buys into the vision of a community that is tightly interlinked and connected to similar aspirations for the future.

Burnaby Heights

Similar things can also be said for other BIAs in metropolitan Vancouver. For example, the Burnaby Heights Business Improvement Association, through member communication, beautification initiatives and projects, community events, and lobbying efforts has been quite successful both in transforming the physical look of the community and in establishing a strong civic sense of place and community. The Heights' legendary, merchant-sponsored, annual "Hats Off Day" is a one-day celebration that brings the community together for a parade, street-level festivities, music, dance, good sidewalk food, and fun.

A BIA can therefore clearly help with developing a neighbourhood vibe or changing current perceptions. Another recent example of the latter is the steps taken in the aftermath of the Vancouver riots following the loss by the Vancouver Canucks hockey team to the Boston Bruins in the Stanley Cup game final in 2011. Let's take a closer look at what happened and at what local businesses did in the aftermath.

Downtown Vancouver and the 2011 Stanley Cup Riots

The events of that spring 2011 evening and the images of riot police, tear gas, burning police vehicles, and casual looting causing millions of dollars of damage to hundreds of businesses were broadcast worldwide.

Some speculated that the events of that evening would forever change how others viewed Vancouverites and would have long-term economic impacts, particularly on the tourism economy in Vancouver, a sector that has struggled in the last few years. In the early days of the aftermath, the Downtown Vancouver BIA was instrumental in organizing volunteer clean-up groups and in piloting initiatives to show support for the downtown core, build community pride, and change perceptions about Vancouver and Vancouverites. Although some of the local media chose to cover the "feel-good" stories following the riots, by that point most of the international media had moved on to cover other sensational news somewhere else.

It is unclear to what degree the Vancouver riots actually damaged the long-term reputation of downtown Vancouver and the metropolitan region as a whole, or to what degree groups such as the Downtown Vancouver BIA were successful in recasting the events of that night in a more positive light. It is difficult to attribute lower tourism rates to a single factor such as the riot, particularly since other factors have also been influential in the slow decline of the tourism economy in metropolitan Vancouver: these include, among others, higher fuel prices, the overall decline in consumer confidence, the weakening currency exchange relative to the Canadian dollar (which for a time increased the cost of travel to Canada from key markets), increased border security and documentation requirements, and the Olympic aversion, up to February 2010.

Regardless of the challenges, there is no doubt that today downtown Vancouver is as popular a destination as ever. It is a vibrant neighbourhood that still attracts many locals and regional tourists looking for great food, shopping, and other sociocultural experiences. Downtown Vancouver remains the strong economic core of the metropolitan Vancouver area.

A Major Takeaway from the Three Cases: Authenticity Matters

Whether in Langley, Burnaby, Downtown Vancouver, Harrison Hot Springs, or anywhere else within the metropolitan Vancouver region, it is critical for place-making to be authentic and feel "grassroots"-based, just like the CED principles that inspire it. There is always a degree to which culture on a community level can be packaged and marketed, but authentic community "vibe" and street culture are priceless – intangible qualities that are very hard to re-create and imitate.

The paradox is that we all know and can feel authenticity when we see it. Some communities and some neighbourhoods just seem to have more of "it." However, as has just been shown, there are things within the CED tool kit that metropolitan Vancouver communities have used and that have supported stronger community place-making, even in the face of adversity and rioting.

Making It Work: Proactive Public-Private Initiatives

Fostering local economic development and getting it "right" are not easy things to achieve. They depend on a process that the small business community within the metropolitan Vancouver region is still struggling to understand. The process requires strong leadership and a willingness to take a certain amount of risk. Community initiatives struggle with issues of timeliness, relevance, and measurability, especially when economic conditions change all the time.

Although reactive economic responses are certainly needed when a community faces a crisis, proactive initiatives are more likely to be effective than reactive ones. For proactive action to be possible, it is important for the business community to be in tune with the rest of the community. When economic development schemes proceed without community buy-in, they quickly lose their relevance for the community, and economic development organizations become out of touch with those they are attempting to serve. Community business leaders must be good organizers and communicators. The primary role of economic development officers is as liaisons between various community groups and stakeholders and local governments; but local business leaders also need to be receptive to new development ideas and to understand the correlation between sustainable communities and the positive business climate.

Just as community buy-in is important, so is accountability. Usually, local economic development offices produce economic plans with set goals and measurable outcomes that need to be regularly updated. These plans and reports measure both the performance of the organization and the general health of the local economy. But for these plans to be valuable they need to be implemented, and the business community in the region needs to be the strongest advocate for such plans.

One of the lessons drawn from the Vancouver metropolitan region is that business leaders need to hold their local governments accountable. Small, locally based business needs to push for more than just the establishment of economic development offices or local investment corporations, as these can often become just cosmetic initiatives.

Unless local economic development and sustainability principles are made the basis of all local government operations (from zoning to overzealous parking ticket enforcement), the desired goals are unlikely to be achieved. It is also important that the roles and responsibilities of economic development offices and their staff be clearly defined. This is crucial, since so many economic development initiatives often depend on external funding and most local governments simply do not have the financial ability to fund all of the initiatives they may need or want.

As things stand, local governments, with their limited revenue sources, often scramble to balance the books while providing reasonable levels of public services. Understandably, the communities that are most in need of local economic development often do not have access to the initial capital required to start the strategic planning process. Even if the initial funding for planning is found, communities may still struggle to find the funds for implementation, which can be even more costly. Because of this, local economic development programs are often dependent on grants or other one-time financial transfers from senior levels of government – a vulnerability that may render many programs financially unstable. In the face of these realities, communities have started to explore ways to raise economic development funds internally – for example, through community corporations.

Local economic development processes are not ends in themselves but rather a means to achieving a better community for all. Viewed in this way, funding alone cannot solve all the problems of traditional, top-down economic development policies that have largely failed. Funding is only part of the puzzle.

More important is adherence to the basic principles laid out by CED: participation, inclusion, diversity, and creativity. Place-making and community building to develop a collective identity and authentic notions of self are not just a fad. We have seen how in downtown Langley this approach can work. Inevitably, local economic development is about partnerships and cooperation. Historically, one of the most important partnerships for local governments has been with the local business community, and it is a partnership that is explored all over the metropolitan Vancouver region at forums on a theoretical level as well as daily on the community level.

Back at the Local B&B in Harrison Hot Springs

Back in Harrison Hot Springs, the bed and breakfast run by Robert and Sonja Reyerse is completely booked. For the metropolitan Vancouver region and its small-scale entrepreneurs, the future may very well depend on looking further inward to identify local assets that are worth exploring and developing. To be sure, there is also an increasing interest in looking further westward, towards Asia. But with the decline in the global economy and increasing transportation and fuel costs, maybe what will bring foreign tourists to these areas is also what allows local residents to enjoy local living; a vibrant, independent and diverse collection of businesses that are locally owned and independently run, often by people who live in the communities they serve. By providing something unique and non-replicable to their customers, independent small-scale entrepreneurs (as if guided by an "invisible hand") ensure the long-term viability of the communities in which they live and work.

Vancouver Postscript

The process of writing this book has been very lengthy. Reflecting on what has been written more than two years after the fact, I am reminded how relevant this conversation about bottom-up place-making in the context of community economic development really is. The intent of this chapter, and of the book as a whole, has been to spur an open dialogue about what makes some locations and neighbourhoods successful socio-economically as complete communities where people can and want to live, shop, work, and play. Intuitively, we often know when we are in one of these neighbourhoods that have "it" – that certain factor that makes them desirable, liveable, and successful. However, this "it" factor is often hard to imitate and duplicate because it is context-specific and takes just the right mixture of planning and organic, bottom-up social interactions to establish.

As our indoor living spaces shrink because of population growth in ever denser urban environments, the discussion about community place-making will become more important. In our ever-evolving roles as urban space developers, residents, investors, customers, employees, and business creators we are all trying to find a niche that is unique but also familiar and comfortable – a place that is both community and home. Ultimately, I believe that community economic development is more about community than economics.

5 The View from Main Street Toronto: A Case of the Bottom-Up, Top-Down Conundrum[1]

Toronto, as we have seen from our introduction, was the birthplace of the first-ever modern Business Improvement Area. It is somewhat fitting, then, to end our city-based evaluation of local economic development and small business activity with a closer look at the place in which the BIA movement was born. On the surface at least, the portrait that emerges is one of unbridled success. Toronto is home to the world's largest concentration of BIAs, and the pace of that growth, for the moment at least, appears unabated. A number of major BIA-led revitalization projects, such as those on Bloor Street and Roncesvalles Avenue, have had a positive transformational effect on the texture of daily life both in those neighbourhoods and in providing an example for the city as a whole. And yet, there is much that rests just beneath this surface that requires exploration.

In particular, why is Toronto often viewed by both its residents and experts as revered as Jane Jacobs as somehow less than the sum of its parts? What is it about Toronto that simultaneously makes it a cradle of bottom-up innovation and also a place where newness and novelty are feared?

The story of how local entrepreneurs have defined a "city of neighbourhoods" and the rise of BIAs as major actors within the city will evoke some of these same themes but will also help us better understand this bottom-up, top-down dichotomy.

The Toronto We All Know ... and Love?

The best way to explore Toronto is to dispense with an official tourist guide and instead ask local residents to name a destination they would visit in *their* neighbourhood on a typical weekday. The locally generated suggestions will most likely produce a welcome surprise, whereas the officially sanctioned recommendations could probably be experienced in most cities a well-travelled person has already visited.

It is this quality – the contrast between "official" and "unofficial" Toronto – that was first remarked on by Jane Jacobs in an interview with the CBC in 1969.[2] Less than one year after her move to Toronto she compared Canada's two largest cities – Toronto and Montreal – and, in her words, found that unlike Montreal "[Toronto had] much less creativity at the top than at the bottom." She drew attention to things locals took for granted, like the ingenuity of Toronto's local entrepreneurs who could transform former residential front yards into storefronts, as can still be found in Kensington Market and along Baldwin Street. "It seems to me," Jacobs commented, "that Toronto has a split personality, a civic schizophrenia. On one level is the spirit of the individual and small groups who get together to do things, what you might call the 'vernacular spirit.' This is all informal, ingenious, quite romantic and full of fun ... a great deal of fun. It seems to me that the official spirit of Toronto is to stamp out fun. It is pompous and impressed with mediocrity so long as it's big and expensive."

It usually takes an outsider with a keen eye to notice obvious yet often unarticulated qualities of a city, and it was this transplanted New Yorker who hit the proverbial nail on the head when she noted that most of what was officially sanctioned by Toronto's "authorities" typically meant something tired and utterly predictable. Most of what was authored locally by individuals and groups of individuals working together, however, was more spontaneous, original, and open to outsiders in a way that "official Toronto" of the 1960s never was.

This insular and closed-off quality described by Jacobs may seem surprising to outsiders visiting Toronto today or even current inhabitants of what the United Nations has called the world's most cosmopolitan city. Toronto is, in relation to its size, the most diverse city in the world, more so than London or even similarly diverse New World upstarts like Melbourne or Sydney. One finds as many foreign languages spoken in Toronto, a city of 2.5 million inhabitants, as one would find in New York with its 9 million residents.

How did this come about? Why did people from all corners of the earth come to settle in a place that, officially at least, seemed so closed and content with its place in the world?

Part of the answer, I maintain, lies in Jacobs's realization that what makes Toronto unique is its on-the-ground receptivity to "newness" – whether it be to ideas or people. In particular, and of relevance to this book, the absorptive capacity of the city's small business sector has played a huge role in allowing newcomers to flourish in our city. Toronto has both the "retail environment" (i.e., in the form of relatively low cost and easy to access commercial and retail space) and the "legislative environment" (i.e., in the form of a well-run and efficient municipal regulation and governance system) needed to facilitate entry into the sector. Toronto's current local governance model may be far from perfect (as with Halifax, mentioned in chapter 3, there was a forced amalgamation of five previously independent municipalities in 1998 that the city has not fully recovered from); but relative to the places from where most immigrants hail, it still remains for the most part a transparent place to do business. Shop owners know what the rules are and are pretty much assured of receiving due notice before a major change occurs. This kind of predictability, it turns out, is crucial for a business of any size to thrive.

Toronto is also, in relation to potential revenues, a low-cost place to set up shop. The major reasons are the many retail spaces that are still available to a small-scale enterprise and their accessibility; they are often situated on main streets with access to parking and an in-built local customer base. They may not be "pretty" from a traditional urban planning perspective, but the storefronts of Toronto, especially those of between 500 and 2,500 square feet located throughout the city, are plentiful and provide a local window into the tangible outcomes of a globalized economy. In BJ's Market, for example, one of the many independently owned and operated shops located along Gerrard Street East, one finds a fresh mango sourced directly from an Indian farm. In Highland Farms, one of Toronto's largest independently owned grocery stores, which competes with large national retailers like Loblaw's and Metro, one can find authentic Maria cookies made in my father's home of Aguilar de Campoo, a small town located in northern Spain.[3]

Small-Scale Entrepreneurs and the Most Diverse City in the World

So is there a link between small business and the evolution of such a diverse city? We think so. The connection is partly the result of the difficulty that new immigrants face when entering the labour force and

securing a paid job. Often, even among skilled immigrants, foreign credentials go unrecognized by governments and employers alike, leaving
as the only viable option small-scale entrepreneurship – one that in
Toronto, despite the recent proliferation of large American-style big-
box store chains, is still a reasonably profitable affair. The fact is that
most of the start-ups in any given main street in the city are opened by
foreign-born persons – a notable difference from the circumstances in
low-migrant Halifax. The shopkeepers of Toronto have largely come
from abroad, which explains why the areas that now figure prominently in the obligatory tourist maps all typically bear the stamp of that
immigration: Greek Town, Korea Town, Little Italy, Little India, Little
Portugal, or any one of our three Chinatowns. Interspersed are neighbourhoods with diverse and sizeable numbers of ethnic enterprises established by Maltese, Poles, Sri Lankans, Filipinos, Iranians, Japanese,
Hispanics, and people from Africa and the Caribbean.

Plan of the Chapter

This chapter provides a snapshot into several of Toronto's most iconic –
yet probably unfamiliar to an outsider – neighbourhoods and small
businesses. The choice is eclectic reflecting the haphazard, unplanned
way in which most of Toronto's neighbourhoods (save for one notable
exception in Don Mills) and retail districts have evolved (see exhibit 5.1).
But the selection is not random. Each choice grew first out of earlier research into the growth and development of business improvement areas
(BIAs) in the city. The cases presented here are therefore reflective of an
archetype of many more businesses that go unmentioned in these pages
but that are frequented and known to many Toronto residents and even,
if they're lucky, some foreign visitors.

The other important selection criterion is the connection that each
chosen small business has with its particular geographic setting. The
neighbourhood in which the independently owned shop is located is as
much a focal point of attraction as the business itself. Toronto, it can be
said, is nothing but its neighbourhoods, and those neighbourhoods are
often defined by their locally based entrepreneurs. Much like individual consciousness, which can be described as an "emergent property"
of many individual synaptic events in our brains, a neighbourhood
achieves its overall "feel" and "sense of place" based on the many decisions of small scale-entrepreneurs and the moments shared with customers that occur inside their establishments at a specific time and place.

The instances accumulate and become embedded in memories, or are transmitted orally to others across space and time, or perhaps are captured in a news story, book, or magazine article. These "bits" of knowledge constitute the living, breathing memory of a business location in the city. The chapter therefore intends, through observation and documentation, to elicit some more universal themes about the nature of how small, independent businesses survive in Canada's largest city and why it is that they remain such a vital component of the urban experience.

East, West, and over the Lake

The city of Toronto has a primary east-west orientation. I recall my high-school geography teacher attributing this to the location of Lake Ontario, which borders the city on the south. A city like Chicago, whose lakefront is located at the western end of the city, has a more north-south flow. Cities like London, where the river Thames snakes its way horizontally through the middle of the city, can have two orientations – north-south as well as east-west. The television show *EastEnders* would never have existed had the city not cultivated a culture unique to the east "end" of the city. These separations occur because of geographic distance, but they are primarily housed in the psyche of individuals residing in these cities. They are further reinforced by cultural patterns of development and natural patterns of traffic and transit links. People can grow up their entire lives in the east end of Toronto, for example, and rarely travel west of the central Yonge Street artery, or vice versa.

Following that natural east-west flow of the city, we have decided to document several spots in Toronto where attempts to revive neighbourhood business areas has led to more citizens trying out and sampling "tastes" from locations they would have been unlikely to visit in previous times. Much of this has been fostered by a renaissance in city touring, "psychogeography," and "flâneurism"[4] and also by the promotion of city-based attractions in local weekly newspapers such as *Now* magazine and *Eye Weekly*, which began offering free information with strong urban content in the late 1980s and early 1990s. This trend has continued and has prefigured the recent success of locally themed books such as *Toronto: A City Becoming*, or *City of Words: Toronto through Her Writers' Eyes* (I never knew Toronto was a "she" until I read this book), or the series dedicated to analysing Toronto titled *uTOpia*.

The exotic, it turns out in these books, is often just a short walk or bus ride away.

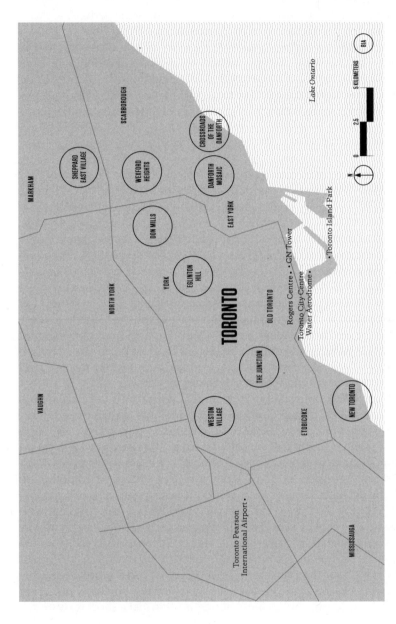

Exhibit 5.1: The city of Toronto, post amalgamation, which includes all the old cities of what was once known as Metro Toronto. The areas highlighted include some of the neighbourhoods profiled in this chapter.

The Best Pizza in Town!

A case in point was my own personal acquaintance with one of the best pizzerias/Italian restaurants in the city. We (my wife and I) were living near the intersection of Coxwell and Gerrard, which is known as Little India, though a more appropriate term would be Little Kashmir, as there seem to be as many Pakistani flags on the street as Indian. The north end of this neighbourhood is bounded by Danforth Avenue, which is the eastern continuation of Bloor Street. The name change occurs west of something called the Bloor Street viaduct, which, as some may know, is featured prominently in Michael Ondaatje's *In the Skin of a Lion*. The viaduct, built in the late 1920s, spans a wide stretch of the Don Valley and was crucial to the establishment of modern Toronto, offering the first substantial connection between the east and west sides of the city.

The Danforth-Coxwell end of the neighbourhood is quite distinct both in terms of street design and with respect to the businesses based there. There is no unique or centralizing characteristic unifying shops in the area – hence the name of the local business improvement area, the "Danforth Mosaic." There is also no surface streetcar route for this neighbourhood, as there is along Gerrard. Instead the subway zips by underneath and leaves a four lane roadway (with a fifth lane in the middle used for turning) that is not as pedestrian friendly as its southern street comparator.

It was in this stretch of Danforth, between Coxwell and Greenwood, that one of the city's best pizzerias was identified by *Now* magazine. This ranking has appeared multiple times, most recently in their 2010 year-end top-ten issue. Both my wife and I were a bit puzzled when we first came across the entry. Not only is the city of Toronto filled to the rafters with pizza parlours, this was an area of the neighbourhood that we drove by almost every day and yet we had never noticed this particular restaurant. Moreover, it had a very peculiar name, given its location on Danforth Avenue: "Gerrard Spaghetti & Pizza." Why was Gerrard Pizza (as it is known to locals) located at 1528 Danforth? Why had we never visited one of the city's best pizzerias, which was only a ten-minute walk from our home? These were questions that required answering, and more to the point, pizza that required eating.

Upon entering Gerrard Pizza for the first time one is struck by its clean and unpretentious atmosphere. You are likely to find the adjective "homey" added to most reviews and descriptions of the restaurant, and it is appropriate. The establishment looks and feels like a perfectly pre-served Italian restaurant from the 1970s, authentic and reassuring.[5] The first time we visited, we were greeted by the owner, Vito Greco, and his nephew, who was waiting tables. The back kitchen was staffed by Vito and what looked like family members, which indeed turned out to be the case (his sister and each of their kids work in the restaurant). Gerrard Pizza is a third-generation family-owned business that, according to the restaurant's Facebook page, "has been preparing great-tasting Italian food using family recipes brought from patriarch Joe Greco's hometown of San Vito, Italy. Yep, Vito is named after the saint!"

In Gerrard Pizza one senses the most elusive yet indispensable attri-bute of a local neighbourhood institution – authenticity. So "authentic" is perhaps the second adjective that comes to mind when describing the restaurant. Vito even imports and spices his very own olive oil from the old country (from Calabria, a region of Italy).

And what about the main attraction?

Well the pizza lived up to the review, and our family have been regu-lars ever since, though our trips as a family are less frequent now that we have moved northwest of the neighbourhood to an area of the city known as Don Mills, which will be documented later on in this chapter.

Small Business and the Creation of Social Connections

I have been to Gerrard Pizza several times since that initial visit, mostly on "business trips" for this book. What is interesting about Gerrard Pizza is the back-story, and, indeed, the riddle of the name was the first to be resolved. It turns out the original business was founded in 1966 by Vito's uncle. That original establishment was located on Gerrard Street to the south. Ten years later his father, who took ownership of the busi-ness in 1972, moved the restaurant north to then fast-growing Danforth east, which was at that time still a strong east-end Italian-immigrant enclave. Starting in the mid-to-late 1980s, however, the Italian popu-lation slowly started migrating northwest of the city to a community known as Woodbridge. The homes were bigger there (a theme we shall see repeated in other city neighbourhoods), and the community invest-ed its hard-won prosperity in more space and larger lot sizes. The east end around Danforth is still known for its small postwar bungalows and semi-detached houses.

How did Vito's restaurant cope with the loss of its Italian customer base? "It was a challenge," according to Vito, "but our clientele now is really the same as it always was; it is made up of local residents whose homes are walking distance from the shop ... it's just that twenty years ago those customers were Italian and now they're from a variety of ethnicities." This is a key to the success of any small business that starts out with an ethnic niche; it must open its doors eventually to a wider customer base if it is to survive. Those initial ethnic customers inevitably do one of two things: they assimilate or they migrate. Fortunately for Vito, his business not only had a loyal following in the neighbourhood, Italian cuisine has been a Canadian (and worldwide) staple for some time. And yet that popularity turns out to be a double-edged sword.

Because of the popularity of Italian food, and pizza especially, there are many competitors in the city. One need only look down the street, just a few blocks south of Vito's pizzeria, to find a large, family-owned, Italian eatery located on the corner. And we have not even mentioned the endless parade of chain stores delivering pizza in twenty minutes or less! How does a small business like Gerrard Pizza compete? The key, according to Vito, is quality and consistency: "We don't serve pizza in twenty minutes or less. Everything we do is from scratch. Everyone here stresses quality and attention to detail in everything we do ... a chain store can lose a hundred customers with inconsistent service because they can add ten times that amount over the course of a year. For my business, it may take me a year to add a single new customer. Because of that, I need to keep that customer satisfied and coming back."

His business, not surprisingly, has a strong reputation in the community. There are true regulars, people who dine there once or twice a week. They come in and have a table reserved for them, and the first and second courses are served without need for an order. This was a ritual I had observed in many establishments before setting foot in Gerrard Pizza, mostly in Europe. People sometimes forget that all of the great cities of Europe – such as London, Madrid, Paris, and Amsterdam – have essentially grown up around local neighbourhoods. And by local, we mean one or two streets' worth of walking distance.

The cities of Europe are denser than their North American counterparts and have more of the necessities of life packed into smaller areas, so that local residents have no real need to venture farther afield as long as the quality is dependable and the price affordable. This is what I immediately noticed at Gerrard Pizza. In subsequent visits I bumped into local politicians (such as local councillor Janet Davis, whom I had worked with in a separate project in the neighbourhood), old friends, neighbours, and people I'd never met but knew by sight, perhaps walking a dog or playing in a local park. The restaurant is a quintessential "third space" that acts as a local "attractor," and its small size facilitates interpersonal recognition and communication. In short, it contributes to a neighbourhood's social fabric in a way that no chain store can because, unlike a chain outlet, Gerrard Pizza can be found in no other place but where it is.

The Long-Time Owner and the New BIA

There is one sore spot in Vito's relationship with the neighbourhood, however, and that is the local business improvement area, the aforementioned Danforth Mosaic. Established in 2008, the BIA is one of the city's newest, and, stretching as it does for nearly three kilometres between Westlake Avenue in the east and Jones Avenue in the west, also one of the longest. The website spells out the "mission statement" and description of the BIA as follows:

> Our community is rich in diversity, which is the reason we proudly brand ourselves a "mosaic" of many cultures. Celebrating various ethnicities in the Danforth Mosaic BIA makes the choice of local restaurants, shops, services, and nightlife a treat for all. We are very pleased with the wide array of family owned shops and services that reside in our BIA, as they add a personal touch to the service provided to each welcomed visitor to the Heart of the Danforth.[6]

It certainly sounds inviting, but what rankles Vito slightly is the lack of follow-through and prioritizing of goals by BIA administrators and boards. According to Vito, the BIA has been fixated for far too long on parking issues such as the time and cost of parking on the street and the access potential customers have to local public parking spaces. In Toronto, parking is indeed an important issue, and Vito acknowledges as much, but in his words a more important priority would be "giving people a reason to come to the area for the first time. Once they make a decision to come they will find a way to get here and parking issues can then get sorted out more easily because we'll understand the scale of the problem. But they [the BIA members] just want to talk about parking without relating that problem to a bigger issue of client attraction."

To paraphrase Vito, not enough community building and local branding efforts (or place-making) get worked on by the BIA. "The holiday decorations that line the street and the flower pots and tree planters along the sidewalk were an initial success, but lately the quality of the decorations and flowers has declined and people take notice," says Vito. Vito would like to see the BIA sponsor more events like the mini jazz festival, which used to take place across the street in a local parkette and which attracted lots of people to the area but was missed this year by his customers and local residents.

Although it was never expressly stated in our conversation, one of the major problems that Vito, like many entrepreneurs, has with a delegated and democratic BIA structure is its inability to act quickly and decisively to meet a market need or solve a customer problem. Of course, a large and far-removed city department would probably be worse in that respect, but the BIA nevertheless is run like any membership-based organization, by consensus and due process. And sometimes that consensus is never reached as quickly as someone used to identifying a problem and fixing it the next day would like.

With those last caveats about balancing individual entrepreneurship with membership in a communal BIA in mind, we move just a few kilometres east of Gerrard Pizza and the Danforth Mosaic, to the last BIA along the eastern end of the Danforth strip, a place called the Crossroads at the Danforth, where some unlikely champions of neighbourhood revitalization have emerged.

A BIA at the Crossroads

Jose (Joe) Murillo works at 3323 Danforth Avenue, in a shop with an iconic small business name, Tip Top Collision. The appellation "Tip Top" is akin to the "ACME Co." of small business names. The name brings to mind a wonderful film by Robert Benjamin, *Nobody's Fool*, which features a grizzled Paul Newman working in a small town as an independent contractor and dealing with the slightly more successful owner of Tip Top Construction, played by a decidedly unglamorous Bruce Willis. The movie rings true because it pays attention to the details of small business and small town life. And there is a message embedded in the film that is relevant to our theme. The small town is something many wax nostalgic for, even if many of us have never set foot in a small town, let alone grown up in one. Yet the town, being too small to attract any large-scale business, is akin to a neighbourhood whose independent businesses service a local niche clientele too small to be of interest to a large corporation.

Such is the case with Joe Murillo's business, which he characterizes as having an "individual flavour." He has fostered excellent relationships with two groups, one of them being the insurance companies that send/recommend customers following an accident, and also the individual customers, some of whom have now entered their third generation, who have called Tip Top their auto body repair shop and used-car dealership for decades.

As with Gerrard Pizza, this is a business which has remained in the family. It was started in 1971 by Joe's father, Jose Senior, and Joe started working there full-time in 1987. His wife has been working part-time, managing the books, for the last ten to twelve years.

Tip Top Collision's business has evolved in an interesting way. The initial focus on the customer – the ultimate customer being not the insurer but the owner of the car – was something that was the key for Joe's father when he started his business. The focus on the customer was drilled into Joe's head and has now become a mantra for Tip Top employees; they must make every reasonable effort to extend personalized care to their customers.

But Joe attributes his own success to efforts that perhaps his father's generation of independent entrepreneurs might not have thought necessary: community engagement. It may seem strange that an auto body repair shop would prioritize community engagement as a key to business success, but Joe feels especially proud of his efforts at community involvement. For instance, Tip Top employees volunteer their time helping to organize and run annual community events that the local BIA sponsors.

So what's in it for him? First, Tip Top's reputation has benefited from its association with the BIA. Joe admits that the community was initially not very happy with the setting up of Tip Top's shop.

As Joe puts it, "they [the local residents] felt that having a dirty, greasy body shop in their community would contribute to the overall impression among people that the area was low-class, cheap and seedy." That impression gradually began to change when Joe Senior was in charge; people came to see the commitment that his family had shown to the neighbourhood, often employing local residents and growing the business using local resources and services. But he sees the establishment of the BIA in 2008 as the real turning point.

Joe and his friend and fellow independent business owner, Dan Glazier, were the biggest advocates for the creation of the Crossroads of the Danforth BIA. Dan, who is the co-owner (together with his sister Renee) of Frontier Sales Furniture, always wanted to improve the image of their community among people living and working in the area. The Frontier Sales Furniture business was started by Dan's grandmother, Grace, in 1981, based on her vision of reusing and repurposing quality furnishings at budget-friendly prices. It wasn't long before Grace's concept caught on, and the company quickly began to grow. Grace enlisted the marketing and retail skills of daughter Donna (Dan and Renee's mother) and their aunt. In 1998, Dan and Renee became the third generation of owners and, greatly helped by the dedication and enthusiasm of the original team of employees, the company has not only survived but has grown.[7]

Personality Matters

Dan has served as chairman of the Crossroads BIA since its inception, and this is where both Joe and Dan have found common cause. The area had a number of challenges when they took over their respective family-run businesses – among them the perception that the neighbourhood was dirty and crime ridden and lacking in interesting things to buy, see, or do.

Much like our story of the then nascent Bloor West Village BIA, the BIA began with small improvements and then quickly moved to improve the lighting standards and add banners and other signage indicating the area's identity as the place where the two Danforths – Danforth Road and Danforth Avenue – merge to become one arterial route at the Crossroads. The BIA recognized that the neighbourhood needed a sense of place and a "rebranded image" if it was to engage local residents and also attract new customers from nearby areas of the city. The name of the BIA is interesting, as it both describes the actual geography of the neighbourhood and evokes the sense of the neighbourhood's transition from an anonymous place with a few longstanding businesses to a neighbourhood that engages its residents and attracts newcomers.

How this happened illustrates the capacity for a "small group of committed individuals" to make profound changes.[8] First, the BIA sponsored several annual community festivals and immediately set out to provide a signage strategy that would help local small businesses make improvements to their storefronts. Second, they also acted as mini inward-investment brokers, finding out if a local entrepreneur was interested in opening up a retail store in the east end and then matching the owners of vacant properties to these prospective entrepreneurs.

The two entrepreneurs, Dan and Joe, have forged a close partnership and are especially proud of the role they have played, through the BIA, as local information disseminators. In early 2008 the City of Toronto came to them with plans for a rapid transit program that would run along Victoria Park from Danforth in the south to Lawrence Avenue in the north. Joe personally attended all the information meetings organized by the Toronto Transit Commission (TTC). He then reported back to the community about what was being proposed and discussed at these meetings. According to Joe, many residents would otherwise have been unaware of it all, so to help spread the word, Joe personally paid for the printing of hundreds of fliers detailing the proposal. Community feedback was also aired at several town hall meetings.

In Joe's words, "They [TTC] wanted to do here what they did [on] St. Clair West, which was a disaster for the surrounding businesses. They wanted to block two centre lanes with solid medians." At BIA-sponsored meetings for the community Joe proposed a better solution: "Just run more buses along dedicated HOV lanes. That wouldn't hurt emergency services or cause greater traffic congestion. Otherwise, with solid medians running down the centre of the street residents would not be able to turn onto their own driveways. Three schools would have had a heavy traffic problem."

Joe felt that the local community had not been properly consulted in the TTC's initial proposal for the project. Regarding how his involvement in the transit fight bolstered his standing in the community, Joe says, "This whole street here are friends of ours; they weren't before. Now I talk to them on their lawn whereas before it was 'Oh, it's that greasy body shop up the road!' We needed to change people's perception of business in the area." Today, whenever there is a proposed community change or building project, large or small, the BIA is informed about the change immediately, and Joe and Dan then use their positions as heads of long-standing independent enterprises to spread the word about these developments.

At the close of the warm end-of-summer day when our interview and walk through the neighbourhood took place, Enbridge Gas handed their gas plans for the area over to Dan and the BIA. The BIA then told residents of the area that "the sidewalks will be torn up in late August," so that they could plan accordingly. The BIA also took a lead in making sure that all the city's by-laws were being properly enforced by the gas company. There is a depleted and hollowed out core of city oversight that used to be enforced by five different municipal governments, but that, since amalgamation in 1998, has been handled by only one City of Toronto administration. The reality is that our city has less capacity to enforce by-laws now than it did prior to 1998, leaving the BIAs, where they can, to pick up the slack.

A Tale of Two East-End BIAs

So in two east-end areas we have seen how small businesses can survive by focusing on a loyal customer base and tailoring their activities to the neighbourhoods in which they are located. We also witnessed how a new BIA can emerge and engage local entrepreneurs and residents, as has happened in the Crossroads. However, if tangible investments in community engagement are not sustained, a BIA can also alienate long-standing businesses with deep roots in the neighbourhood, as was the case with Vito and the Danforth Mosaic.

For a less personalized and perhaps more dispassionate view of what BIAs do (or don't do), what their members look like, and how they are formed we can turn to the findings of surveys carried out among actual BIA members. In the late summer and early fall of 2008, we were asked to survey local businesses along Lawrence Avenue East and Kennedy Road in order to provide feedback to the BIA membership about the activities and feelings of BIA members.

The Wexford neighbourhood where the survey with the larger response rate took place lies about ten kilometres north of the Crossroads of the Danforth and it is there that we travel next.

Can a BIA Survive in the Suburbs?

The Wexford Heights BIA was formed in 2004. The BIA idea was a long-standing dream of many old-time businesses in the area, such as the family-run Wexford Restaurant, which has been in business since the mid-1950s, operated by four generations of Greek Macedonian immigrants. As Tony Kiriakou, second-generation owner of the restaurant, once bluntly put it, "We needed to put Wexford on the map!"

What truly helped spur the creation of one of the longest BIA's in the city was the concerted action of a (then) largely unknown and newly elected city councillor named Michael Thompson.

Formerly a businessperson himself, Councillor Thompson recognized that the area had suffered through a pretty rough recession in the 1990s, with a consequent lack of public investment and residential engagement. When the city amalgamated in 1998, many of the city's suburban neighbourhoods felt left out and alienated from the concerns of the newly enlarged City Hall in downtown Toronto.[9] When he was elected to Toronto City Council in 2004, as the councillor for Ward 37, Michael set about to change that feeling and decided to form the second-ever BIA in Scarborough. What convinced Councillor Thompson that a BIA could work in such a geographically dispersed and car-oriented area of the city? Well, according to Michael, it had to be done because otherwise there was going to be an ever-growing stagnation and frustration among both the residents and the business owners in his ward. He also had the successful model of Kennedy Road BIA, which was also in his ward, to follow.

The Heart of Wexford

The Wexford community's heart resides along the spine of Lawrence Avenue East, a six-lane roadway fringed by an extremely varied and eclectic selection of one- and two-storey strip malls. The stores are set back from the sidewalks, with free parking located at the front of each shop, and the ownership is sometimes shared; that is, each store has its own owner and the mall is just an amalgam of independent property/business owners. In other cases, the mall has one landlord, and the retailers rent from this single landlord.

The dynamics of these two types of malls are quite different, given that, while only property owners must pay the BIA levy,[10] all store owners are voting members, regardless of whether they rent or own. Sometimes streetscape improvements are welcomed by owners of buildings but not so much by renters, as they eventually can lead to hikes in rent that may not be matched by consequent increases in customer foot traffic, at least not immediately.

This is perhaps why one of the first things the BIA set out to do was to organize a street festival along this multilane roadway. Bringing new customers to the area would be of benefit to all businesses, whether rented or owned.

At first, people were sceptical that the city would even allow such a large car-carrying roadway to be closed. But the city did allow it and, seven years on, the festival now attracts close to 250,000 visitors over its three-day period. In part to gauge member satisfaction with the festival and BIA activities more generally, a survey of BIA members in Wexford was undertaken by the author in late fall 2008. The questions ranged from basic demographic descriptions of business owners and their establishments to questions about the extent of business owners' involvement in the BIA and the community. It was, in a strict sense, a fact-finding mission for the BIA, which had never surveyed its own members since its inception. For us as researchers it offered a unique window into a sector that is unfortunately not accurately captured by SME designations or representative bodies such as the Confederation of Independent Business.

What we found in our microscopic look was that most businesses were indeed small, employing on average just under three employees, and that they were "truly" local in the sense that the employees were largely drawn from the neighbourhood. The lower pay and lack of benefits associated with firm size is, as theory would predict, partly compensated for by the ease of commute for local employees.

The average commute for a business owner was surprisingly low; less than twenty minutes. This is roughly half as long as the average time spent travelling to work by most commuters, which in 2010 averaged forty minutes.[11] Business revenues were also made up of local inputs; residents accounted for 80 per cent of the customer traffic, according to the business owners surveyed.

These results nicely demonstrate how small businesses can collectively, even in what is otherwise a suburban part of the city, act as the commercial and service hub of a sustainable, environmentally committed community. The use of local amenities is one of the few ways most citizens can compensate for rising fuel costs. The Wexford BIA survey demonstrates that consumers are embracing local shopping, which allows them to make efficient use of their time while hunting for value. Wexford's small businesses, located accessibly along both sides of Lawrence Avenue, also showcase that the drawbacks of a suburban model predicated on car use can be mitigated if local shopping districts offer consumers the ability to meet their needs while driving only short distances. If we are not yet seeing a pronounced decline in vehicle use, changing consumer tastes and an aging society are pointing towards increased use of alternative ways of using transportation resources. Locally owned small businesses are ideally poised to benefit from this shift. The Wexford BIA demonstrates this.

Though there is more to uncover from the Wexford BIA survey and others undertaken as part of the larger BIA project in the late 2000s, we shall stop here for the moment and focus our attention on the idea of local production and consumption. About five kilometres west of the

Wexford BIA, Lawrence Avenue crosses the large expanse of the Don Valley and enters the heart of the former city of North York. It is here that one comes across an interesting experiment in urban commercial redevelopment known as "The Shops at Don Mills."

Between Main Street and the Mall

Built on the site of what was once the Don Mills Centre, an enclosed mid-sized mall that ceased operating in 2005, The Shops have returned the area into an open-air shopping mall or what the developers, Cadillac Fairview, refer to as Ontario's "first urban village." Much has been written by urban designers and modernist architecture enthusiasts about the community of Don Mills – signs adorning the neighbourhood proudly refer to it as Canada's "first planned community (see exhibit 5.2)."[12] Although it is not our intent to delve deeply into that residential and architectural history, a few lines of context are required.

The community of Don Mills gained its reputation as the "ideal suburb" in part because, unlike many later suburban developments, it was built in the 1950s to meet local needs. What post-Don Mills suburbs copied were the trappings of suburban life such as wide lots, cul-de-sacs, curved roads, and a mix of bungalow and two-storey housing. What they failed to pick up on was that the Don Mills neighbourhood was designed in that way to mesh with the local topography. In an effort to preserve the oldest trees in the neighbourhood and ensure that all the small eskers, drumlins, and moraines were not flattened, housing was built around these "natural barriers," hence the snake-like street design. The development also incorporated a mix of public and private buildings to serve the needs of the population, including rental apartments, accommodation for the elderly, elementary schools, a library, and a centrally located shopping district with a public square, all within walking distance of nearly every resident. In short, it was suburban development that did not require local residents to drive long distances in order to get from the grocery store to the post office and back home.

In spring 2009, the outdoor shopping arcade was officially reopened with a new, more contemporary design, and it is still in the process of evolving, with many – roughly a third by last count in early 2014 – of the storefronts still not having found retailers. One reason for the vacancies has been the timing of the mall's opening: following the worst recession in modern history, not many new stores were about to open in a somewhat "untested" open-air mall. A second reason is that the

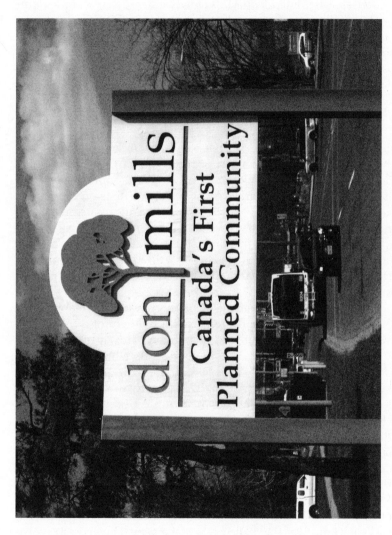

Exhibit 5.2. The local Don Mills Residents' Association placed these signs up along the entry points to the neighbourhood in 2005. *Photo by Todd Harris © 2014.*

eventual building of condominiums surrounding the mall (most are slated to open in the next three to five years) has perhaps generated a wait-and-see approach on the part of potential start-up businesses. As a more densely populated Don Mills slowly emerges, so will the number of potential stores catering to this yet-to-arrive urban customer base. But still, the lack of a complete retail offering several years after the official opening was one reason I was intrigued by the story of a local business owner's difficulty in leasing a storefront from the owners, Cadillac Fairview.

The Icing on the Cake

The business in question is Ice 'n Cake, a stylish-looking gelato and dessert shop located right in the heart of the Shops at Don Mills, which includes the central Town Square and a Douglas Coupland-designed clock tower. Two of the co-owners, husband and wife team Jim Turpin and Sue Le, are there most days of the week.[13] Sue takes care of the "on-the-ground" operations such as the actual preparation of the gelato and the ordering of ingredients, while Jim handles relations with co-owners and, crucially, the landlord. It turns out lengthy discussions had to be undertaken before Cadillac Fairview were convinced that Ice 'n Cake was worthy of a place in the prime central square location.

Unlike the surrounding "franchise" or "corporate chain store" outlets, the restaurant is unique, designed with the help of a friend and built with local contractors and a local architect. This, it turns out, is a classic independently owned and operated store, which just happens to be located in a sea of chains. To be fair, the mall owners did offer space to all former tenants of the mall, and many of the stores in the Shops are indeed independently owned or are first-time franchises. But what was unique about the Ice 'n Cake opening was how much work had to be done by the owners on the "look and feel" of the store to ensure that it matched and maintained the integrity of the overall mall design. A similar requirement, I have been told, applies to all tenants in the mall, even the Canada Trust bank branch that was the mall's first official tenant.

"One of the good things to come out of that [the lengthy negotiations] exercise," says Jim, "was that it did prepare their small business to evolve should it consider expansion or franchising." They essentially had to take on the look, feel, and operation of a well-established brand, despite being less than a year old from conception to grand opening. The trick for Ice 'n Cake will be to do what other successful small businesses have done – establish a connection with customers and local residents.

The other good thing to come from the lengthy negotiations with Cadillac Fairview was the relationship forged with their landlord, which in turn has got to know its retailers much better and has tried to create events that are tailored for shop owners all year round, especially around the town square, thus attracting people and potential new customers for shops like Ice 'n Cake.

What is interesting to note is that this is all activity that, in the absence of a single, large, corporate landlord like Cadillac Fairview, would be undertaken in other parts of the city by the business owners themselves, often by consensus and by taxing themselves with the BIA levy. Which model proves more successful may play out over the next several years as the Shops of Don Mills expands its retail offerings and new residents begin to populate the active condo community opening up alongside the mall.

A West-End Turning Point

Leaving Don Mills and travelling west yet again along Lawrence Avenue, across the entire breadth of North York, we enter the former city of York and the intersection of Lawrence Avenue West and Weston Road. This, it turns out, is one of Toronto's most westerly located neighbourhoods, appropriately named Weston Village. The intersection of Weston Road and Lawrence Avenue serves as the gateway to the core of old "Weston Village." The symbol one sees atop all Weston Village signage is an old-fashioned bicycle. This was appropriated from the area's history of manufacturing bicycles at the old CCM plant on Lawrence Avenue just east of Weston Road.

It certainly does not look like a village anymore, at least at first blush, but this is one city neighbourhood where the village tag line actually applies. Though the intersection is now marred by what some in Toronto might describe as a "brutalist 1970s building spree,"[14] only a few hundred metres north on Weston Road one finds the original settlement of Weston Village, where one can begin to see what the area must have looked like in its heyday from the late 1800s to the mid-1940s when it boasted its own town hall, theatre (both no longer standing), and library (still standing).

Weston Village was originally settled by British and Scottish immigrants and for many years had a very stable population and civic identity. In fact, as recounted by Suri Weinberg-Linsky, the first business owner to greet us, the area was actually settled by Europeans several decades before the founding of what came to be known as Toronto. In 1792, John Countryman, a member of Lord Simcoe's original survey crew sent to map the Humber River, was so pleased with the oak and pine bush in the area that he built a sawmill on the west bank of the river. More settlers followed, attracted by the drop in the river that offered excellent power for saw and grist mills. The hamlet was eventually incorporated as a village in 1881, and in 1915 the busy, bustling village became a town (see exhibit 5.3).

There is a deep sense of pride among Westonites in what they still refer to as their "town." As pointed out by Suri, who is also a resident of Weston, one really does feel quite apart from the mainstream of city life on Weston Road. Toronto could be a world away if you live, work, and shop in the area. Indeed, for many years it was the old city of York that was the natural point of reference for Westonites, not Toronto. This meant that if they required anything from "city hall" it was the City of York, whose administrative buildings were located just a few kilometres southeast of Weston on Eglinton Avenue, rather than Toronto, that they turned to. The Weston Village BIA was formed in 1979, so this also makes Weston one of the oldest BIAs in the city.

This is all prefatory to what Suri refers to as the current challenges facing the area; but first we must delve into why Suri is here in Weston in the first place. Suri, it turns out, is co-owner of one of the longest-standing independently owned establishments in the city, Squibb's Stationers, which was founded in 1927 by Arthur and Cary Squibb, immigrants from England who began their careers as proprietors of a stationery outlet in the late 1800s. They set up shop on what was then 48 Main Street (now 1974 Weston Rd). The shop changed hands several times, until Suri's parents, Jack and Marilyn Weinberg, bought the store in the early 1980s. Suri, like many entrepreneurs, "grew up in retail," living above her parents' first store, which meant that from the age of one to her teenage years, she was surrounded by small business life. When her dad became ill in 2000, Suri took over the day-to-day running of the Squibb's operation. So Suri follows in a long line of family-owned businesses that pass along the reputation and loyal customer base of a well-respected retailer to the next generation.

Exhibit 5.3: The Weston Village moniker, buffeted as the village is on either side by two large 1970s residential tower blocks, may seem strange at the entrance to the main street, but a short stroll up Weston Road reveals the area's past glory. *Photo by Todd Harris © 2014.*

Surviving in an Era of Box-Store Growth and Market Decline

But how does a business dealing in paper and stationery survive in an era of big-box stores, the increasing move to digitization, and the phasing out of the use of notebooks and textbooks? The answer, once again, revolves around themes of personal engagement, an understanding of the local community, and catering to a loyal customer base – many of the same themes that we saw earlier along the Danforth. In Squibb's case, the business would not exist without the store's close relationship with schools, both local and outside the Weston area. Suri and her husband have developed a solid reputation and long-standing relationships with many teachers from all across the GTA. When teachers need to purchase school supplies for their classes they go to Squibb's because, according to Suri, "They know that they will get the most efficient, fast, and personalized service."

At this point one might be tempted to ask, "Teachers buy school supplies? Don't schools and boards make those purchase decisions?" Apparently not. According to Suri, schools rarely allocate enough resources to meet the stationery needs of teachers and their students. So, many teachers reach into their own pockets to make up the shortfall.

According to Suri, "they [teachers] know from experience that they can trust [her] with their orders." Sometimes, Suri explained, "parents of students will want to order their children's school materials somewhere else. Usually the teachers will try to convince them [parents] to instead do business with Squibb's." Often the parents who order elsewhere will find that the store or distributor will delay placing their order, not inform them of complications, and, in general, "be more trouble than they are worth." Suri often hears customers complain that they had trouble getting their order from some online company and that "from now on they will stick with her because they know that they are dependable. They [Squibb's] are sometimes put in the position of having to fix someone else's mess!" Suri's husband at this point chimes in with the observation, "This business has survived because of relationships, [because] if this store only relied on walk-in retail business, we wouldn't be here."

Building Loyalty, Trust, and Brand Capital ... One Customer at a Time

The fact that the store has cultivated relationships with teachers and schools is the primary reason for the success of Squibb's. No less important, however, according to Suri, "are the very good relationships cultivated with people in the neighbourhood, who come in and shop on a recurring basis." This customer retention extends to "people who don't live here, but who know of our store and come great distances to shop." But "of course," says Suri, "if we were relying on only walk-in type of business, we wouldn't exist; it's just not that type of business anymore." Or perhaps it never really was.

If there is one thing that unites niche neighbourhood players it is their focus on attracting and retaining the *loyal customer.* The customer base need not be large or dependent on drop-in traffic for a small independent business to survive, so long as the frequency of purchases from loyal customers matches the much smaller overhead that independent ownership affords. Given franchise costs, even an independently owned franchisee cannot survive without some significant "drop-in" customer traffic – even more so if they are located in a mall. Not so the independent small-scale entrepreneur with a committed clientele.

Indeed, even Suri and other small-scale entrepreneurs like herself who have fashioned iconic shops in neighbourhoods are sometimes unaware of the value locked up in shaping neighbourhood identities. In some sense this is akin to the "intangible assets," "brand equity," or "goodwill" that one hears management experts speak about when they are referring to large corporations. Markets place a value on these intangibles under the banner of "brand equity," which can often be more valuable than all of the tangible assets a firm owns. That is why, for example, a company like Nike, with very few tangible assets to sell if it were to declare bankruptcy, nevertheless trades at a multiple of its earnings far greater than a company like General Motors, which owns many more tangible things (e.g., machinery, cars, factories, land, etc.) but has not cultivated (or in the case of GM has lost) buyer loyalty.

Former Coca-Cola CEO Robert Goizueta (the guy who introduced New Coke to North America and inadvertently caused a consumer backlash and traditional Coke love-in that saved Coca-Cola from being overtaken by Pepsi) famously stated that Coca-Cola could survive the destruction of every single bottling plant but would be out of business the next day if consumers suffered from collective memory loss. It was a perceptive observation because, as blind taste testing has indeed shown, Coke, with its bitter aftertaste, is not the preferred cola even among self-ascribed Coca-Cola loyalists! Everything of value to Coke as a company is actually locked up inside people's minds. From a child's very first recollection of a birthday when the pop drink was served to the red and white colours of Santa's outfits that match perfectly with the iconic Coke logo, these instances and more make up what Coke "owns" and what shareholders have monetized.

Small businesses like Squibb's are similarly the physical embodiments of relationships forged with customer and community, and in this sense they too have "intangible" assets of value. They may not be as great as Coca-Cola's, but they can be realized when the firm is handed down to the next generation or is sold to a new owner intent on trading under the same name and location. The value of retaining the Squibb's name and location, over successive generations and transfers of ownership, is I think a major part of Suri's survival story.

As Suri later recounts, "I have people who, you know, come [to Weston] for a funeral, and they have to walk the main street just to see who's around, and they almost burst into tears, because they haven't been here for thirty, forty years, and they go, 'Oh my god, you're still here, I can't believe it! I can't believe you're still in business.'" But although Suri, perhaps more than anyone interviewed, is aware of the relationship between community building and customer loyalty and acknowledges that it is gratifying to hear the words of former residents, she still knows that nice sentiments are not enough to run a business. The visiting customer who once lived in the neighbourhood does not, according to Suri, " necessarily buy anything; they just want to see if it smells the same way it did thirty-seven years ago. It's all a sentimental journey, and [unfortunately that] doesn't pay the bills."

While true, it does however mobilize a committed group of loyal customers to be your free "guerrilla marketers," something major corporations are always trying to obtain.

On the Way out the Door

Before we leave Squibb's, Suri offers some perceptive comments about the socio-economic divide in the neighbourhood between long-time residents living in the residential enclave on the northwest side of the railway tracks, which is one of the oldest parts of Weston, and those residents who have recently arrived from abroad (places like Somalia, Ethiopia, and Ghana) and who populate the south end of the neighbourhood where the large seventies apartment blocks house numerous renters. The "old" Weston west of the tracks, although of mixed ethnicity, is nevertheless stable and includes "people that have lived in their homes for forty to fifty years. In many cases, their children live here as well."

Fortunately, according to Suri, this ethnic and economic divide has not produced any tension or violence: "There are no ethnic problems in this community. Knock on wood. We all get along." But that social and spatial divide has created a stigma in the community, whereby "the people who are part of the old guard of Weston do not like to come down to [the] main street, because they do not necessarily understand or like the new guard." By the "new guard," Suri is referring to the many new shops and restaurants that have sprung up in the last decade to cater to this newest wave of immigration – a mostly East African clientele. Her wish is that Weston's old-time residents will get over their fears and re-engage with their main street. But she knows that even if this were to happen, it would take a long time.

And what about the area's longstanding BIA? Suri, as one would imagine, has been actively involved in the past, but lately her involvement has waned. Although not expressing some of her obvious frustration, she does add that, while she may not be happy with some of the current BIA priorities, her absence from the board means that "[she] can't [very well] steer the agenda."

The Local Barber Shop's Place in a Neighbourhood

Not far down the road from Squibb's, along a curious side street called John Street, is Pete's Barber Shop. Like many long-standing neighbourhood barber shops, it is the quintessential male environment. In this case, the shop is laden with hockey paraphernalia. A quick Google search reveals that many of hockey's greatest players have shown up at Pete's shop and have had their pictures taken there. If you are a Toronto Maple Leaf of any renown and have not entered Pete's for the obligatory photo-op, then your credentials in "Leaf Nation" are severely diminished.

Not surprisingly, the owner of Pete's Barber Shop is none other than Peter Kalamaris, a first-generation Westonite who took over the running of the shop from his father, Pantelis (Peter) Kalamaris, Senior, who passed away just after our first interview in the fall of 2011. Readers of this book may want to have a look at the store's website and the wonderful eulogy written by Peter, Junior, about his dad. Like many immigrants arriving in Canada in the early 1960s, Pete found that his hairdressing credentials from Greece were not initially recognized, so he opened his shop a decade or so later, after toiling away in many part-time jobs.

And what about Peter the son?

Peter's story reads like a scene from the Frank Capra movie *It's a Wonderful Life*, in which George Bailey, played by Jimmy Stewart, puts aside his own aspirations for college and world travel in order to take over his father's small-town savings-and-loan company. In the late 1990s, Peter put aside his own teaching career in order to help his father manage the barber shop. Judging by how enthusiastic Peter is about his neighbourhood, his shop, and what he thinks needs to be done to turn Weston's fortunes around, it seems he has no regrets about leaving his teaching career behind. And after spending just a few minutes in his dad's barber shop, one can see why.

The place is like a miniature Hockey Hall of Fame, and the customers are as big a part of the ambiance as Peter or the shop's iconic contents. Only a few minutes after starting our conversation, a customer receiving a close shave pipes up to explain the enduring appeal of Pete's establishment: "Sure he's a half decent barber [sarcastically] but you can get a haircut and a close shave anywhere in the city ... but not in a place like this!" The customer gestures towards the walls covered in hockey memorabilia.

The customer then adds his own take on the shop's vibe: "It's like hanging out at your friend's house. You have fun ... and then he cuts your hair!"

After receiving a haircut, the customer and Pete proceed to play a spirited game of table hockey, during which Pete taunts the customer, repeatedly boasting that he is going to beat him. Pete clearly displays a highly personalized and irreverent style of customer service: "I don't provide any customer service! My customers get abuse!" he says. Then, more seriously, Pete sums up his own business philosophy: "Talking to the people, listening to what they have to say, [and] not ripping them off!" That's the key to staying in business.

This is very similar to Joe, Junior's, explanation for the success of Tip Top Collision or Vito's philosophy for his east end pizzeria.

Small Business and the Intergenerational Transfer of Knowledge

It seems that, whatever the sector, the lessons passed on from one generation of successful small business owners to the next remain remarkably similar. Quality and customer care more often than not trump expansion and greater potential revenues – at least for multi-generational entrepreneurs rooted in a specific location. "We had the opportunity to buy another store, but we didn't," says Pete.

When asked about the reasons for not expanding the business, Pete adds, "It allowed me to be more involved in local activities. I'm the School Council president at my daughter's school."

Some of the projects he helped organize while serving on the council included school dances, milk and lunch programs, and planting trees in the area. These were positive changes for the community and the school, and this was all made possible "because I have remained a small business. Otherwise I couldn't do that," says Pete. "I'm not looking to drive a Ferrari. I just wanna pay the bills, and have some money for a rainy day."

Sometimes Staying Small Is the Point

Pete believes that, had he expanded by employing more barbers or becoming a larger chain-style business, he would not have had the flexibility in his work schedule to get involved in as many worthwhile community activities.

Pete's freedom also allowed him to be able to take better care of his ailing father. "I can be at the barbershop, then take off when I need to. I can take better care of my parents. Being that I'm an only child I need to be free to do the things that I need to. If I was working for a large organization, I couldn't do that."

Twenty minutes into the interview, Pete closes down the shop, but continues to chat. During that time, he turns down a regular customer who is knocking on his door.

He says that he feels bad about it, because he knows the guy, who works at a construction site near Dufferin Street and St Clair Avenue, and knows that he makes a special trip to get down to his shop. However, today is a busy day for Pete, who after our interview will go to the hospital to visit his ailing father. While we talk, he receives a call from someone in his family who demands to know why he hasn't left the store yet. Peter clearly is very connected to his family and works hard to achieve a healthy balance between personal and business responsibilities.

But like his father before him, he feels a strong sense of personal commitment to his customers.

He explains, "I never go on holidays. Dad never took a holiday. You wanna be here for people that make a long trip to get here." Pete is very proud of the personalized service he provides: "Ninety-nine per cent of people who come in here don't have to say a word about how they want their hair cut." Much like the meal that is ready to be served to locals without a menu at Gerrard Pizza, the regulars who come into Pete's barber shop know they merely have to sit back and relax in the chair and the rest, as they say, is up to the man holding the blades.

His father taught him that, after two visits, he should know a customer's hair-cut preference. "If you don't, then you are in the wrong business." Pete adds that customer preferences are more important to know than names. "I don't know all their [customers'] names, you know. But I recognize their faces and hairstyle ... and [of course] they definitely know me." The male customers' hair-cut preferences tend to stay remarkably stable over time. The exceptions are the seasonal hair-cuts (winter versus summer) that cause people to modify the basic cut a bit. And wedding haircuts, for example, involve just a light trim, "to clean things up a bit," according to Pete.

Battling over BIA Identity

Before departing I wanted to learn just a little more about the store's hockey motif. It turns out the hockey-laden ambiance of Pete's barber shop is not a mere vanity project for the owner. The hockey theme is actually rooted in the area's rich history as a source of many of the National Hockey League's (NHL) greatest players and coaches. As an example, Pete points to the rather touching story of the late Roger Neilson, who wanted to visit the shop, but was unable to do so before he passed away. However, while in hospital, he sent Pete a letter expressing his interest in the shop and connecting it to the fact that he had started his career playing junior hockey in Weston. Pete treasures this memory and had the handwritten letter framed and placed on his wall.

This story touches a nerve with Pete, who begins once again to draw on a larger point. "Why is there no advertising highlighting the Weston hockey connection? Many hockey stars were born here, yet you don't see any signage advertising the fact!" He believes signs leading into the Weston area should prominently display the hockey heritage: "You are now entering Weston, proud home of this and that hockey legend."

So why hasn't this happened?

The answer can be linked back to those "old"-style bikes that are located above the BIA signage welcoming visitors into Weston Village.

Apparently, every time Pete has tried to promote the idea of Weston as Toronto's hockey mecca, he has met with stubborn resistance: "The BIA board feels that if the area is to be branded, it should be around the theme of bikes and bike riding. But you don't see anything much to do with bikes around here anymore!" says Pete, now clearly animated. He feels that the area's signage should be redesigned to highlight a vintage hockey feel. "What I would do is improve the signage. Make it retro. But nobody wants to put up the money for it … The old timers have great hockey memories." If the hockey heritage was highlighted in the area, he believes, it would help draw people to the Weston area. "Because right now, there is no single draw, and that's what we really need, something to give people a reason to visit Weston."

Small Business and the Large Anchor Tenant

Pete, it should be pointed out, graduated with a BA degree in urban planning and history. So he is particularly well equipped to critique the area's marketing and design failings. Indeed, Pete's final set of observations about the decline of local businesses along Weston Village's main street speaks to the more complex association independent businesses often have with larger more (financially) successful chains. It is not always the case that independent entrepreneurs want to keep corporate giants out of a neighbourhood. Building on a theme touched on by Suri, the more affluent long-time local residents of Weston rarely shop along Weston Road anymore, and the reason, according to Pete, is that all the well-known chains have moved out of the area.

"There was a good car dealership, a Canadian Tire, but they all relocated. Years earlier, when the factories were employing people, things were different. People would come and shop on their lunch breaks. Weston and John Street used to be so busy. You should have seen it. But when the factories closed, the surrounding businesses were really hit hard, and they never recovered." The companies that Pete is referring to included Kodak, CCM, Dominion Bridge, and Moffat.

"Loblaws was here, men's clothing stores, movie theatres, all these things are gone. Is it any wonder the small guys are suffering? There are no anchors to draw people in. All people know about Weston are the bad things, that's why people stay away."

In the absence of an "anchor," many in the area are now pinning their hopes on the one stop to be included in the new rail link that will connect the airport, ten kilometres from Weston, to Union Station in downtown Toronto. Although Weston was chosen as the only station between downtown and the airport, according to Pete this is not a reason to celebrate.

The trains are diesel-powered, not electric, for one thing. Pete points out that this would be fine if the trains passed two or three times a day, but having them run every twenty minutes will only add to the public perception that Weston is a dirty and unhealthy area. Still, Pete does admit that the train station is an unknown quantity. If the trains run on clean-burning fuel or are eventually electrified, it could improve Weston's fortunes.

"But don't count on it happening any time soon," says Pete. In order for the area to capitalize on the promise of the airport link, there must be an urban plan in place to rejuvenate the area. In this city, however, "all the planning … is cut and paste and … not unified under a grander vision of city building and neighbourhood-specific input." This is something which drives Peter "crazy!"

Again, one can't help recalling Jane Jacobs's forty-year-old lament, which started our chapter off, in which creative bottom-up Toronto seems to clash with the official top-down vision (or lack thereof) of the city's larger institutions. Paradoxically, this is why I come away feeling that Weston, despite its challenges, may well end up taking advantage of its eventual new train station. So long, of course, as small business owners like Pete stick it out, maintain their independent presence in the neighbourhood, and stay involved in community life.

Speaking of stops along the way, our last stop in Weston Village takes us to a fashion retailer just down the road from Pete. If you thought purveyors of stationery had a struggle in today's economy, how does a seller of clothing stay in business with competition from the likes of Wal-Mart and Winners?

Well, that's just what we're about to find out next.

The Local Fashion Retailer: A Dying Breed?

Feeling Fine is owned and operated by Sam Kleinman, a frank-talking entrepreneur who started his career as a project engineer at Dupont. He then worked in consulting and, in the late 1980s, finally took over his father's small business. In 1988 he opened up his current shop, Feeling Fine, which deals in women's fashion.

The name was inspired by another business that had a similarly upbeat moniker. Sam noted that if he ever opened up his own business he would use something like it. In Sam's words, "I want people to feel good when they are shopping in my store, because clothing is a luxury."

"Women buy clothes to feel good about themselves ... they look at the price of an item, and if they like it they say I'm worth it." And having never noted the connection between careful shopping habits and personal longevity, Sam reveals an obvious truth that had eluded me about the gender divide: "The reason women live so long is because they take care of themselves. Men [on the other hand] shop very differently; they look for clothes that are more functional. And they buy much less clothing in general." According to Sam he couldn't run the store selling clothes to men: "I just wouldn't make any money."

So how does an engineer summon the *chutzpah* to become a ladies fashion mogul?

According to Sam he always knew he had a knack for sales, and in the early years from 1988 to 1992, business was indeed good. It wasn't until the hated Goods and Services Tax (GST) was introduced that sales stalled, and it was at that time that the area also started to deteriorate. Business has been slowly and consistently declining ever since.

At this point the business is surviving because of Sam's love for sales and retail fashion. In fact, Sam feels that new store owners often lack the basic skills of how to sell, which is why there is so much turnover in the industry. He is clearly proud of his self-taught salesmanship and attributes his knowledge to having read up on the subject and having attended the sales seminars put on by the Retail Council of Canada. He is particularly fond of Paco Underhill's book *Why We Buy: The Science of Shopping*, which was the primary text that he used to shape his understanding of salesmanship and retail.

"It should be mandatory for all retailers to attend a good sales seminar. At low cost you could improve every single main street retailer in the city." At this point Sam lets loose one of his many ideas for how to improve the small business sector: "In fact, why doesn't every BIA in the city use some of that levy money and offer 'free' seminars to its retailers?"

Why not indeed?

According to Sam, retail involves very specific knowledge that the best salespersons have developed over time, but that can nevertheless be effectively taught. For example, "Before you try to attend to a new customer, you have to train retailers to be polite, and say 'Hello,' 'Good morning,' with a smile to everyone that walks in your door." Another simple but often neglected axiom of good salesmanship is that "It's easier to sell to an existing customer than to a new customer."

On marketing and impression management, Sam notes that "maintaining uniformity of image is the key. Knowing how to make your street displays look 'clean' is as simple as cleaning your windows every morning, and changing the window display often. This one action gives you ten per cent of your sales."

And this final pearl of fashion retail wisdom: "A good salesman doesn't sell an item, he sells a wardrobe."

Despite a clear love for what he does, Sam is planning to retire in a few years (when he reaches sixty-two or sixty-five years of age, depending on how the markets do). Indeed if his retirement time horizon were not approaching so fast, he would have closed the shop already and turned to a new endeavour. This is sad to hear from a small business owner brimming with ideas and local knowledge.

But Sam is busy with family these days; he has older parents, and if he has to close the store one day to take his father to the doctor, he has the freedom to do so, echoing the statements made by Pete the barber just up the street. But, of course, every time he has to close up shop, it negatively affects the business. His daughter has triplets, which he also, along with his wife, helps to take care of.

The Causes of Boutique Fashion Store Decline

After a short digression on the falling price of clothing based on the entrance of Asian suppliers, we start talking about the causes of the small-scale fashion retailer's decline.

First, businesses like his were aimed squarely at the middle-class consumer, something which, in Weston and in many other parts of the city, has all but disappeared. It started with those bastions of Canadian middle-income retail, the department store giants Eaton's and Simpsons, which were the first casualties of the simultaneous move up and down the retail clothing food chain. In place of quality at an affordable price, the essence of middle-income purchasing activity, retail now offers largely unaffordable luxury at one end or cheap disposable fashion at the other. Ironically, smaller retailers like Feeling Fine have managed to hang on longer than department store chains like Eaton's because of loyal customers and lower overhead. But as Sam readily admits, that model is coming to an end. "Not enough new people are walking into the store. As my customers get older, they need stuff less. I'm not replacing them with new customers."

And remember our observations about the need to replace an ethnic customer base when it either moves or assimilates. That's another reason behind Feeling Fine's dwindling fortunes. Since the early1990s an exodus has occurred in Weston. There was a solid base of upwardly mobile first-generation Italian, Spanish, Portuguese, and Jamaican residents who made up the bulk of the neighbourhood's customer base. But, as Sam notes, "they [the early immigrants] did better for themselves, and they moved away to places like Woodbridge." Some of those customers, many from the outlying 905 area of Greater Toronto, still come back, however. "I know the people's names, I know their family. I'm their psychiatrist. I know what they need."

In fashion retailing, according to Sam, "the secret to business success is knowing where and how to buy your product and then knowing what your clientele wants ... and most importantly of all, understanding what they also *need*." For people who don't have fashion sense, Sam offers free wardrobe advice, helping undecided customers pick out the right clothes. Anticipating fancy social networking applications offered by Amazon or Facebook, Sam has been linking customer tastes to their fashion wants for two decades: "When I know that I have clothes that my customers will like," says Sam, "I call them up and tell them about it. I know what they like and what will look good on them."

Sam then quite perceptively rhymes off a number of other social changes that have affected the boutique fashion scene: The trend towards "dress down Fridays" has shifted the incentive away from buying nice dress clothes. Also, fewer people now attend church, which has meant that "fewer people need dressy clothes." And just as I was about to leave Sam's shop feeling "not so fine" about the state of Toronto's many small retailers, I heard Sam utter the following: "Winners just up the road called me up one day and asked if I wanted to work for them as a general manager at one of their stores."

So what's the competition doing calling up and offering a job to someone like Sam? Well, it turns out customers who shopped at both stores noticed a big difference between how the two establishments treated their customers and displayed their clothes. Soon those same customers started badgering Winners store managers to make changes to the store to make its layout and operation more similar to that of Feeling Fine. After a while it seems, someone higher up in the personnel department at Winners caught wind of this and called Sam personally and asked him if he wanted to work for them.

When asked why he didn't jump at the opportunity, Sam shrugs: the difference between his store and a chain like Winners is "personalized service" and his "sensibility for the organization of his business."

"One day," Sam comments as I pack up my bag and put on my coat to leave, "people may come to realize that small business service is a value. But by then we may be all gone."

With that final lament burning a small hole in my gut, I leave Weston Village and prepare for the long (rush hour) drive back east to Don Mills. There is just one more stop left in our tour of "bottom-up" Toronto, to a store with seemingly even less of a chance of survival than Feeling Fine's fashion retail.

Eglinton Hill BIA and the Concept of "Local Mayor"

Driving south along Weston Road we turn east along Eglinton Avenue and arrive at Keele Street at the western entrance of the Eglinton Hill BIA. It turns out the person I am going to visit, Steve Tasses, is the long-time owner of, of all things, a video store called Variety and Video. He also happens to be the founder of the area's BIA.

I first met Steve in the summer of 2008 when we were conducting interviews with local BIA founders across the city. What immediately struck me at the time was how integral Variety and Video was to the functioning of that short strip of Eglinton Avenue West. People didn't just come in to rent movies; they came in to chat, reminisce, drop off and pick up items, and to just say "Hi." In fact, a minute did not go by during that initial interview without a local business person, former neighbour, long-time customer, or random pedestrian walking in and, on a first-name basis, engaging in a short conversation with Steve.

Most impressive was Steve's knowledge of Jamaican patois, which I witnessed as the local owner of a curry and roti restaurant proceeded to ask Steve a question that I was unable to understand. To my amazement, Steve motioned and responded, "Just over there behind the root beer," and the owner carefully found what he had asked for, a large two-litre jug of Pepsi-Cola.

This was evidence, at least to me, that there is more than a single mayor in a city like Toronto. In reality, there are as many "mayors" as there are diverse main street neighbourhoods. Much like the street-level world "of fun and spontaneity" described by Jacobs, Steve's inter-actions with residents were emblematic of the community engagement that is so critical to small business success but also, critically, to the success of a neighbourhood.

Steve seemed to be plugged into all that was Eglinton Hill- and Ward 12-related.

After a rash of shootings in 2009, for example, Steve was quoted extensively in a *Toronto Star* article that focused on the use of special officers to monitor community events and force criminals out of local parks.

"A lot of people said they were happy with police getting rid of the bad guys," said Steve, but "[the residents] wanted the program to keep running – they didn't want the gangsters to come back." It was this desire to not only make his store a success but to improve the fortunes of the neighbourhood that he had worked in for over twenty-six years that prompted Steve to run for office in 2010 as councillor for Ward 12.

Given what I had seen in my initial meeting, I can't say that I was surprised by his run at local politics a few years later, but I was surprised by the outcome. Steve eventually lost, which is perhaps why I couldn't help but feel that the interview this time around was not as animated as the first time we spoke. But then again, his incumbent, Frank Di Giorgio, has served as a local councillor for twenty-two of the past twenty-five years, so it would have been a tall order for a first-time rival like Steve to win.

Still, Steve seems as engaged as ever in the local neighbourhood and, like the other entrepreneurs whom we have met, has a fountain of knowledge about the area's history and fortunes. As Steve puts it, "Job opportunities are lacking in the area." As was the case with Weston up the road, "Kodak used to be a big employer, so when they closed, it left a vacuum. Kodak's position in the community was equivalent to GM in Oshawa. When Kodak was here, business was booming. We need to get more businesses like that in the area."

The Diversity of Business Offerings and Main Street Success

With Kodak now sadly filing for bankruptcy, it seems unlikely that this end of the city will ever get a manufacturer like that again, but some of Steve's other ideas are more doable. Taking a page out of what seems like a Tyler Brûlé *Monocle* article on the keys to urban main street success, Steve points to the need for "retail balance" if a neighbourhood is to succeed in engaging its local residents as customers. Specifically, he argues that "there's simply too much duplication of business in the area. Do we really need ten hair salons ... are people's hairstyles in such bad shape?"

"What one needs," according to Steve, "[are] stores that complement each other." Quite sensibly "if local residents continue to by-pass Eglinton Hill's main street shops," Steve asserts, echoing the same concern voiced in Weston Village, "then we as a group of businesses have failed to offer them [the residents] what they require to shop here. We need a meat store, a bakery, a grocery store, and a fish market" – the basic building blocks of a complete diet made manifest on the storefronts of Eglinton West.

Though he "treats his customers like gold" and many of his best customers now "span three generations," the traffic in his shop for video rentals has slowed considerably.

As to his own store's fortunes as a "video purveyor," Steve is under no illusions.

In the early 1980s, during the height of the VHS era, Steve used to rent 1,100 videos a week. Now he rents 300 in a month if he's lucky. His Variety and Video store's main business is now "confectionery, Lotto, cigarettes, and TTC tickets," and, since the local Coffee Time closed, "a lot of coffee."

"Adapt with the times or go the way of the dodo bird" seems to be the message as we wrap up the conversation.

As I am about to leave Variety and Video, not sure if I am a little less or a little more hopeful about the viability of small-scale entrepreneurship than when I arrived, Steve offers one last quotable line: "If Bob Rae had had a second term, he would have extended the subways out here to Eglinton West and beyond to the airport more than a decade ago. We are the only city in an industrialized country that doesn't have that!"

Indeed, I cannot help but think that our local mayor is once again correct.

What Toronto Teaches Us about Small Business and the Success of a City

As I sit down to write the concluding words for this chapter, I do so from the corner table of a locally owned cafe adjoining my university college and its residence. Bar Mercurio is owned and operated by the Mercurio family. Some of the staff members have been working with the family for over a decade. In an industry with high turnover, Bar Mercurio's waiters and waitresses recognize most of their customers, and we recognize them. The bar serves great food and great coffee and is always busy. Perhaps this is why I feel a sense of hope for the widely engaging local entrepreneurs and the neighbourhoods that I visited as part of this research project.

But what will happen a decade from now? Will Toronto's small-scale entrepreneurs be able to keep up with the many challenges facing their sector?

My hunch is that, so long as locally situated storefronts are still in existence, there will be owners like Vito, Joe, Dan, Tony, Sue, Jim, Suri, Pete, Sam, and Steve who care passionately about their businesses and the customers they serve. I come away more certain than ever that locally owned and operated shops will continue to function as the authentic social and economic anchors of the areas they inhabit and will go on doing so long after their original owners have moved on and many once-mighty brand names have disappeared.

What this selection of small business vignettes perhaps best illustrates is how Toronto, by accident more than by design, has evolved in some unique and world-envying ways since Jane Jacobs arrived in 1968. An influx of more newcomers from every part of the globe has helped make the city an infinitely more vibrant place than it was when my own parents emigrated from Spain, or when Peter's father emigrated here from Greece in the early 1960s. This is in no small measure because of the energy and ambition of Toronto's independently owned and operated businesses, which have helped revitalize many of its neighbourhoods, or as was the case with a number of the areas we visited, are at least in the process of trying.

Toronto Postscript

It is said that business is always changing, and this is confirmed by the fact that, since our conversations with small-scale entrepreneurs on the streets of Toronto, a number of things have altered. The city has added several new BIAs since the chapter was first drafted, adding to its impressive status as the city with most BIAs in the world. And as the book goes into copy-editing, a vote on whether to establish a new BIA is being held in an area known as "Ossington Avenue" in the city's west end. Some business owners profiled here have sold their interests in businesses they helped found, while others are now in the process of retiring from their life's work. But what is remarkable amid all this change is that Toronto neighbourhoods can still bank on seeing new stores pop up opened by small-scale entrepreneurs in the hope of making it stick this time around.

PART II

Unlocking the Potential
of Small-Scale Enterprise

6 The "Art and Science" of Small Business Survival: Lessons in BIA Practice

As seen in Part I of *Small Business and the City*, Canadian BIAs are struggling to represent their members' interests while at the same time meeting the challenges of twenty-first-century living. They are also highly diverse, covering the full gamut of socio-economic and geographic diversity. In Toronto, for example, they range from the Fifth Avenue-style affluence of Yorkville to the bohemianism of Queen Street West, to the emerging suburban BIAs of Scarborough and North York. In the Vancouver region they range from a single downtown business district not too dissimilar from the downtown BIA found in Halifax to the spa town of Harrison Hot Springs, over an hour's drive from central Vancouver. Among the examples presented in Part I, there is probably something that will resonate with readers living and working in a range of urban environments.

In research conducted prior to the start of *Small Business and the City* we found that, while many BIAs are dealing with a range of localized issues (e.g., getting local business buy-in for new investments, competition from other BIAs and retailers, organizational capacity building, etc.), a recurring theme among many of those interviewed was concern over a lack of coordination between economic development activities and support for small business – a theme that was also apparent from our look at Vancouver in chapter 4. From the street-level perspective of small-scale entrepreneurs, their local knowledge allows them to identify policies of government departments and actions of big business that often seem at odds with the goal of promoting entrepreneurship and bettering local amenities. Our intention in this chapter is to highlight these challenges in order to propose some solutions.

Our Part I examination of the birth of the BIA movement and of the challenges facing entrepreneurs in three of Canada's major cities showed how the urban regions we live in are defined by the number, quality, and character of their small, locally owned, independently operated businesses. Large urban centres are not, by implication, defined by the large chain stores or corporations that are often lured with generous public tax breaks to set up shop on our streetscapes. There is no doubt that local residents – even those who oppose the entry of a corporate chain – benefit from the range of choice and dependability of an anchor store. But these gains are very much attenuated when smaller independents are lost and a main street is eviscerated in the process. Large cities require diversity to thrive and survive.

The three business qualifiers used often in this book (i.e., small, local, and independent) all matter because they are what make cities worth caring about (if you are a resident) and worth visiting (if you are a tourist). Neighbourhoods are defined not by features that are common and ubiquitous but by those that are unique.

In this chapter, we explore more generally how the city – as an agglomeration of consumers, workers, and entrepreneurs – relates to small business success and how small businesses in turn add to the vibrancy of our urban regions. First, some evidence as to the nature of these interrelationships.

BIAs and Neighbourhood Rankings

In the spring of 2013 *Toronto Life* magazine presented what it billed as "the ultimate ranking of the city's neighbourhoods." The magazine examined ten factors across 140 neighbourhoods that the city draws from its census tract definitions, assigning them a score out of 100. The categories included housing (which considers year-over-year appreciation and the ratio of average price to household income), crime, transit, shopping, health and environment, entertainment, community engagement (which factors in voter turnout and beautification projects), diversity, schools, and employment. After averaging the scores of these ten items (weighted based on what *Toronto Life* readers listed as the most important factors), the survey produced an overall score and a ranked list of the 140 neighbourhoods.

A team of researchers at University of Toronto's Martin Prosperity Institute helped crunch the data, drawing on a wealth of sources – including Statistics Canada, the city's exhaustive statistical research, the

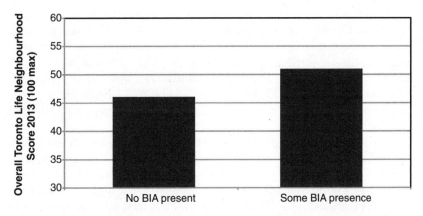

Presence of BIAs within or near neighbourhood borders

Exhibit 6.1: Overall *Toronto Life* Neighbourhood Ranking Scores (out of 100) split by BIA presence, 2013. *Source:* Author calculations based on data from *Toronto Life* website

Toronto Police Service, the Centre for Research on Inner City Health, and the Fraser Institute. The results proved controversial in that the top ten did not include the most likely candidates and instead were spread across the city, ranging from some of the wealthiest neighbourhoods to some of the most modest.

While one could quibble with allowing a non-random sample of *Toronto Life* readers to determine the weighting of the index items, the ranking itself, in our estimation, was easily one of the most objective to be conducted by a popular magazine. The ranking was much less subjective than the typical editorialized opinions about what neighbourhoods are "coolest" or most "up-and-coming" found on countless other lists. However, had the researchers grouped neighbourhoods by a variable that was surprisingly absent in the *Toronto Life* rankings, it would have found that small businesses were implicated in this ranking, too.

By matching the proximity of the seventy-plus existing BIAs in the city of Toronto to the 140 neighbourhoods in the *Toronto Life* list, we created an additional variable that links neighbourhoods to BIAs. In Exhibit 6.1 we compare neighbourhoods with no single BIA within or near their borders to neighbourhoods with some BIA presence. We find that there is a small but significant four-point boost in overall neighbourhood scores associated with BIA presence. If we treat BIA presence a little more finely and split the variable into three categories (low, modest, and high BIA presence) and compare once again to the non-BIA referent neighbourhoods, we see in exhibit 6.2 a discernible increase in the relationship. Neighbourhoods with modest-to-high BIA presence draw the largest benefits, having close to an eight-point advantage as compared to those with no BIAs.

This effect is amplified even further when we compare across the ten sub-components of the overall score. It is clear that a neighbourhood benefits from having a vibrant and active small business on its doorstep. The ranking in exhibit 6.3 is ordered from the highest to the lowest BIA relationships. At the top of the list, not surprisingly – and confirming findings of other research related to BIA presence – were housing valuations, availability of shopping, and crime level reduction. In each case the boost to these scores was 12.9, 12.2, and 8.5 points, respectively, when at least one BIA was located within or near the boundary of a neighbourhood. In the middle were scores for community engagement (8.3), entertainment (6.9), transit (3.4), and employment (2.8). Our BIA case studies show that there is clearly a feedback process associated with some of these categories. For example, in the case of transit, a BIA can add an "institutional voice" to push for increased bus or streetcar frequency. Equally, a BIA is likely to spring up when consumers have easy access to business offerings. At the low end of the BIA and neighbourhood rankings were schools, health and environment, and diversity – all of which were non-significant save for diversity, which was negatively related. It seems that BIAs are associated with neighbourhoods that are more homogeneous, again not surprisingly, given the dominance of Little Italy, Chinatown, and Greektown BIAs in many cities.

Some Basic Theory on Cities, Size of Establishment, and Business Variety

Up to now, we have described how small firms and large urban environments become co-dependent upon each other's success. We have also shown, using 2013 data from Canada's largest city (Toronto), that there is a discernible statistical correlation between the positive attributes of city neighbourhoods and the presence of an active and engaged small business community in the form of a BIA presence.

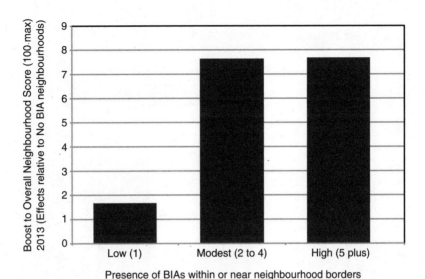

Exhibit 6.2: Effect of BIA presence on Overall *Toronto Life* Neighbourhood Ranking Score (mean 48.5), 2013. *Source:* Author calculations based on data from *Toronto Life* website

The links between city and small business, however, are not merely natural ones unaffected by forces such as state action – or inaction, as the case may be. The main idea explored below is that as the size – measured in people and activities – of the city grows in *scale*, large corporate employers begin to matter less to the viability of a local region. This is because the *scope* of individual needs expands with city size as do the opportunities for innovation and a start-up culture to take hold. This is a non-recursive process in which positive feedback ensures that as cities grow so do the opportunities for small-scale entrepreneurship.

Take, for example, the recent collapse of the financial sector in Britain following the Great Recession of 2008. The loss of an estimated 300,000 jobs in the financial sector, located mainly in the city of London, proved crippling for the government's budget balances and indeed brought Britain's rather torrid economic growth of the preceding decade to a screeching halt. But in London, one of the epicentres of the financial meltdown, the regional outlook was, relatively speaking, brighter than in most other parts of the United Kingdom.[1] The reason is

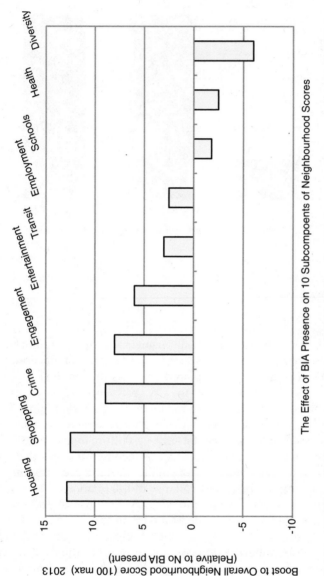

The Effect of BIA Presence on 10 Subcompoents of Neighbourhood Scores

Exhibit 6.3: Effect of BIA presence on *Toronto Life* Neighbourhood Sub-component Scores (mean 48.5), 2013.

Source: Author calculations based on data from *Toronto Life* website

that Greater London is a diverse economic region of 12 million inhabitants, in which several industries and sectors support a diversity of economic activity. It would take the collapse of several industries all at once to knock London off the economic map.

Contrast the London experience with that of other cities that did not achieve this critical level of size, density, or diversification – cities like, say, Detroit or Windsor, that rely heavily on employment in the auto sector – and we see how a comparable level of job losses has meant, in Detroit's case especially, the wholesale abandonment of entire neighbourhoods. The city in many places is reverting back to agricultural food production and, in some cases, forest.

What Determines Whether You Get to See the Next Foreign-Language Oscar-Winning Film?

The idea that population (or market) size is the limiting factor in supporting a greater variety of niche tastes was a feature of economic life first noted in Adam Smith's *Wealth of Nations*, and it makes highly intuitive sense.[2] A personal taste for French films would likely be hard to satisfy for someone living in rural British Columbia. But someone living in Vancouver can enjoy its annual French Film Festival (now in its fourth season) sponsored by the union of local independent cinemas known as Festival Cinemas. So, in a seemingly straightforward relationship, the larger the city we live in, the greater the variety of small businesses it is likely to support, for the commercial viability of catering to niche tastes occurs only when there are sufficient numbers of other niche-loving consumers with the same tastes.

Complementary explanations for the same phenomenon abound. Chad Syverson, from the University of Chicago, for example, proposes a model in which large markets with many producers allow consumers to easily switch their patronage, thus increasing competition and leading to smaller but more efficient firms.[3] Another argument is that, where transport costs are high, there must be enough demand in a small enough space to support a variety of product offerings. This general idea was tested in a study of restaurant diversity by Glaeser, Kolko, and Saiz, who note that "the advantages from scale economies and specialization are ... clear in the restaurant business where large cities will have restaurants that specialize in a wide range of cuisines – scale economies mean that specialized retail can only be supported in places large enough to have a critical mass of consumers."[4] In this same vein,

Waldfogel notes that, "some products are produced and consumed lo-cally, so that provision requires not only a large group favoring the product but a large number [of small businesses] nearby."[5]

In short, what Smith's original idea suggests and modern research confirms is that cities large enough and dense enough will support much more small-scale diversity than smaller, less urban environments. They can do so because individual entrepreneurs, though small in scale, will nevertheless find enough demand for their niche offerings.

The Proportion of Independent Businesses and City Size

If we were to graph the relationship between city size and local entre-preneurial variety, it might look like the rising straight line (*a*) in ex-hibit 6.4, with city size on the horizontal axis going from small to large and with relative enterprise diversity (measured as the number of small independent enterprises as a fraction of the total) running from low to high on the vertical axis. This we can term the "linear hypothesis" of city size and business variety, in which increases in city size (as mea-sured by the number of people) lead to greater business variety (as measured by the number of independent businesses).

But this is not the whole story. In very small towns that are geo-graphically isolated, we also see small independent businesses thriv-ing. The family-owned general store, selling everything from fresh produce to gas, is still a feature found in many rural locations. There are also numerous self-employed tradespeople and operators who supply many of the needs of the community in small towns with sev-eral thousand inhabitants or less. But when the small town grows be-yond its very small borders, becoming something in between a large town and a small city, or when the once-distant edge of a larger urban environment creeps closer to the "rural" fringe, the "depopulation" of independent enterprise begins. In such cases, the opening of a nearby (in some cases an hour's drive is close enough) big-box store or power centre can quite powerfully reshape the retail and commercial land-scape of the small town.

Traditional urban economic textbooks often depict these ideas visu-ally with the growth of concentric circles of the type shown below (see exhibit 6.5), where a central business district in a small town separated geographically from the suburban fringe of a larger urban environment is able to survive (the dark solid-line circles) at time *t*. In fact, both

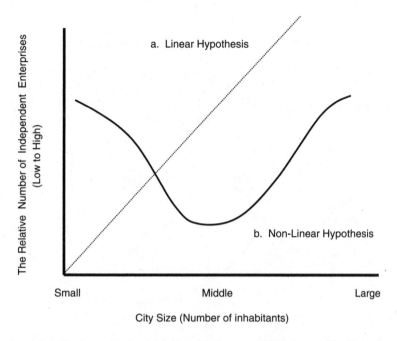

Exhibit 6.4: The hypothesized relationship between city size and independent entrepreneurship

central business districts (in the city and town) do well in serving their respective local populations. But as the suburban fringe of the city expands and/or the town grows at time *t+1* (as depicted by the dotted-line circles), the ability for small town merchants to stay afloat in the central business district begins to decline, as perhaps would the central business district in the large centre, as well, given that both populations can be equally served by a retail park located halfway between them.

So our relationship turns out to be a double-humped shape, as in line *b* in exhibit 6.4. From zero inhabitants to very low levels of population size, we get a potential market size not worth the effort of supplying by big firms – hence the viability of small independent ownership in geographically isolated towns. As the small town size grows, however, it is still not large enough to cater to niche tastes (those customer segments are too small in absolute size) and so the "long tail" of consumer niche tastes is still not serviced, while the mass-market consumer becomes an

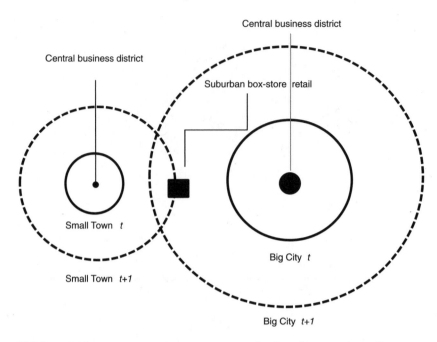

Exhibit 6.5: The expansion of a town or city suburban fringe and its effect on local retail offerings

ideal candidate for a large corporate chain, which can wipe out a main street shopping district. The small-to-medium-sized urban environment is therefore ripe for annexation by well-organized corporate retail giants, a fact that accounts for the proliferation of these modes of commercial space in mid-size cities and modern suburbs with a concen-. trated population size of between 50,000 and 250,000 inhabitants. It is only as city size continues to grow, often well beyond the million person mark, that the size of a niche customer segment is large enough, in the presence of positive transportation costs, to once again support a small, independent, and diversified business sector.[6]

Urban Built Form as a Moderator of the Independent Business–City Size Relationship

There is one added factor that can alter the relationship described above, and this comes into stark relief when one travels outside of

North America. It turns out that the capital of New Zealand, Wellington, is roughly the same size as Kingston, Ontario. Yet, the two cities could not be farther from each other in terms of their look and feel and, more importantly for this book, in terms of the number and vibrancy of small independent businesses that one finds in downtown Wellington versus downtown Kingston.

On one level this is strange, since both Wellington and Kingston were settled by similar Protestant immigrants of Scottish-British origin who were very loyal to king and country. The cultural origins and timing of settlement are therefore quite similar, and both cities have a harbour and a large waterfront. Yet, there is an important geographic difference. Wellington is bounded by large hills and sits on a relatively small, open, valley plain where a majority of the city's residents, amenities, public buildings, and workplaces have to be concentrated. Kingston lies on a flat estuary plain, with nothing north of its original port and fort settlement to constrain its growth. Kingston has therefore sprawled over a much wider area, whereas Wellington (hemmed in by geography) has not. Consequently, Wellington's central core feels "like a big city," with lots of unique offerings for tourists and residents alike, despite its relatively small population, whereas Kingston's main downtown streets feel like those of a small town even though its population is relatively large.

The missing "moderator" of the city size and independent ownership relation is the "density of people and compact urban form." Two metropolitan areas of equal size but varying urban densities can produce a different configuration of enterprise and local amenities. The density of a city, as a consequence, moderates the effects of size on diversity of business offerings.

Bringing persons with particular tastes in closer proximity to each other makes small, independent local supply viable at a much lower population break-even point. This is a fact clearly observed if one plots the number of restaurants in any given city against the population size of that city. The relationship is essentially log-linear, which means that for every 1 per cent increase in population, cities gain 1 per cent more restaurant offerings. However, if the type of cuisine is instead measured against the size of city, the line, though still positive, becomes flatter, with more variance. This shows how a city's product diversity fluctuates with changes in overall city density.[7]

And how well does this amended density model stack up to the evidence?

Evidence from a Study of Restaurant Cuisine

As mentioned above, restaurant data provide a nice test of what happens to product variety under differing urban conditions. University of British Columbia Sauder School of Business Professor Nathan Schiff recently found that cities that concentrate people into smaller areas have more choice of independent food retailers, holding the size of the city constant. This is because the increase in the number of consumers demanding specific varieties in turn increases the likelihood that a small firm will find sufficient demand for its niche product. In Schiff's case, he collected information about restaurants across U.S. cities and found that larger and denser cities have both *greater* and *rarer* varieties of restaurants.

According to Schiff, "varieties that appeal to fewer people are much more likely to be found in denser cities because spatial aggregation becomes more important when demand is limited." The presence of ethnic neighbourhoods or other geographic clusterings of tastes facilitates the spatial aggregation of demand and can significantly increase the likelihood that a market will support a particular set of locally owned independent businesses.[8]

Overall, our own observations about the contrast between Wellington, New Zealand, and Canada's Kingston, Ontario, coupled with the empirical results of Schiff's paper, show a definite link between a denser city structure and greater product differentiation. The observations also provide empirical evidence for one of the theoretically important benefits of greater agglomerations of people and small-scale entrepreneurs: greater consumer choice.

Capturing the Density Effect

Our graph needs modifying, therefore, to show how, for a given city size, the low-density and high-density scenarios differ in their prediction of how many local offerings consumers will have access to. This is done in exhibit 6.6, which shows that in urban forms where people and industry are farther apart, holding constant the size of population at some middle range, there is less diversity of business enterprise at point *d* and a tilt towards the larger chain and corporate giant. By contrast, in cities where people and firms are clustered together more closely, they tolerate greater diversity (as seen at point *c*), with greater numbers of smaller firms under independent ownership able to survive.

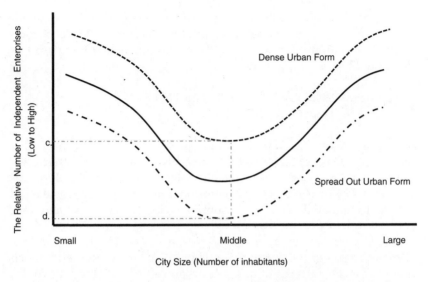

Exhibit 6.6: The moderating effect of urban form on share of independent entrepreneurship

One of the key findings to press home is that the physical and socio-economic characteristics of a neighbourhood affect the returns to small-scale entrepreneurship, both directly through their impact on local demand and indirectly through their role in facilitating the accumulation of social capital – a term that captures the extent to which social relations offer individuals real practical benefits, or what the World Bank has defined as "the institutions, relationships, and norms that shape the quality and quantity of a community's social interactions."[9]

The physical characteristics of a neighbourhood (e.g., its urban design) can affect the "the quality and quantity of social interactions" and hence the performance of entrepreneurs in a number of ways. For instance, the social capital required to succeed in a small business is more easily formed within more highly populous, highly integrated, and economically clustered urban areas. The reason may be as simple as the fact that the chance of interacting and meeting peers who share complementary business products, services, skills, or interests is greater in these areas. Greater proximity also promotes clusters of spin-off service enterprises, offers valuable opportunities for interaction, and acts as a catalyst to small-scale innovation and the sharing of information.

Finally, as Ciccone and Hall[10] first observed in the mid-1990s, neighbourhoods with higher population densities and greater levels of commercial concentration generate higher levels of demand for the services of the small-scale business owner.

Is There Any Evidence in the BIA Data That Density Affects Diversity?

If we take present-day Toronto as our benchmark, since it currently has the largest number of BIAs and the longest history with their presence, we can see that, based on the original metropolitan city boundaries, the greatest number of BIAs (45 out of 73) are concentrated in what was the old City of Toronto, followed by the suburban cities of Etobicoke and York (19), North York (5), and Scarborough (4). This is shown in exhibit 6.7

And if we reshuffle the deck, so to speak, and identify more precisely the areas of the current city where BIAs are located and match them to (a) the patterns of original urban settlement (1800–1900); (b) early suburban development based on the extension of the tram lines in the early twentieth century (1901–45); and then (c) to postwar suburban (1946–present) expansion, the portrait of greater urban density favouring clusters of small independent businesses emerges even more clearly.

As seen in exhibit 6.8, of the seventy-three BIAs in Toronto in 2012, forty-three are located in the urban core, twenty-three are located in the early suburbs, which maintain many of the features of traditional urbanism (narrow residential neighbourhoods feeding onto one or more main streets), and only seven are located in the postwar suburbs, despite the fact that the area encompassed by the newer suburban fringe is three times as large as that of the original urban form covered by the pre-war city.

This analysis looks at only a few aspects affecting how and why BIA activity may differ, namely the numerical presence of BIAs based on features of the particular local urban landscape. Other dimensions of BIA activity for which we luckily have some data are also worth exploring. It is to these other relationships that we now turn.

A BIA Segmentation Analysis: What Accounts for BIA Diversity and Success?

What we want to discuss now are some of the typologies that emerged from our three inter-city on-the-ground narratives. That is, we wish to

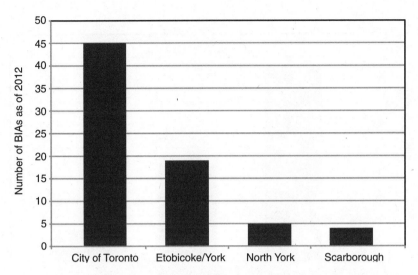

Exhibit 6.7: The number of BIAs in the city of Toronto by pre-amalgamation municipal boundaries, 2012. *Source:* Author calculations based on data from TABIA website.

examine which dimensions of the BIAs differed from area to area and what consequences this has for shopkeepers and residents and for a city more generally?

We can identify five clear markers of BIA segmentation. These are listed below, followed by a short explanation of their significance. Later we shall complement these typologies with a few tests of conjectures against actual data, again gleaned mainly from Toronto, since it has the largest number of BIAs to use in comparing and contrasting our observations and predictions.

The Size of the BIA (as Measured by Membership)

The first segmenting variable is the size of a BIA as measured by membership rather than geography (that will come later). Some BIAs have a large membership base while others are small. Using data from the TABIA website, we see that the median size of a BIA is 200 members and the average is not too far off at 250 members, suggesting that a few large BIAs are pulling the average higher. Those well above the median we would deem large while those well below we would identify as small.

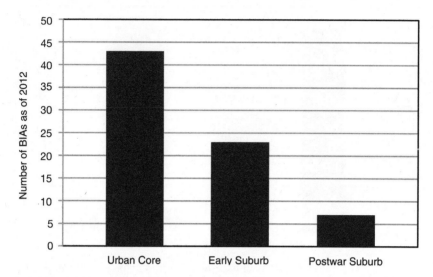

Exhibit 6.8: The number of BIAs in the city of Toronto by timing of urban development, 2012. *Source:* TABIA website.

On this scale, the largest is the Yonge Street BIA, with close to 800 members. Harbord, with just over 60 members, is at the small end of the scale. Size, however, does not appear to be a determining factor in the success or failure of a BIA, at least over the range observed in a city like Toronto. In a city like Montreal, which is not discussed in our book but which was included in a study carried out earlier by the authors, the creation of an SDC (Société de développement commercial) is more of a top-down affair. The boundaries can therefore be quite large, because what an SDC does is brand a specific area of the city, which could include several blocks but also several main streets. As a result some BIAs in Montreal have more than 1,800 members, and this has raised the issue of a representation void, with some members, typically smaller ones, feeling left out of the planning and budgeting process.

The Age of the BIA (as Measured in Years since Formation)

The second dimension is age. The median age of BIAs in the city of Toronto is thirteen years, which, given the forty-year history with the

BIA concept, shows the explosive growth over the past decade of the BIA movement. An example of an "old" BIA is Bloordale, which unfortunately has been on the losing end of Bloor street revival. The area is historic, and so is the BIA. But the neighbourhood it inhabits has had a poor reputation for many years. The small businesses that lined the main street first suffered at the hands of Dufferin Mall, which drew customers away from the street, much as Yorkdale did to Bloor West Village. Only in Bloordale's case, those customers never returned in the same numbers. As old businesses faded or closed down there was no renewal from a younger generation of entrepreneurs. Having said this, things are starting to look up. With the help of young and dynamic local leaders, the perception of the area is starting to change.

A very new BIA, College Promenade, actually has a long connection to the Portuguese community. It has very strong local resident buy-in, and its primary purpose was to begin to emulate the success of Little Italy located just east along College Street. The priority, agreed to by a majority of members, was streetscape improvement. There is little threat from competition, since it caters to very specific local needs and the residents are staying put. Indeed, this is a BIA born not out of need but out of opportunity. The creation of the BIA has strengthened existing bonds among business owners and ties to the neighbouring residents. The area's natural advantages of safety and peace and quiet will likely lead to a successful niche. Again, age is not a discernible factor in making or breaking a BIA.

The Urban-Suburban Orientation of the BIA
(as Measured by Its Location and Density)

The next dimension is geography, which is a composite criterion that blends the area's urban form (suburban or urban) and, by implication, its physical size (the distance encompassed by the BIA's borders). In the original pre-amalgamated city of Toronto, apart from a couple of BIAs along Yonge Street and Bloor Street, BIAs are smaller because they were built around the compact urban form that predates the full-scale introduction of the car into the city, unlike the outlying suburbs built after the 1950s, where the car was assumed to be king and distances along major streets are much greater. A neighbourhood BIA like Wexford Heights has the same number of businesses as Danforth Mosaic, yet it covers nearly double the physical distance.

What's interesting is that these early postwar suburbs no longer form the outer ring of residential and commercial development; rather they are encased by the much newer suburbs of Markham and Vaughan to the north, Brampton to the northwest, Pickering, Ajax, and Whitby to the east, and Mississauga, Burlington, and Oakville to the west. This is why Toronto's older suburbs today are closer to the core and even appear compact as compared to the hyper-dislocation of post-1980s suburbs.

There is some benefit to being relatively compact as a BIA, in that information and knowledge of BIA activities are more quickly transmitted and shared in less spatially segregated neighbourhoods. It is also easier to make the case for streetscape improvements when the benefits are closer to one's doorstep. On the other hand, a more geographically spread out BIA can have a greater net impact on a city if its efforts to clean up a main street shopping district and satisfy local customer needs spills over into the neighbourhood as a whole, something that we saw in the case of the *Toronto Life* neighbourhood ranking data. Just being near a BIA makes for a better and more highly desirable place to live and bring up a family.

The Homogeneity/Heterogeneity of a BIA (as Measured by Diversity of Offerings Available to Shoppers)

Another dimension is whether the businesses in an area are clustered around similar socio-economic elements or whether the BIA encompasses lots of variety. In short, is the BIA homogeneous or heterogeneous?

A heterogeneous BIA such as Bloorcourt (the neighbourhood to the west of Bloordale mentioned above) contains all kinds of business types and people. There are mixtures of age, ethnicity, stores, public services, and restaurants. There are plenty of local convenience stores and a destination store named Long and McQuade, which serves a musical community by selling and renting guitars (mainly) and other musical instruments. Contrast this with a BIA like Liberty Village that is unique in servicing only professional tenants in reconverted warehouses and storage facilities. Some live and work in the Liberty Village area, but many others do not. Neither the heterogeneous or homogenous model is globally better than the other, but rather, it is a question of which is best suited to its particular environment.

This sets up the next dimension of variation.

*Is the BIA Locally Oriented for Residents or
Is It a Destination for Visitors?*

Does the BIA cater primarily to its residents or does it function as a destination for both local residents and visitors from outside the neighbourhood? An excellent example of catering to residents is Roncesvalles Avenue, which, in conjunction with city public works and economic development, has recently completed a facelift of the neighbourhood's main street that took nearly five years. Streetcars, buses, bike lanes, cars, street parking, storefronts, and people have somehow been squeezed onto this traditionally narrow street in what can only be described as a seamless intervention. (Of course, don't tell the residents and businesses that lived through the construction phase for nearly half a decade that the process was seamless, but here we are referring to the outcome.) A walk down Roncesvalles Avenue, the area's main street, merits attention, for Roncesvalles today, more than ever, is a great example of a healthy, vibrant balance of old and new. It is locally sustainable and can cater to most local needs, and at the same time is inviting to someone living outside of the BIA.

A "Destination BIA," on the other hand, can present difficulties for visitors, locals, and business owners. Little Italy has become known more as College Street in recent years, as it increasingly is host to hipster bars, restaurants, and clubs with little connection to the Italian heritage of the area. Moreover, its main street no longer provides the variety of amenities required to serve the local needs of residents. The noise and late evening revelry that come with being an "entertainment" destination have caused frictions between College Street businesses and local residents.

One would presume by this example that the Destination BIA would be intimately linked with the homogeneity/heterogeneity distinction; the implication being that as soon as a BIA turns a corner and switches from local residents' needs to catering to visitors it loses its capacity to be diverse. Think again. Small business owners and BIAs can improvise and innovate in ways that confound our expectations (especially as researchers rooted in the positive social sciences would tend to predict). The Korea Town BIA, located just west of Mirvish Village (one of the smallest Destination BIAs), caters to all of life's needs, from grocery stores to travel agents to dentists, and also has plenty of Korean restaurants serving Korean food. Yet the bulk of its customer base comes from outside the neighbourhood. Toronto's Korean community is geographically spread out, though if it is clustered anywhere, it is most concentrated in the east end of the city where many of the community's churches and its major community centre are located. The Korean community nevertheless recognizes the value of this west-end agglomeration of ethnically tailored products and services, and its members frequently make the trek from across the city to shop and seek recreation in this central city neighbourhood.

Do a Majority of BIA Members Participate in the Activities and Decision-Making Process of the BIA?

There is one last segment that is neither visible on a surface visit to a BIA nor available in city descriptions of individual BIA activities. It comes from an analysis of survey data and interviews with BIA members across a range of neighbourhoods and cities. What we have observed as the single most important ingredient of BIA success is the degree of local member "buy-in." If BIA members appear disaffected and disillusioned by the BIA process then the BIA is not harnessing the potential of its membership base. Worse still, if BIA members are ignorant of the BIA's presence, which is possible if they are part of a numerically large or geographically spread-out organization, then this really lessens the impact of BIA activity.

In our three city case studies in chapters 3, 4, and 5, we found many BIAs whose real problem was not external (i.e., not with the city or with competing box-store developments) but with themselves. They failed to get a majority of local businesses on board and participating in the BIA's decision-making process.

Why is this important? As an experienced union leader once told me, if your own members aren't part of the process then you cannot honestly broker with management and you will have less influence with both the company and your membership base. There is a strong parallel here, already noted, between formally organized (i.e., dues-paying) representative and membership-based organizations, of which trade unions and BIAs are two examples, and their need to engage the membership in order to be successful in their dealings (in the case of BIAs with customers and government and in the case of unions with their employers). BIAs need and require the input and implicit support of their members if they are to prove successful in achieving their goals.

Fortunately, based on some detailed survey analysis conducted in 2008 for several BIAs in the city of Toronto, we were able to identify several factors that lead to greater BIA member participation. In rank order of strength of association, as measured by frequency of attendance at annual general meetings (AGMs) and general knowledge of BIA activities, we found that:

- Being the owner and operator of the building and business increased the likelihood that a member was a regular participant in BIA meetings and had a good knowledge of BIA activities (owners were just over 20 per cent more likely to be regular BIA participants than non-owners);
- BIA members who lived relatively close to their place of work were more likely to participate in and have knowledge of BIA member activities (each additional ten minutes of driving lowered the participation rate by just under 20 per cent);
- Next in importance was age of business: more established businesses, as measured by years in operation, had higher rates of participation and knowledge;
- The last significant predictor was size: having more than two employees increased the likelihood of participation and knowledge.

These factors and our earlier qualitative analysis clearly show that certain BIAs, either because of their composition (i.e., they have more members who are owners of their buildings and businesses and who live nearby, are longer-tenured, and are larger) or because of their design (they are small and compact), have a greater participation rate. Those BIAs that lack these characteristics, such as those in the suburban fringes of the urban core, have a lower participation rate. Fortunately, they have advantages that may be exploited to offset their challenges, and it is to these that we turn next.

The City as Tourist Attraction: A Case of Comparative Advantage

An aspect mentioned in chapter 4 in the context of Vancouver's mostly successful "place-making" efforts, and that is touched upon more generally in Part II of this book, is the growth and importance of city-based tourism that attracts visitors both local and external. The link with small business and BIAs comes from the classic idea that underlies why countries engage in trade – the concept of *comparative advantage*. That is, as nations benefit from trading with each other in categories of goods or services where one or the other has a comparative advantage, so cities benefit from neighbourhoods that provide a diversity rather than a duplication of goods and services.

If our urban neighbourhoods had identical chain stores and restaurants (as many new urban environments certainly do) there would be very little to be gained by a trip across town for dinner or a weekend visit to a neighbouring city for shopping and dining. BIA-influenced neighbourhoods such as Bloor West Village and Kensington Market have, for more than three decades now, preserved and fostered the survival of local independent businesses. This, in turn, has ensured the desirability of these neighbourhoods for local residents and workers, as demonstrated by higher-than-average residential property prices and earnings. They have also provided the vitality needed to draw in visitors and new, non-local entrepreneurs. This is a point that it is valuable to emphasize to local business leaders and politicians.

Making It Work Suburban Style: The Case of Strip Malls

The dilemma for city officials is whether the benefits of BIA "place-making" can be extended to parts of the city that we normally tend to think of as not all that interesting.

We think they can. With an advertising campaign that aligns expectations correctly, such a strategy can be made to work. Take, for example, the early suburban strip mall. Strip malls not only constitute a unique architectural imprint in North American cities, but also give life to new ideas and house a rich diversity of cultures and shop owners from around the globe. Walking tours such as Jane's Walk – an annual neighbourhood walk that started in 2007 and now takes place in more than 100 cities around the world on Jane Jacobs's birthday in May – serve to document and expose this rich diversity and highlight alternative tourist destinations for local residents and foreign visitors alike. People wishing to explore the vibrant, unconventional nodes of urban life housed within the city's seemingly anonymous strip malls can now find lots of places to look for information. For example, in Toronto, magazines such as *Spacing* and websites such as *Torontoist* do much to heighten the profile of successful suburban BIA street parties such as the Taste of Lawrence Festival.

Models may be found in initiatives such as a recent Moroccan tourism campaign in Europe that focused on the "exotic aspects" of the Arab *souk*, or covered street market, where tourists can find authentic non-branded foods and street merchants. If an entire country can base a major marketing campaign – to a very sophisticated global tourist market – on an authentic non-branded market-based experience, certainly cities like Halifax, Vancouver, and Toronto can do the same with their own suburban version of the Arab *souk* – the strip mall. It is not a stretch to say that many strip malls in cities like Toronto are more diverse than anything found in Morocco – or any other country in the world, for that matter. Where else can one find a Chinese herbal tea store next door to a Lebanese pastry shop? Or a curry shop from Trinidad beside a dry cleaner from Afghanistan (see exhibit 6.9)?

Because many of the city's strip malls are now approaching fifty and sixty years of age, not only do they house a wide variety of authentic cuisines and products from around the world, but they are also architecturally interesting, exhibiting some of the same design features found in the early Las Vegas strip (now largely torn down).

One area of Toronto with just such a diversity of tastes and experiences is in west Scarborough. Along four major routes in Scarborough – Kingston Road, Eglinton Avenue East, Lawrence Avenue East, and Victoria Park Avenue – one can find the world in microcosm. Some malls have remained effectively unchanged for half a century, while in others new businesses pop up all the time, offering an incentive to revisit an area to find out what's new.

A key recommendation, then, coming out of the place-making playbook, is for BIAs to partner with their local transit commissions and other institutions to create and offer guided tours of strip malls or other features of their local area. In earlier work we suggested how to brand these journeys using the typography and names of bus routes in the chosen areas. The so-called 54east project, based on the Lawrence Avenue 54 bus, was one of these ideas (see exhibit 6.10).

Though ideas such as this, and a myriad of other opportunities that a BIA can promote, provide reason for optimism, we know from our city-based interviews that all is not perfect with the small-scale entrepreneur in major urban environments. Independent business owners have major concerns. We end this chapter, therefore, with a list of common challenges and a few words about the potential future of the BIA concept.

Exhibit 6.9: A suburban strip mall in Scarborough, in Toronto's east end. *Photo by Rafael Gomez and Phillip Romain. Courtesy ThinkTankToronto © 2004*

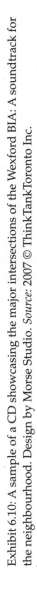

Exhibit 6.10: A sample of a CD showcasing the major intersections of the Wexford BIA: A soundtrack for the neighbourhood. Design by Morse Studio. *Source:* 2007 © ThinkTankToronto Inc.

Current Challenges Facing BIAs

While all BIAs deal with a range of local issues (e.g., getting local business buy-in for new investments, competition from other BIAs and retailers, organizational capacity building etc.), a recurring concern raised by many of those interviewed for this book was related to the lack of coordination between city economic development offices providing support for BIAs (which most entrepreneurs were happy with) and the actions of other city departments that seemed at odds with measures to promote local economic development. Frequently cited problems included the following:

- The perceived overzealousness of parking enforcement officers that discourages people from visiting main street shopping areas;
- High business property taxes, especially relative to neighbouring jurisdictions, that contribute to the demise of independent shops, which give way to generic and bland chain stores or, in the worst cases, empty storefronts;
- Uncoordinated and often unwanted city infrastructure enhancements that undermine BIA street design plans; and
- Poor consultation by various city departments with BIAs on issues that directly affect them (e.g., proposed bus route changes or disruptions related to sidewalk repairs) and on which they can provide constructive input.

It should be noted that this lack of a proper consultative process is not a uniquely small business concern but is characteristic of large city governments that have lost their local council representation (i.e., Halifax and Toronto, in particular, following amalgamation and the loss of their metro-wide governance models in the 1990s). Groups such as People Plan Toronto (PPT) and Dave Meslin's highly engaging Fourth Wall exhibit are worthy examples of initiatives highlighting the desire of local business and citizens to participate and have a say in local affairs.[11]

Beyond the need for more engagement, there are challenges from farther afield that are affecting small-scale entrepreneurs across the country. The effects of the Great Recession of 2008, as it is now known, are still with us. And while the recession is reshaping business in ways our interviews and surveys could not have captured, the best course for most BIAs, we have seen, is to re-examine priorities rigorously, to invest more in business and customer attraction, and to work harder on their initial goals as BIAs – that is, to improve the chances of small business success and to enhance the local streetscape environment. To be competitive, successful districts need, first of all, to be convenient. They need more reasons for people to be there, clear directions, and simple parking arrangements. Those BIAs that have up to now focused mainly on being successful purveyors of clean sidewalks will now need to focus their attention more firmly on *people* – employees, visitors, shoppers, and residents.

Final Observations and Lessons

What has emerged from our study of cities and BIAs is that, even at their least effective (i.e., BIAs lacking engaged members and without a clear focus), they generally have a positive impact on their surrounding communities. This includes, of course, economic benefits such as increased foot traffic, increased revenues for local businesses and ultimately government, and a heightened awareness of the unique impact of BIAs outside their immediate vicinity. But there are other very important contributions made by BIAs that go beyond just fostering greater local economic development. For example they provide:

- *An improved sense of place* – We have seen how BIAs have improved the aesthetic quality of many commercial and retail strips in Halifax, Vancouver, and Toronto by providing unique and distinctive design touches that differentiate them from other neighbourhoods in the city.
- *Community building* – We found that BIAs with strong links to community groups and other local organizations were more likely to instil a sense of pride through a variety of special events. Also noteworthy were the countless examples of intercultural relationship building that occurred at a local level through BIA-sponsored activities such as street festivals and social work.

From a policy-making standpoint, the positive effect of such place-making and social outcomes should not be underestimated. In the aggregate they contribute in very real ways to making a city a more attractive place to live and invest. A large part of the success of the BIA movement lies in its grassroots approach to local issues, which is often the antithesis of big bureaucracy (public or private). Viewed from this perspective, even relatively modest investments in BIAs by governments at all levels will likely produce significant dividends in both economic and social capital, as we demonstrate in subsequent chapters.

The Future of the BIA Concept

What is the future of the BIA concept? We caution that the continued resilience of BIAs should not be taken for granted. As was noted in chapters 3 to 5, a number of those interviewed expressed very real frustration with the lack of consultation or consideration by government agencies related to the concerns of small-scale entrepreneurs. If governments want BIAs and the small businesses that flourish in them to thrive, they need to consider how poor planning decisions, high property tax rates, overzealous by-law enforcement, and policing practices, among other issues, can undermine their future success. The local intelligence and commitment to community building embodied in BIAs needs to be effectively channelled. In short, governments at all levels need to establish mechanisms for taking seriously the input of BIAs when developing and implementing initiatives that significantly affect citizens at the local level.

7 Of People, Profits, and Place: Lessons in Local Economic Development

Boston, U.S.A.

In early 2011, Boston's Jamaica Plain neighbourhood witnessed the closure of a beloved landmark, a forty-seven-year-old Latin grocery store, ushering in the arrival of a Whole Foods Market.[1] Immediately, a large backlash against Whole Foods erupted from within the local community, a unique mix of Latino immigrants, African Americans, university students, and young white professionals.[2] The most public organization formed to stop Whole Foods from establishing itself in Jamaica Plain was an all-volunteer organization known as "Whose Foods/Whose Community?: The Coalition Against Gentrification."[3] Among the organization's criticisms of Whole Foods were its high prices, out of the reach of poorer residents in the area, and the unavailability of products the local community desired, such as Latin foods.[4]

Bristol, England

Thousands have been campaigning and even rioting since 2010 to stop the British supermarket chain Tesco from opening a giant store in the Stokes Croft area of Bristol, a city in the southwest of England.[5] According to activists, the reasons for not wanting a Tesco in their community range from the impact on local shops and farmers through to deep concerns about how the dominance of the supermarket model could affect the future availability of food.[6] More than 2,500 petition cards were sent to Bristol City Council objecting to Tesco, and 96 per cent of local residents recently surveyed said they wanted more variety and didn't want another supermarket chain in their neighbourhood.[7]

Toronto, Canada

Toronto's mayor was forced to withdraw a proposal to transform a vast swathe of the city's lakefront into a huge mega-mall, replete with large American retailers like Macy's and Nordstrom's. The development plan would have included the world's largest Ferris wheel and a monorail connecting the mall to the western part of the city centre. The climbdown came after an unprecedented torrent of criticism and opposition, "which dismissed the plan as an outdated, last-century vision concocted in secret without consultation with residents and city councillors."[8] The fight against the mall saw community protest groups spring up across the city, with prominent Toronto architects, academics, and planners also petitioning against the plan.[9] The opposition was motivated not only by the development's impact on local neighbourhoods and businesses but also by environmental concerns about the effects such a development could have on efforts to re-naturalize the nearby mouth of the Don River.

Three cities and three conflicts related to the place of independent business in the urban fabric. Three cities, three countries, and three protests, but by no means isolated. Events like those that unfolded in Boston, Bristol, and Toronto are occurring in towns, villages, and cities across the globe. Just prior to the drafting of this book, the "Occupy" movement was making waves on both sides of the Atlantic, with its attack on big finance, political corruption, and soaring inequality.

All these distinct and disparate responses display, at their heart, an exhaustion with the economic dogma of the past thirty years – a dogma symbolized by the repeated mantras of twenty-four-hour news media: "global supply chains," "flexible labour markets," "mergers and acquisitions," "freer trade," and so on. Notwithstanding the adherence of governments to these well-worn nostrums, global capitalism continues to lurch from crisis to crisis and is increasingly unable to deliver the most basic of economic goods, such as a job or a decent wage. The evident malaise is further compounded by the frightening realization that many of our political and business elites are out their depth in dealing with the global economy's downturn and the increasingly insurmountable problems of sovereign debt, unemployment, and environmental degradation.

How did we get here?

That seemingly daunting question is addressed in this chapter, which distils ideas in local economic policy that emerge from our narrative of the BIA movement (chapter 2) and from the study of small business in three of Canada's major cities (chapters 3, 4, and 5). In so doing we identify nine major lessons for local economic policy that arise from our street-level look at small business and the city in Part I.

Lesson One: We Ignore the Human Scale at Our Peril

Part of the answer to the economic problems faced by many countries at the moment is undoubtedly a crisis of bigness, as Paul Kingsworth recently argued in Britain's *Guardian* newspaper. Observing the world's present banking and debt woes, Kingsworth writes:

> Banks grew so big that their collapse would have brought down the entire global economy. To prevent this, they were bailed out with huge tranches of public money, which in turn is precipitating social crises on the streets of western nations. The European Union has grown so big, and so unaccountable, that it threatens to collapse in on itself. Corporations have grown so big that they are overwhelming democracies and building a global plutocracy to serve their own interests.[10]

In making his case, Kingsworth alludes to the little-known Austrian political thinker Leopold Kohr. Kohr's message was quite succinctly summed up in the opening pages of his 1957 book, *The Breakdown of Nations*: "wherever something is wrong, something is too big."[11] Kohr's claim was that society's problems were not caused by particular forms of social or economic organization but by their size. Socialism, anarchism, capitalism, democracy, monarchy – all could work well on what he called "the human scale": a scale that allowed people to play a part in the systems that governed their lives.[12]

Drawing from history, Kohr argued that when people have too much power, under any system, they abuse it. The task according to Kohr, therefore, was to limit the amount of power that any individual, organization, or government should have access to. To some extent, "the human scale" that Kohr discussed was in much better shape in the early part of the postwar period than now. Comparing the pluralistic sociopolitical culture of the 1950s and early 1960s – with its varying poles of political, bureaucratic, labour, and business power – to the current period, one can't help but be astounded by how far we've diverged from what the great political scientist Charles. E. Lindblom described as America's (and Canada's) "polyarchy." That is, a state in which no one group or stakeholder controls society and where various elites engage in a productive competition that helps sustain a healthy market democracy. In later works, such as *Politics and Markets*, Lindblom would detail how labour, small business, and other stakeholders would be effectively marginalized and then excluded from the body politic, as a result of the growing size and power of large concentrated private interests. Simply put, in Lindblom's view, "The large private corporation fits oddly into democratic theory and vision. Indeed, it does not fit."[13]

Staying Small and Avoiding the "Too Large to Fail" Syndrome

Fast forwarding to 2011, Kohr's and Lindblom's perspective is certainly shared by former chairman of the U.S. Federal Reserve Paul A. Volcker, who, in his 2011 William Taylor Memorial Lecture, titled "Three Years Later: Unfinished Business in Financial Reform," highlights the perils of institutions that are too large and interconnected to be allowed to fail.[14] Identifying this as the gravest structural challenge facing the financial system, Volcker compellingly advocates a radical shrinkage of "the risks these companies pose, whether by reducing their size, curtailing their interconnections or limiting their activities."[15]

Though he was speaking about banking and finance, Volcker's words could apply to any number of sectors of the economy, from automotive manufacturing to retail. The North American auto bailout is an obvious case in point. It cost U.S. and Canadian taxpayers billions of dollars and forced two national governments to take on a staggering 73 per cent equity stake in General Motors, hence the popular moniker at the time, "Government Motors."[16] While a robust case could be made that the money spent on the bailout should have been directed to areas like transportation infrastructure or support for new and emerging high-growth SMEs, one can understand the dilemma the collapse of a company like GM poses for politicians.

There is the direct and indirect loss of thousands of jobs in the car manufacturing process and the supply chains it sustains, not to speak of the potentially devastating social and economic impacts on cities like Oshawa and Windsor. But looking at the success of the more diverse Japanese auto industry, with its Mazda, Subaru, Toyota, Nissan, Honda, and Mitsubishi brands, one can only speculate about what

North America's auto industry might have looked like today if independent firms such as Buick and Chevrolet had continued to flourish on their own.

Likewise, big retail is in crisis and continuing to face major contractions throughout North America. In 2011 alone, well over a thousand major retail outlets shut their doors in the United States, including 405 and 633 stores respectively from the now-defunct book and video rental chains Borders and Blockbuster.[17] Apart from the massive job losses associated with the closures, what is troubling is that they often occur all at once in super-sized suburban big-box stores that have been harmful to small-business-oriented main streets and downtowns. The net effect is that communities are deprived not only of jobs but of any nearby basic amenities such as restaurants, coffee shops, and grocery stores, which brings us to lesson two.

Lesson Two: Save Some Space for Upstarts and the Little Guys

This dynamic is vividly captured in a 2009 study by economists at Loyola University's Centre for Urban Research and Learning in Chicago. They found that "the opening of a Wal-Mart on the West Side of Chicago in 2006 led to the closure of about one-quarter of the local businesses within a four-mile radius."[18] They monitored 306 businesses, evaluating their status prior to Wal-Mart's arrival and one and two years after.[19] By year two, 82 of the businesses had closed.[20] The study observed that businesses within close proximity of Wal-Mart had a 40 per cent chance of closing, with the probability of going out of business falling 6 per cent with each mile away from Wal-Mart.[21] In the end, these closures eliminated the equivalent of 300 full-time jobs, about as many as Wal-Mart added to the area. Indeed, sales tax and employment data provided by the state of Illinois for Wal-Mart's zip code and surrounding zip codes confirmed that overall sales and employment in the neighbourhood did not increase but actually dipped from the trend line.[22]

The Loyola study also exposes another rationale for preserving spaces where small-scale retail enterprise can serve a local population. The reason is rooted in what happens when a large discount chain displaces local retailers. The loss of a few shops directly affected by the new event can snowball and weaken an entire business district. As shoppers lessen their need to buy one thing along a retail strip, they begin to make fewer trips to the area. Existing businesses initially unaffected by the entry of a Wal-Mart (i.e., the hairstylist or health food store) begin to see their customer traffic also drop. A perfectly competitive market adjustment would be for rents to fall in line with the reduced demand and thereby preserve the "zero-sum" adjustment, allowing some firms to remain and perhaps allowing new ones filling different lower-cost niches to move in.

Unfortunately markets (let alone property markets) are hardly perfect. A commercial lease, like any contract, is often signed with long lead times and costly opt-out clauses. Many renters are also at the mercy of local property owners, who often have sizeable investments in neighbouring properties; these forces, taken together, make any downward pressure on rents not enough to offset the decline in local demand. As a result, what was an initial displacement of small-scale clothing stores in favour of a larger, newer retailer turns into a full-scale collapse in main street shopping and a decline in neighbourhood fortunes.

This would not occur if a new, innovative, clothing store were to enter the market or a new hip bar were to open at the end of a street noted for its nightlife. In either case the new entrant would cause, at worst, the more tired stores to close down; but at best the new tenant could raise the profile of the neighbourhood and/or increase the net benefit to a customer by providing greater variety and an opportunity to combine several types of consumption in a single visit to the main street.

Similar research from the Greater Toronto Area (GTA) on the impact of selected big-box stores between 1993 and 2002 found that the closure rate for smaller stores located within five kilometres of big-box retailers ranged from 26 to 55 per cent.[23] In the first years of competition, the closure rate was at its highest as the weakest street retailers were forced out of business.[24] The GTA studies also reported a negative impact on the "quality" of the shopping experience in the streets of Toronto because of the loss of independent stores.[25] While the situation was mitigated to some extent by a shift to restaurants, high-end coffee shops, and personal and business services outlets, on the whole, independent clothing and hardware stores disappeared and made way for dollar stores and doughnut shops.[26]

In a study of hundreds of cities over a twenty-year period (1977–2000), Glaeser and Kerr focused on city industries, which are industrial sectors within given metropolitan areas, such as fur manufacturing in New York or computers in Silicon Valley. By controlling for all city-level and industry-level trends, they could test to see whether a city-industry cluster that had a greater number of small, independent firms (relative to both the metropolitan-area norm and the industry norm) grew faster than the average. They found that a 10 per cent increase in the number of firms per worker in a metropolitan region (their measure of small-ness) was associated with a 9 per cent increase in employment growth in that region between 1977 and 2000. Likewise, Glaeser and Kerr found that a 10 per cent increase in average establishment size (their measure of largeness) in 1992 was associated with a 7 per cent decline in subsequent employment growth due to new start-ups.[27]

All this is to say that, whether it's the Occupy movement fighting big finance or residents fearing the arrival of big retail, there is much to be concerned about when firms become too big to fail and when only a few players dominate any one sector of the economy. More often than not, their decisions are made without the remotest concern for those most directly affected, namely, local workers and residents, and smaller enterprises. As well, one should not understate the undue and often corrupting influence on our political system of these vast "industrial complexes," whether in the military, financial, automotive, construction, or big oil sectors.

Not surprisingly, at the same time that people are directing their anger at seemingly remote government officials and large corporate interests, small and medium-sized enterprises (SMEs), according to countless polls, enjoy a high degree of popularity among the public at large – a fact reflected in the active, but mostly rhetorical, courting of this sector by all of Canada's major political parties.

So a legitimate question is whether this value placed on small business is warranted on more than just pure economic grounds? This concern is addressed below.

Lesson Three: Strong Local Businesses Make Communities More Resilient

In making the economic case for small, locally owned enterprises, it is useful to highlight their remarkable resilience, in terms both of recovering from economic downturns and of responding to changing market conditions. This resilience, in turn, helps local, regional, and national economies weather the inevitable booms, busts, and shocks of large-scale global capitalism.

Contrary to the hubristic statements of the 2000s from U.S. Federal Reserve Chairman Alan Greenspan and the U.K.'s Gordon Brown (Britain's chancellor of the exchequer from 1997 until 2007 and prime minister from 2007 to 2010), we didn't step into a "new paradigm" of economic development nor did we see the "end of boom and bust." The reality was depressingly familiar: a major international financial crisis presaging a subsequent global recession, economic turmoil, and social unrest.

One of the earliest casualties of the 2008 crisis was the small country of Iceland. As seen in the Academy Award-winning documentary film *Inside Job*, Iceland went from a modest but comfortable existence sustained by a large fishery, tourism, and related businesses to becoming a global epicentre for online banking and finance. At the height of its boom in 2007, Iceland's banking sector had assets worth eleven times the country's total gross domestic product (GDP).[28] Relative to the size of Iceland's economy, the subsequent collapse of its financial sector would be the biggest banking failure in history.[29]

For years, the business press and many economists were praising the boldness of what the *Economist* magazine described as the "Thatcherite zeal" with which its former prime minister went "about privatising most of the banking system and floating the currency, the krona."[30] Here was a classic example of specialization, finding your comparative advantage and running with it, and, by implication, generating larger scale and supposedly greater efficiencies. But in the end, it was just another cautionary tale of what happens when countries, regions – and cities, for that matter – put all their eggs in one very large economic basket and tie their fortunes to the mammoth, unstable, and highly interconnected firms so feared by Paul Volcker.

Fortunately for Canada, its economy was able to survive the effects of the 2008 crisis in somewhat better shape than other major economies for a variety of reasons, including the federal government's fiscal stimulus and its decision to prevent our five major banks from merging in the early 2000s. But, as we shall see, our vibrant small-business sector contributed as well.

From a Canadian perspective, the experience of Iceland, though extreme, should compel us to think about how we can inject a high degree of local resilience into our own economy. This means ensuring that we have a diverse and balanced economic base that is not wholly dependent on large organizations, whether in the natural resources, financial services, retail, or government sector.

Some interesting thinking on this notion of "resilience" has been developed by the U.K.-based think tank Centre for Local Economic Strategies (CLES). It defines the idea of resilience as "the ability of a place to respond to the challenges that it faces; what enables some areas to respond effectively from [sic] shocks, whether they be economic, social, political or environmental, whilst other areas falter and decline."[31] Based on their research in such English regions as Manchester and Oxfordshire, they note that when an economy becomes too reliant on any one sector, either public or commercial, place-resilience can be vulnerable and brittle and susceptible to external shocks.[32] Among the gravest weaknesses they point to in many governmental economic strategies is an inadequacy of basic metrics, such as good measures of *business diversity*, to foster a culture of innovation, creativity, and entrepreneurship.[33]

Innovating during Downturns

Distant and more recent history provides an indication of how economies spring back after being hit by major shocks. More often than not, it is due to what CLES defines as that "local culture of innovation, creativity and entrepreneurship." Though it is easy to be downbeat about the future, past economic crises have witnessed the development of transformative technologies including commercial aircraft production, television, personal computers and the Internet, all of which laid the groundwork for future growth. As the economic historian Alexander J. Field observed, the Depression era of the 1930s constituted "the most technologically progressive decade of the century."[34] And helping lead the charge for innovation in the aftermath of serious economic tumult have been small independent firms, particularly new business start-ups. These are often established by out-of-work employees – many of them laid off from larger firms – who are able to identify market opportunities for new solutions or improved goods and services.

And while many small firms fail during these downturns, in the aggregate there tend to be relatively more small businesses in existence after recessions and depressions than before.[35] Indeed, a 2009 study sponsored by the Kauffman Foundation in the United States found that more than half of the companies on the 2009 Fortune 500 list, including well-known companies such as Microsoft, Apple, and CNN, were launched in the wake of a recession or a bear market.[36]

Canada's experience coming out of the recessionary period of the early 1990s is testimony to the spectacular job-creating capacity of SMEs. From 1993 to 2003, SMEs accounted for nearly 80 per cent of net job creation in a period during which large firms (of 500-plus employees), despite high economic growth, were actually shedding jobs.[37]

This pattern was repeated after the recession of 2008–9, which saw the Canadian economy lose more than 300,000 jobs, with virtually all of those reductions coming from large corporations.[38] Canadian SMEs, on the other hand, not only made it through the recent recession with less damage than in any other postwar recession, they did so while outperforming their more established peers.[39] For example, SME employment remained steady during the first six months of 2009 as compared to a 10 per cent drop among larger companies.[40] And, peering into the future, a report from the Bank of Nova Scotia predicted that "highly entrepreneurial small-and medium-sized businesses in rapid-growth areas will likely be a key source of Canadian job creation over the next decade."[41]

Finding and Exploiting a Niche

The resilience of Canada's smaller-scaled enterprises – operating in both local and global economies –manifests itself in their capacity to adapt to competitive pressures. As a recent study on creative clusters in the city of Toronto notes, individual cultural entrepreneurs, small firms, and high-tech support services are increasing at the same time as employment in the large-scale reproduction and manufacturing of cultural goods is on the decline.[42]

Similarly, it is fascinating to see small record and video retailers succeed in the face of the decline and demise of big storefront retailers such as HMV and Blockbuster. They do so by identifying a unique niche (obscure foreign films, hard-to-find vinyl, etc.) not served by the existing marketplace, combined with a strong attention to specific customer needs and wants.

This is not unlike Germany's small- and medium-sized business sector, which focuses on extremely specialized products – particularly in machinery and engineering – that are almost custom-made for the client.[43] German firms secure long-term contracts with customers that are in a sense monopolistic, given that the client does not have any other suppliers who can produce the same good or service at any price, let alone the lowest.[44]

The contributions of SMEs primarily operating in local economies are therefore a critical source of economic resilience, given that they are more likely to acquire a greater proportion of their procurement, such as in services, from their home community.[45] Incidentally, this is one of the primary reasons why the recruitment and retention of headquartered firms is considered such a desirable economic development practice.[46]

Having firms tapped into local markets and supply chains also makes the economy less vulnerable to the negative effects of external events, whether they be financial crises in the Eurozone or natural disasters such as the earthquake and tsunami that devastated Japan in 2011.

Lesson Four: When Giants Fall, Don't Cushion the Blow ... Find New Places to Grow

Knowing the value of SMEs makes it all the more troubling to see the "reverse multiplier effect"[47] ripple through local economies when an elephantine big-box retailer like Wal-Mart moves in. Wiped out are the local designers, advertisers, wholesalers, accountants, and logistics specialists that support local store owners and the opportunities for innovative entrepreneurs in the community to get shelf space for their products.[48] Wal-Mart's enormous efficiency lies in the global reach of its supply chain and its ability to concentrate back office and supporting functions in one place, Bentonville, Arkansas, or to off-shore them to China or India.[49] Understandably, under this kind of business model, sourcing such services locally simply wouldn't make sense.[50]

Crucially, therefore, the survival and growth of small enterprises in Canada supports the fiscal resilience of Canadian governments at all levels. Accounting for about 53 per cent of the GDP produced by non-agricultural businesses in Canada,[51] SMEs are a major source of tax revenues for federal, provincial, and municipal governments.

At a municipal level, we have seen how small businesses are particularly vital when organized as Business Improvement Areas (BIAs), which help local revenues in a number of ways. For example, the work small-scale entrepreneurs undertake to improve the condition of their properties and facades raises the assessed value of the properties, which in turn increases revenues from a range of taxes. Moreover, with sluggish job growth in larger firms and government, new enterprises and small businesses save governments millions of dollars in social spending and jobless benefits, offsetting the costs of tax credits and subsidies directed to SMEs. We see this to some extent in Japan, where a weak welfare state is complemented by the vast numbers of people employed in small shops and farms, which are preserved courtesy of stringent regulations in the agricultural and retail sectors, effectively barring the entry of foreign firms.[52]

The resilience and dynamism of small, locally based enterprise is clearly evident in our urban centres, and it is here where we can learn a great deal about how to spur sustainable and long-term economic growth. In a global economy where economic activity is increasingly clustered around agglomerated city-regions, those with the greatest number and density of small and medium-sized enterprises are most likely to succeed. Analysing U.S. economic data from the late 1970s to 2000, Harvard economists Ed Glaeser and William Kerr found that "that an abundance of small, independent firms is one of the best predictors of urban growth"[53] – a piece of evidence, the authors pointedly note, that should give pause for thought to politicians intent on luring or bailing out big established firms through lavish tax breaks and subsidies. Instead we need to set the stage for new firms to arise.

Lesson Five: Save Space for Small-Scale Clustering … It Makes You Richer

An added question posed by Glaeser and Kerr in their research paper is this: Given the very real and strong relationship between the prevalence of smaller firms and economic vibrancy, why then are some places more entrepreneurial than others?[54] In attempting to answer this question they draw on the ground-breaking work of Anna Lee Saxenian and Benjamin Chinitz in their studies of business formation in Silicon Valley and New York.[55]

In her study of Silicon Valley, Anna Lee Saxenian observed that its abundance of small independent firms facilitated "further entrepreneurship by lowering the effective cost of entry through the development of independent suppliers, venture capitalists, and an entrepreneurial culture."[56] Similarly, as far back as 1961, Benjamin Chinitz maintained "that the presence of small, independent suppliers was particularly crucial for understanding why New York was so much more entrepreneurial than Pittsburgh, where the economy [at the time] was dominated by major vertically integrated steel companies."[57]

Echoing this work, is a 2011 study by economists Stephan Goetz and David Fleming, "Does Local Firm Ownership Matter?," published in the journal *Economic Development Quarterly*.[58] Goetz and Fleming analysed 2,953 counties in the United States, including both rural and urban places.[59] They found that counties with a higher density of small, locally owned businesses experienced greater per capita income growth between 2000 and 2007. Non-local businesses had a negative effect on incomes. The authors reported that even after controlling for other economic variables, "the non-resident-owned medium and large firms consistently and statistically depress economic growth rates."[60] The other major result was that resident-owned small firms had a "statistically significant and relatively large positive effect" on income growth.[61]

Stepping back even further and looking at nineteenth- and early-twentieth-century capitalism, one sees how Britain was able to become the "workshop of the world" through a vast network of SMEs clustered around the growing cities of Manchester, Birmingham, and Newcastle. Much like Silicon Valley and New York, British cities became magnets for entrepreneurs from around the world, including Karl Marx's German bankroller and fellow traveller Friedrich Engels.

But despite the obvious shortcomings of "too big to fail" business models and what evidence tells us about the role SMEs play in helping engineer economic recoveries, supporters of the status quo are not about to surrender without a fight. This brings us to lesson six.

Lesson Six: The Perception That Bigger Is (Always) Better Should Be Countered

At a 2011 recent Senate committee hearing on pricing and inflation, Canada's then central bank governor, Mark Carney, bemoaned the fact that Canada's retail market is underserved relative to that in the United States, noting that Canada has fourteen square feet of mall space per person while the United States has twenty-three square feet per person.[62]

Meanwhile, the *Toronto Star*'s respected business writer David Olive, in a 2011 column, launched a barrage of broadsides at Canadian small and medium-sized enterprise. Dismissively caricaturing the sector as a non-exporting, low-innovation, "low-wage, low benefits ghetto," consisting mainly of accountants, travel and real estate agents, and beauticians, Olive went on to argue that it was not worthy of the allegedly generous tax treatment and subsidies it receives from government.[63]

Curiously, Carney's comments before the Senate committee and Olive's belief in "bigger is better" exhibit the same line of reasoning proffered by Toronto's Mayor Rob Ford in his failed mall-by-the-lake vision for Toronto's waterfront. Luckily, the argument that a city like Toronto needs more plus-sized malls was effectively skewered in an open letter to Toronto Council by some of the city's leading academics and planners, including Richard Florida, director of the Martin Prosperity Institute at the University of Toronto, and former Toronto chief planner, Paul Bedford. On this issue they pointed out that:

in the U.S. 20% of the 2,000 malls are failing and a staggering half a billion square feet of retail space lies empty. Even Wal-Mart has abandoned 400 stores across the U.S. The great irony in our current debate is that in many of these U.S. locations planning efforts are underway to convert dead malls into mixed use centres with lots of residential development! Here the proposal is to do the reverse. While the Toronto economy is certainly stronger than in many parts of the U.S., no logical evidence has been presented as to why this proposal for constructing massive amounts of new retail space is warranted, either as an economic development or an urban development strategy. [64]

Instead of gravitating towards the grandiose and tacky, the city's politicians would be well advised to take lessons from the ideas seen in Part I of this book – namely, the recently revived neighbourhoods of Spring Garden in Halifax or of longstanding successes like Bloor West Village in Toronto. Here they would see how smaller-scale, independent businesses can generate economic benefits much greater in scope and sustainability than those offered by the mega-malls and big-box stores. Combined with cultural institutions, a city's unique mix and density of small, independent, high-quality eateries, bars, galleries, and stores give shape to a more sophisticated urban brand that increasingly attracts more and more international interest.

In 2011, no less an icon than the weekend *New York Times* gave Toronto's Roncesvalles district a full page of coverage in its popular Sunday edition. Waxing rhapsodic, the *Times* described the area as "a hub of local design and casual-hip dining," and went on to profile five of Roncesvalles's most innovative small business owners.[65] As they say, "you can't buy that kind of publicity," especially if you want to attract affluent and well-heeled travellers. In economic terms this is not chump change. In 2010, overseas (as opposed to North American) tourists pumped $3-billion into the Toronto economy, much of it from increasingly sophisticated and higher-spending travellers,[66] many of whom, it would be safe to say, were not lured to Toronto by the prospect of visiting Canada's largest lakefront mall in the city's east end.

Lesson Seven: A Focus on Improving Amenities Attracts Talented People and Fosters Increased Local Consumption

The neighbourhood stories of Halifax, Vancouver, and Toronto have been replicated worldwide from Brooklyn, New York, to Manchester's Northern Quarter, to Pittsburgh's East Liberty, in a remarkably consistent pattern. As documented by Richard Florida and his colleagues, the process works something like this: artistic and creativity-based small business start-ups are the first to move into areas in decline, subsequently attracting more people and investment, public and private, in their wake. Obviously, the more of these areas a city has, the more growth and jobs it will generate and the more attractive it will become for people and businesses considering changing locations.

This perspective is shared by Ed Glaeser and Harvard colleagues Jed Kolko and Albert Saiz, who observe that higher-amenity cities (i.e., those with a richer variety of restaurants, galleries, and theatres, and that are relatively easy to get around in) generate more economic growth than those deficient in such features.[67] Among the most successful American cities in this regard were New York, Boston, and San Francisco as well as mid-western cities such as Chicago and Pittsburgh.[68] As with Canada's major urban centres, which also score high on a range of international rankings, these are cities with relatively successful industries that have done well in the information economy.[69] They all have fairly high levels of human capital and interesting architectural endowments, combined with a rich set of consumption activities.[70]

The aforementioned city of San Francisco is an exemplar of high-value and locally based consumption. The city is a stronghold of small, locally owned businesses, generating sizable benefits for the city's economy, having been a high performer even during the recession and slow-paced recovery. A 2007 report prepared by the U.S. think tank Civic Economics, using San Francisco as a case study, calculated market shares for independents and chains in several categories: bookstores, sporting goods stores, toy stores, and casual dining restaurants.[71] In all four categories, small locally based, independent businesses captured more than half of the sales within the city of San Francisco, a much larger share than the average for the United States.[72]

In examining the economic impact of small, locally owned businesses versus big chains, Civic Economics researchers found that local businesses buy more goods and services in their communities and employ more people locally per unit of sales than non-local firms. The reason is actually quite straightforward: they have no headquartered staff elsewhere.[73] Every $1 million spent at local bookstores, for example, created $321,000 in additional economic activity in the area, including $119,000 in wages paid to local employees.[74] That same $1 million spent at chain bookstores generated just over half the value (or $188,000) in local economic activity and less than half ($71,000) in local wages.[75]

The story was much the same in other categories. For every $1 million in sales, independent toy stores created 2.22 local jobs, while chains created just 1.31. Another important finding came from economic modelling the researchers undertook looking at what would occur if residents were to redirect just 10 per cent of their spending from chains to local businesses.[76] The effect was impressive: $192 million in additional economic activity in San Francisco and almost 1,300 new jobs.

Lesson Eight: Lower Productivity Is a Real Problem but Not Necessarily a Small Business Problem

To return to the typical criticisms aimed at small business: as with any stereotype, there is sometimes a shred of truth. Yes, there are SMEs, often operating on small margins, that pay their workers minimum wages with limited or no benefits; but sadly that is an unfortunate facet of today's business world, big and small. We see this in the airline industry, where employers are trying to get flight attendants to accept lower wages, in some cases barely above minimum wage, and with limited or no benefits. The fact is that real wages for most Canadians have been on a downward trajectory for years, accompanied by a steep growth in income inequality. The causes, which are not just a function of firm size and are a matter of considerable debate, include the following: declining productivity, increased global competition, automation, the weakening of unions, and changing social norms with respect to executive and worker compensation.

It is much the same story concerning the low levels of innovation, productivity, and R&D within Canadian business. Indeed, the issue has bedevilled Canadian policy makers for years, despite one of the most generous R&D tax credit regimes in the world. Doubtless, it is valid to say that a small firm with fewer than ten employees is likely to spend less money on R&D than a larger firm. But inadequate R&D spending in Canada is a problem that afflicts firms of all sizes, to varying degrees. The real question is why this occurs across all businesses in Canada.

In part, this might be a function of Canada's vast resource wealth, which creates a relatively complacent and risk-averse business culture, a kind of "path dependence" legacy from our traditional role as "hewers of wood and drawers of water." It could also be argued that years of government budget and tax cuts, as well as lagging public investment in energy, transportation, and communications infrastructure are significantly reducing our competitiveness. Certainly, if we look at any number of international rankings measuring innovation, levels of R&D, and competitiveness, Canada falls well below such high tax jurisdictions as Denmark, Finland, Germany, and Sweden. These issues of declining wages, inequality, and low productivity are serious and hamper future economic growth. Tackling these problems means looking at ways of encouraging businesses, big and small (and governments, as well), to invest more in human and physical capital. In short, productivity decline is a problem attributable not to the "smallness" of our firms but, rather, to the *small-mindedness* that fuels our collective economic decision making.

Lesson Nine: Variety Should Be Something We Value and Try to Protect

As for countering the perception that independent accountants, real estate agents, beauticians, and other small-scale service providers are drags on economic efficiency, it's difficult to know where to begin. For a start, take a small accountancy providing strategic advice on financing to a budding entrepreneur, or a local real estate agent offering intelligence on available employment lands to a small business owner looking to expand: both provide invaluable services that help sustain and improve the productivity of local economies. And in light of what we know about "the beauty premium" for women and men in the workforce (something which in an ideal world I'm sure we all wish did not exist), even beauticians play a role in this process, by helping workers better compete in the job market.[77]

It is also worth mentioning that, at street-level, independent professionals provide an important presence in occupying office and retail space in areas not attractive to blue-chip consultancies and big retail chains, contributing a not-insignificant amount of social capital to local communities.

On a personal level, we can certainly attest to the value-added contributions of small independent accounting firms. Located above an adult video store and a drapery outlet in a tiny strip mall, my accountant's office would never be mistaken for the headquarters of KPMG. Nevertheless, for well over twenty years he has provided affordable and valuable financial advice to the local community. He helped set up my consultancy and supports other family members in managing their business affairs. His clientele is made up of local residents and the countless small manufacturing, retail, and service businesses that dot the landscape of Toronto's east end.

What also needs to be challenged is the lazy stereotyping of small entrepreneurs. While they include both beauticians and the beloved "mom and pop shops" of yore, they are also represented by a growing number of "cultural entrepreneurs" as described in a recent Martin Prosperity report on creative clusters.

Typically, these cultural enterprises include independent artists, musicians, and graphic designers as well as producers, directors, and film-makers in a variety of firm mixes, from sole proprietorships to high-growth start-ups to second stage companies.[78] These entrepreneurs help drive the city's cultural sector, which generates $9 billion of Toronto's GDP, employs 83,000 people, and is growing faster than manufacturing and financial services.[79]

Just as many cultural entrepreneurs provide expert goods and services for public- and private-sector media giants such as the CBC and CTV, small and medium -scale advanced manufacturing firms play a similar role in supply chains for big firms in the aerospace and automotive sectors. Along with engineering, architectural, and energy and environmental services firms, they are an integral part of the economy, providing the kind of high-value-added goods and services that are increasingly in demand across the globe. Certainly, whole sectors of our economy – from mining, to oil and gas, to construction – benefit from the expertise of small and medium-sized players.

But to return to the earlier example of Germany: in spite of chronic problems in the Eurozone, its small and mid-size firms are the backbone of its economy and continue to make it a global exporting power. SMEs make up the bulk of Germany's economy, accounting for an astounding 99 per cent of all companies and more than 70 per cent of all employees.[80] While the tendency is to think that SMEs are too small to benefit from economies of scale and globalization, Germany's small, independently owned firms prove otherwise, driving both innovation and exports.[81] It should be noted that the innovation associated with the small business sector originates from small manufacturing firms integrated in production and research networks including other small, medium, and large firms. These "network effects" are what allow these SMEs to compete in national and global markets, which brings us to lesson ten.

Lesson Ten: Small, Locally Based Firms Can Foster Social Cohesion

In looking at the role of SME's in our communities, we can't just focus on economic measures such as GDP, jobs created, and productivity.

Clearly, the environment, social cohesion, and happiness are just as important to our individual and collective well-being. The examples of community fight-backs in Boston, London, and Toronto noted at the start of this chapter illustrate the strong emotional attachment people have to their physical locations and to the individuals that make up the small businesses ensconced in the streetscapes of our towns and cities.

In Boston's Jamaica Plain neighbourhood, not even the arrival of Whole Foods – the most "politically correct" of grocery chains, with its wide selection of organic produce and artisanal cheeses – could shake locals' loyalty to their ramshackle 1960s-vintage supermarket. Though definitely not the "customer experience" touted by retail experts, it was infinitely more human, with all its imperfections and idiosyncrasies.

This is something E.F. Schumacher, British economist and former pupil of the aforementioned Leopold Kohr, understood intuitively when he published his wildly popular 1973 collection of essays, *Small Is Beautiful: Economics as if People Mattered*. What underpinned his work was a core belief that modern society was losing touch with basic human needs and values – and in doing so failing both the planet and its people.[82]

In search of profit and technological gains, Schumacher argued, modern economic policies were generating rampant environmental degradation and dehumanizing labour conditions.[83] "Ever bigger machines, entailing ever bigger concentrations of economic power and exerting ever greater violence against the environment, do not represent progress: they are a denial of wisdom. Wisdom demands a new orientation of science and technology towards the organic, the gentle, the non-violent, the elegant and beautiful," Schumacher wrote.[84]

The vision he proposed – a holistic approach to human society, stressing small-scale, localized solutions – flies in the face of "bigger is better" economic orthodoxy.[85] As Schumacher declared "I have no doubt that it is possible to give a new direction to technological development, a direction that shall lead it back to the real needs of man, and that also means: to the actual size of man. Man is small, and, therefore, small is beautiful."[86]

When it comes to cities, where most of us now live and work, Schumacher's philosophy and fears were very much shared by Jane Jacobs in her writings and struggles against the pharaoh-like public works projects of 1960s North American planners. Jacobs's last, prescient work, *Dark Age Ahead*, published in 2004, poses a challenging issue for the future: "At a given time it is hard to tell whether forces of cultural life or death are in the ascendancy. Is suburban sprawl, with its abandonment of traditional community plans, extensive use of land, time, and energy, a sign of decay? Or is the rising interest in means by which we can overcome sprawl a sign of vigour and adaptability in North American culture?"[87] Arguably, while either could turn out to be true, the fostering of local resilience and small-scale entrepreneurship is as good a bet as any against the forces of social and cultural decay.

Lesson 11: Too Many Large, Non-Locally Based Firms Can Destroy Social Capital

Taking a pessimistic slant on Jacobs's question, in parts of Toronto the spread of big-box retail outlets and sprawling parking lots remarkably continues unabated. Laird Avenue in Toronto's Leaside area was (until recently) an eclectic mixture of industrial, residential, and small retail uses, including one of the city's best fish and chip shops (still in operation) and even a Scandinavian deli (recently closed). However,.it is now home to a power centre, with another one under construction just metres away. The current power centre's buildings, their Mediterranean design motif more suited to California or southern Europe than to the modest postwar buildings and housing typical of Leaside, fringe a vast parking lot facing Laird Avenue. At night, the heavily lit and empty complex is testimony to the "wastes of land, time, and energy" that so enraged Jacobs, making a stark contrast to the lively and bustling street scene of 1950s Greenwich Village from where she moved.

Drive a few miles east of Leaside and you see a similar story unfold on a stretch known as the Golden Mile, a mainly industrial quarter patterned on the London suburb of Brentford. The Golden Mile played a critical role in Canada's Second World War efforts (the GECO plant produced more arms than any Commonwealth factory throughout the war) and later became the quintessential industrial park, producing everything from vans to fridges and featuring a Who's Who of international manufacturing – including GM, SKF, GE, Inglis, and Canadian firms like Thermos. But the Golden Mile wasn't just a manufacturing centre.

In the mid-1950s, on the western edge of the Golden Mile, the Eglinton Square Shopping Centre opened, along with the Golden Mile Plaza, the largest shopping centre in Canada at the time, catering to the needs of the booming local population and a growing middle class. Typical of the more human scale of malls from that era, they featured a mix of small independent stores, restaurants, retail chains, and a grand old cinema where teenagers gazed transfixed at such summer film classics as *Top Gun* and the Bond flick *Octopussy*.

By the early 1990s, the distinctive manufacturing and retail character of the Golden Mile would be lost, symbolized by the 1993 closure of the GM van plant and the demolition of the elegant modernist and art-deco influenced Golden Mile sign (see exhibit 7.1). The vagaries of recessions, globalization, technological change, untrammelled sprawl, and government neglect would see one of Toronto's once-great manufacturing and mixed retail hubs morph into the highest concentration of large-format retail stores in Canada, including the nation's biggest Wal-Mart.

But to return to Jacobs's open question in *The Dark Age*: it may not be all doom and gloom on today's Golden Mile. While the Golden Mile Plaza's big-box-store replacement is showing signs of decline and decay – now subdivided into a dollar store, a couple of discount food outlets, and a government welfare office – Eglinton Square, one of the city's first generation of enclosed malls that appeared just post-Yorkdale, continues to flourish.

On a recent shopping trip to the mall, I was struck by how little things had changed from the days of my youth, spent hanging around its environs and searching out the latest record releases by the Smiths in its well-stocked Sam the Record Man. Though Sam's has given way to mobile and smart-phone retailers, the venerable Watt's family restaurant survives, as does an original British bakery. The food court is, as always, a hub of activity with many of the area's retirees enjoying a coffee, along with an abundance of young families sampling the court's varied food offerings. It looks a lot like a textbook case of people "voting with their feet" in search of a sense of community and basic human interaction.

Cumulatively, the loss of these more human-scaled gathering places has a major impact on a community's level of social capital. Or, to put it slightly differently, "social capital is not just the sum of the institutions which underpin a society – it is the glue that holds them together."[88] In this regard, the social interactions that take place among local entrepreneurs and customers represent an important ingredient in the "glue" that sustains social capital.[89] What's striking about the Golden Mile's current power centres is how utterly different they are from the original Golden Mile Plaza or Eglinton Square just down the road. Most notably, they are devoid of any hint of "third-spaces," such as a local barber shop, cafe, or diner, where informal social gatherings and community building can take place.[90]

At street level, the homogeneous format of big-box retail doesn't perform the role of "a social, cultural and economic focus for their surrounding neighbourhoods"[91] played by small-business-dominated

Exhibit 7.1: Two commemorative plaques sit isolated at the edge of a box-store parking lot, in the only parcel of land in the Golden Mile not devoted to car parking. *Photo by Todd Harris © 2014.*

city areas like Kensington Market or College Street West. Moreover, in contrast to early postwar suburban malls and street-based retail strips, big-box retailers fail to offer the range of community-oriented amenities – such as medical clinics, post offices, and libraries – that help to maintain the city's quality of life. Nor do they tend to initiate or sponsor local events such as art fairs, antique shows, and street festivals.[92] In addition, the size and inaccessibility of big boxes make them exhausting and disorienting to navigate, especially for seniors and people with disabilities.[93]

Lesson Twelve: Small Business Can Foster Local Leadership

The departure of locally owned businesses from a neighbourhood and the accompanying loss of social capital also have a very real human impact. There is the obvious demise of that personalized and helpful customer experience one usually gets from a small business – the opposite of today's DIY corporate ethos where consumers are expected to do everything, including scanning and bagging their groceries, filling up their gas tanks, and assembling their furniture.

Even more ominously, the elimination by urban design of small, independent, locally based entrepreneurs means the end of the social relationships, norms, and trust they help build up in their communities over time.[94] They are what sociologists define as the urban "leadership class."[95] Critically, they are people who, on balance, have the public interest of the local community in mind and therefore "understand the interpersonal dynamics of its members and their various networks."[96] Consequently, they are often able to avert conflict and get individuals to cooperate when a local problem requires collective action,[97] as was illustrated in earlier chapters about life on the main streets of Vancouver, Halifax, and Toronto.

Summary

We have seen that the impact of urban planning that facilitates big-box shopping does not fall solely on existing small businesses but also affects the complex and less visible supporting infrastructure within the communities served by these small local retailers. It is an infrastructure that includes legal, accounting, transportation, warehousing and logistics, financial, publishing, and advertising firms that work closely with these small-scale retailers.[98] In particular, local lawyers, accountants, and bankers are typically also community leaders who, in addition to providing essential support services for the small independent retailer, also get engaged in local neighbourhood issues. With "the arrival of Wal-Mart, and the attendant reduction in the demand for their services, they [professionals] leave the community to pursue opportunities elsewhere."[99] Tragically, the social capital they embody is forever lost to the community, along with their entrepreneurial skills and other forms of location-specific human capital.[100]

The leadership and community activism of local entrepreneurs was something clearly observed in chapter 2 on the growth of BIAs in Canada and in the three city-based case studies in chapters 3, 4, and 5. Time and again, whether it was the local pharmacist, realty broker, gallery owner, or furniture store manager, small-scale business leaders were frequently the key intermediaries between the community and government on local issues such as crime, infrastructure enhancements, and the need for public transportation. Impressive as well were the countless examples of their support for local charities and community groups, along with the intercultural relationship building they were able to provide through a variety of initiatives such as street festivals and other special events. This could be called small-scale corporate social responsibility in practice, minus the expensive advertising promoting the "good work done" by corporations.

The negative social and civic consequences of losing these community leaders and businesses was highlighted in a 2006 study titled "Wal-Mart and Social Capital" by Stephan J. Goetz and Anil Rupasingha published in the *American Journal of Agricultural Economics*; the study found that communities that attracted a Wal-Mart had fewer non-profit groups and social-capital-generating associations (such as churches, political organizations, and business groups) per capita than those that did not. Wal-Mart's presence also was associated with lower civic participation and was even associated with reduced voter turnout in presidential elections.[101]

In short, we should not underestimate the role small-business entrepreneurship plays in supporting social cohesion and helping integrate newcomers and minorities into the fabric of a local economy and society. As demonstrated by both our earliest waves of immigration from Britain and Europe and more recent ones from the Caribbean, India, and China, the ability to start up a business has provided groups often shut out of existing commercial and employment networks with a pathway to prosperity and social mobility. The dynamism and vibrancy of

Toronto's "Greektown" and multiple "Chinatowns" are the polar opposites of France's *banlieues*, the bleak suburbs that ring its major cities and that erupted in ethnic-based violent rioting several years ago.[102]

Owning your own business gives you a stake in the success and well-being of the community – a stake that rioting youths in Paris, excluded from any means of making a living, felt they did not have. We need to make every effort to learn from lessons in economic development that highlight the benefits of supporting small-scale entrepreneurship and finding ways to counteract the potentially destructive effects of large-scale, monocultural economic policy making.

8 Small Business and the Main Street Agenda: Lessons in Public Policy

Accustomed as we are to believing that the North American economy is dominated by large enterprises (whether public or private), we may take a sceptical view of one of the basic premises of this book – that the current and future success of contemporary Canadian (and for that matter Western) society depends on numerous small, locally based, and independently owned enterprises operating in highly urbanized environments. This premise, we acknowledge, requires some explaining.

The reason for placing such an emphasis on small enterprise and the city is actually quite simple. It is based on four observations about what small businesses can do given an appropriately designed urban environment (all listed below). These observations, in turn, give rise to what we might term "the Main Street Agenda" – a set of objectives or rules that could guide policy makers in their twin quest to make our national economies less vulnerable to the vagaries of global capitalism and to ensure that our cities stay vibrant and liveable. We begin by outlining the underlying reasons for our focus on policies aimed at small businesses within our largest cities.

Four Reasons Why Small Business Matters as a Public Policy Priority

Reason One: Small Business Employs People, Not Capital

The first reason for emphasizing small-scale enterprise rests on the realization that the primary interest of private corporate organization has been in the use of expensive capital and high technology, and, increasingly, the outsourcing of economic activity. This approach has been successful in simultaneously increasing output while reducing labour and other costs. But this labour-displacing effect also explains why most workers are now employed outside the largest industrial corporations.

This focus on capital and technology at the expense of people is even more pronounced among the largest 200 or so manufacturers (measured in assets), which account for roughly half of manufacturing value in Canada but only one-third of manufacturing employment. In June 2011, the manufacturing sector accounted for 16 per cent of the Canadian labour force, which means, in other words, that the work of only 8 per cent of the labour force is organized within the largest manufacturing corporations. In contrast, there are nearly 2 million sole proprietorships and limited partnerships in the Canadian economy, meaning that almost twice as many people work independently as are employed by corporations.

The belief that the key to our future success is dependent on the very largest industrial enterprises is simply mistaken, at least from the perspective of *where* most of the work of selling, distributing, and servicing gets done. Large enterprises have traditionally been adapted to work in manufacturing, transportation, and public utilities where the minimum efficient scale has typically been quite large and important. But these industries at present account for less than a quarter of the total economy, and even less than that in highly urbanized environments. The secular declines in agriculture and manufacturing employment have been more than offset (until recently) by growth in what used to be termed the "tertiary" sector, or what is now less dismissively referred to as the service sector, which (apart from banks, insurance companies, and retail firms) is made up mostly of small, locally owned players.

There are no doubt issues as they relate to the capacity for small-scale entrepreneurs to expand the economy, in part because small-scale retailers, professional service providers, and restaurateurs do not export (except in the case of tourism or online sales). Nevertheless, local and regional economies create the majority of jobs (the evidence is pretty clear here) and have the capacity to be "economically resilient" in the sense of being less susceptible to the vagaries of global capitalism than multinational enterprises. A vibrant culture of small-scale entrepreneurship servicing local needs shields communities from the closure of a single large employer.

The success of such an entrepreneurial culture requires both an urban market of sufficient size and a "built form" that allows small-scale enterprises to flourish. This type of urban set-up can lessen the likelihood that foreign cost advantages will lead to the outsourcing of jobs, for two reasons. First, because what is being provided cannot be easily outsourced (getting my hair cut from a distance – say, in Bangladesh – is still not an option) and because small-scale enclaves always leave open the possibility that, though one small firm may fail, a new firm offering a novel service or a solution to a problem may take its place, attracting consumers and talent from outside the locality.

Reason Two: Small Players Can (Fruitfully) Disrupt the Economic Status Quo

A second reason for our emphasis on small, independent, and locally owned enterprise is that even within sectors that seem well suited to large corporations, there is always room for disruptive innovation by small start-ups.[1] Joseph Schumpeter referred to this as "creative destruction," but we might refer to it as simply finding newer, better ways of doing things. This role is particularly well suited to small, independent, economic actors that can experiment at relatively low cost and with few negative consequences for society if they fail but big benefits to both the individual entrepreneur and society if the experiment succeeds. In fact, experimentation on a small scale can help ensure the continued efficiency and existence of large players, as we saw in the Toronto chapter, where a large local retailer sought the local customer knowledge of a small business owner in order to stay ahead of the competition.

Established corporations did not *invent* the airplane, the automobile, the telephone, or even the first personal computers, but they assured – through the use of mass production, distribution, and marketing – their widespread adoption. We do not dispute the important role of big business in the process of innovation. But it is important to remember that hugely important innovations have typically come from small pioneering firms, as was the case with Apple, RIM, or, in an earlier era, Ford. And, like an accordion, large enterprises also sometimes have to shrink in order to later expand, as IBM did when it shed computer production in the 1990s and focused on software solutions and information management. It was only after becoming small (relative to its large size at the start of the 1990s) that IBM was able to innovate once again. The recent trend among domestic auto manufacturers towards "rightsizing" senior management and downsizing operations in order to launch new (and more successful) car models also speaks to this facet of innovation.

The lesson here is that economic resilience implies change and adaptation, and that much of that takes place through the formation of enterprises that are, at least initially, small and often independently operated. Simply put, you don't have to worry about breaking any rules when the rule book hasn't even been written.

Reason Three: Distributed (as Opposed to Centralized) Decision Making Is Typically Best

A fundamental characteristic of innovation, stretching back to the dawn of the Industrial Revolution, is that it occurs in a decentralized way in small independent enterprises. This same idea has been cleverly recast under the twin banners of "distributed intelligence" and "Wikinomics" to explain the explosion of economic activity brought about by the digital revolution and new social media.[2] To innovate in the way Western economies have traditionally done, it is necessary to decentralize economic activity – that is, to delegate the authority to make economic decisions to a multitude of actors of diverse size, ownership, internal structure, objectives, and location. To maximize this traditional process of growth in economic output, Western societies have had to accommodate a considerable degree of diffusion of authority and responsibility and have (up to now) limited the pyramiding of managerial hierarchies to cases where such a hierarchy clearly pays off.

Nevertheless, the strength and the sustainability of decentralized economic decision making are chronically underappreciated, if one may judge from the slavish concern with the performance of large enterprise in the popular business press or from the predictions that our Western way of life is being threatened by a new, more centralized form of East-Asian capitalism (i.e., Chinese-style managed economic growth).[3] One should note that these are prophecies that have been repeated ever since Marx and later Schumpeter concurred that capitalism tended towards monopolization, and that still remain unfulfilled.

Reason Four: For Every Goliath There Needs to Be at Least One David

Our fourth and final observation related to public policy for the small-business sector is that conditions that permit the easy formation of new independent enterprises serve to constrain the economic and social power of larger, more established firms. The same tendencies that produce bureaucratic rigidities in mature non-market actors (governments or industrial trade unions) are also at work in mature corporate enterprises, in each case acting to limit innovation and dynamism. In successful economic environments, the forces of change can express themselves in newly established firms that circumvent bureaucratic rigidity and supply older corporate players with incentives (i.e., the need to stay in business) to alter habits that would otherwise lead to obsolescence. Because change is continuously destroying established methods in older lines of business, the new economic activity required to achieve a net advance over the declines must exceed the old activity being displaced.

While this new activity may well arise from the expansion of older businesses or the conversion of some older enterprises to new forms, the creation of new enterprises plays a particularly important role in sustained economic development and growth. This is why, as we saw in chapter 7, a disproportionately high share of new jobs are created in small and newly established firms. Through experiment and innovation (our second factor above), these new firms are born; and while many experiments fail, the firms that do succeed are an important source of dynamism in modern economies. The amount of employment growth directly attributable to new enterprises is therefore quite high.

This is not to say that large firms do nothing but wait to go extinct; on the contrary some large corporate firms work to ensure stable jobs and manage to change with the times. However, small local start-ups are indispensable to overall economic prosperity, because of their role in hiring new labour market entrants and because of the pressure they place on older corporate giants to continue innovating.[4]

All four of the above policy rationales for recognizing the value of small independent enterprises and their contribution to overall economic vibrancy and growth are intimately related to the success of city living. Our final set of observations therefore relates policy and the economic success of our local economies to our urban plans, zoning laws, and city governance structures. But before we get there, two notes of caution on this issue of smallness and start-up prowess are necessary.

Two Notes of Caution and Clarification

Can We Really Compare Steve Jobs to My Local Barber?

Our discussion of high-growth firms that started off small but ended up big players in their respective markets may leave readers with the impression that this is a universal phenomenon or that the lessons for market dominance apply as much to Apple as to the local barber shop. This is clearly not the case. Some of the reasons for high growth from a small base stem from the creation of a product or service that meets a particular need and that no other firm is positioned to exploit (very unlike my local barber). Being one of the first to tap into a latent but largely unmet demand offers huge growth potential. However, from that point of departure there is a stubborn similarity between my local barber and a highly successful company like Apple.

In order to remain a long-run success, any firm (no matter what size) has to be attuned to what buyers want and need.[5] Just as my barber knows my name and can predict what haircut I will ask for from the moment I sit in his chair, firms that have remained large market players have had to find ways of mimicking that small-scale, detailed knowledge of their customers. Had BlackBerry (formerly RIM) been more attuned to its customers and the evolution in their tastes following the move to touch-based devices backed up by impressive software applications, would it have made the same poor business decisions that it did? Note that the period of explosive growth (as measured in revenue and employment) for BlackBerry occurred over the period 2006–8, exactly the period when its market lead in smart phones was starting to be overshadowed by Apple and Samsung.

Leaving aside the outward manifestations of innovation (i.e., flashy new iPads), a look at Apple in 1997, at the time Steve Jobs returned, shows that he first took on the task of transforming the company internally into a series of small-team innovation labs. Each was tasked with different aspects of innovation for the firm, everything from software to hardware to promotion and advertising. The result was much like the famous 1984 advertising campaign and product launch that preceded Apple's foray into personal computing, which was then dominated by IBM, the largest computer hardware maker in the world. Apple in the 2000s redefined what a cell phone could be and what the smart phone would become, leaving established (and bigger at the time) players such as Nokia and BlackBerry flatfooted. Though the success of the iPhone has eclipsed Apple's earlier triumphs, we shouldn't forget also that Apple destroyed another dinosaur of a market leader in the early 2000s with its iPod and iTunes digital music platform. The Walkman brand was synonymous with portable recorded music. Sony was a much larger and more profitable firm at the time Apple entered the market, and yet we now barely remember when the Sony Walkman dominated the cultural and consumer landscape.

This is all to say that one does not have to *be* small to mimic what a small player would do to break into a new market (i.e., take the kind of risks one does when there is no possibility of cannibalizing your own market dominance by a radical innovation). The success of Apple under Steve Jobs's second tenure as CEO is a textbook case of focusing on the end-user and re-establishing a small upstart ethic in order to achieve big results. Granted, my barber is not Steve Jobs, but in his attention to the needs of his customers, the two have a lot in common.

Small Businesses May Create Many Jobs, but Aren't They Low-Paid, Low-Productivity Jobs?

A very well-known predictor of wages is firm size. After differences in such things as age, gender, and type of industry have been controlled for, firm (establishment) size and wages (inclusive of benefits) are robustly and significantly related, although a complicating factor in this relationship is unionization. The firm size premium is more than halved when we include union presence, as most small employers are effectively non-unionized.

That being said, there is still a wage-benefit premium associated with size. Some of this residual premium (after controlling for unionization) is no doubt the result of increased productivity, but another component has to do with Adam Smith's observation in the *Wealth of Nations* that "the agreeableness or disagreeableness" (in Smith's original use)[6] in the work or workplace can cause wages to be different between workers even within the same occupation. These so called "compensating wage differentials" that accrue to a worker in a larger firm exist therefore to offset the "disagreeable" aspects of working in a more impersonal and perhaps less flexible environment. There is evidence in our own study of small business owners as well that people working in larger enterprises travel longer distances to work while those working in smaller, more locally based workplaces travel shorter distances. There is, in short, a trade-off noted by labour economists between the characteristics of a job and the wage paid for it.

The same argument applies to the urban environment. Some of the wage premium associated with living in a more densely packed city, as opposed to a town or suburb, is rooted in productivity gains from sharing knowledge and being in proximity to greater levels of human and physical capital, but some of it is designed to offset the less agreeable aspects of city life such as noise and congestion.

City Life and Small Business: Exploring the Urban Policy Connection to Small Business Success

The success of a small, locally owned business is intimately linked to its proximity to as many people as possible. This is because small enterprises rely primarily on local customers and on human (as opposed to physical) capital. The size and density of cities therefore play particularly important roles in the expansion and the formation of small businesses because they lower the costs of searching for human talent and customers, which for a small business matters a lot. The bigger and denser a city, the more opportunities it gives prospective employees and shoppers to access jobs and services from otherwise hard-to-locate small enterprises. This kind of geographic "clustering" offers advantages to employer and employee alike.

The more interconnected and dense a city or neighbourhood becomes, the more likely it is to be economically vibrant. This notion stands in marked contrast to the major currents of city design and urban planning that emerged during the early postwar era, and that, sadly, are still operative today in most North American cities.

As we saw in Part I, throughout the 1950s and 1960s and even into the 1970s, the problems of "over-crowding" and "slum elimination" were central preoccupations of local governments. And against the warnings of a few dissenting voices (Jane Jacobs being one of the most prominent critics at the time), cities went about eviscerating the heart of lively, well-functioning, though sometimes poor neighbourhoods on the assumption that these places had shoved people and workplaces too closely together.

The evidence reviewed in chapter 2 and in our city case studies points in exactly the opposite direction. Clustering people and commerce closer together in safe, well-designed neighbourhoods is a recipe for economic success, not failure.[7] The ultra-suburban project, on the other hand, with its vast (mostly empty) parking spaces and low density separation-of-use model will soon be (if it isn't already) the economic equivalent of a dinosaur. This is made clear in a number of recent books, among them Chris Turner's *The Leap: How to Survive and Thrive in the Sustainable Economy*, which showcases how successful governments and organizations around the world are doing things differently, eliminating dependence on fossil fuels and still supporting a lifestyle that is both prosperous and durable. In *Green Metropolis*, *New Yorker* staff writer David Owen aptly summarizes how denser cities can meet the challenge of rising energy costs by what he calls "unconscious or built-in efficiencies." He describes the process as follows: "unconscious efficiencies [such as those gained by creating denser urban forms that encourage walking and public transit use] are the most desirable ones, because they require neither enforcement nor personal commitment to cutting back [consumption]. In European cities, as in Manhattan, in other words, the most important efficiencies are built-in."[8]

Cities, Small Business, and Innovation

The policy rationale for thinking that small-scale enterprise and city living go hand-in-hand is also supported by the important role played by small business in generating new innovations. Innovation is sometimes the result of spin-offs from major educational facilities; at other times it is brought into the country by migrants from abroad. In all cases, however, the chance that an innovation will succeed increases with the number of "trials." A city is a natural incubator and generator of experimentation on a local scale. The failures do not impose a great social cost (e.g., the new vegan restaurant in the neighbourhood happened not to make food people enjoyed, so it closed down), but the benefits of success (e.g., the popular organic burger restaurant that expanded to open outlets across the city), if replicable, are huge.[9]

It is one of the paradoxes of modern urban existence that the birth, death, and regeneration of independent business works as well as it does precisely because there is no single actor or "big brother" running the entire operation. In fact, the bigger and more centralized the governance model for local decision making, the worse the outcomes usually are.

The pre-amalgamation governance of cities like Halifax and Toronto – where each federated city in the metropolitan model had a local council and mayor – were much more responsive to local needs and were also less expensive to run – a fact most grating to those who opposed the amalgamated city structures in the late 1990s, which is to say a majority of the citizens of these cities.[10] Having lots of little brothers (local councils) or even baby brothers (local BIAs and residents' associations) governing a city makes for a more democratically run urban government and produces a public realm more attuned to citizens' needs. This is clearly demonstrated by a comparison between the relatively successful place-making approach of the Vancouver region

– which never forced amalgamation on its cities and suburbs but instead expanded its regional metro umbrella – with the difficulties faced by Haligonian and to some extent Toronto business owners under amalgamated city structures.

In another international example, London effectively existed without a central governing authority for most of the past three decades (since Margaret Thatcher broke up what was then seen as a left-of-centre obstacle to public-sector reforms). The central mayor's office was recast in the early 2000s but with the principal, and singular, statutory remit of supervising the greater London transit authority. Most of the decisions about what gets built and serviced throughout London's neighbourhoods are still made in local councils, the equivalent of the old borough and city structures housed within the traditional metro governance model. During this twenty-year period (1988–2008), London emerged as the most successful city in Europe, and perhaps the globe, in terms of attracting new businesses and human talent.

The same benefits that accrue when political governance is decentralized to its most appropriate scale also result from decentralized economic decision making. Despite the apparent ability of centralized systems to transform areas of economic blight overnight with a single factory, casino, or business park, the sustainable path to economic prosperity is typically the result of lots of small decisions by independent actors that cumulatively, over time, create lasting value. Moreover, unlike footloose capital, which is as likely to scale back or close down the moment a better opportunity arises in some other part of the globe, smaller, locally generated investments are more likely to stay put and employ local resources.

Cities, Agglomeration, and the Next Bill Gates

The agglomeration of talented people in a single urban location, where new ideas can be effectively launched and tested by actual consuming participants, also acts to discipline older, well-established corporate giants.

Bill Gates, at the height of Microsoft's dominance of the PC software market in the late 1990s, was quoted as saying that the biggest threat to his company resided not with government anti-trust laws – at the time, Microsoft was under the scrutiny of Congressional law makers – but by the next generation of innovators operating in their basement apartments or household garages. Time has proven that Gates was not far wrong; both Google and Facebook, two of Microsoft's biggest rivals, were started by college students working from the university equivalent of a dense inner-city tenement block – the university residence dorm room. The urbanized city, in short, can be viewed as the equivalent of a Petri dish where new ideas form, evolve, and either survive or die.

At this stage, a fair question is, "What does all this 'small is beautiful' stuff imply for our elected leaders and policymakers? Does public policy have a role, and if so, what is it?"

The Role of Public Policy at all Three Levels of Government

For policy makers at all levels, the answer is that they should recognize what decades-old research amply demonstrates: small, independent, and locally owned enterprises are the main drivers of economic growth and, crucially, of job creation. They are also a key source of social capital and economic resilience in periods of national and global economic distress.

Second, and equally important, our leaders need to acknowledge the major contributions small businesses in our towns and big cities make to personal well-being and quality of life. Small-scale capitalists are both the present and the future of Canada's economic and social health, and public policy needs a strong focus on ensuring their ongoing vitality.

Fortunately, promoting entrepreneurialism is much less about targeted tax breaks and niche policies than it is about ensuring the provision of basic public goods such as favourable zoning, good schools, safe streets, efficient public transport, sound business regulation, and the ability to adapt to changing circumstances.[11]

To quote Glaeser and Kerr once again,

> there is much to be said for the strategy of focusing on the quality of life policies that can attract smart, entrepreneurial people. The best economic development strategy may be to attract smart people and get out of their way. This approach is particularly appealing because the downside is so low. What community ever screwed up by providing too much quality of life?[12]

Establishing the right environment for small-scale enterprise to flourish requires governments at all levels not only to follow traditionally sound macro-economic policies but also to use the many policy levers they already have at their disposal to foster the liveability and dynamism of their cities. In what follows, we offer guidance aimed specifically at each level of government.

What Can the Federal Government Do?

For the federal government, creating a pro-growth macro-economic environment is a priority, especially during a period of weak aggregate demand. How much more severe would the effects of the great recession of 2008 have been without the fiscal and monetary policy stimulus implemented in Canada and a number of other countries? Although this is still an open question, those small-business advocates in Canada who are singularly focused on tax and budget cutting need to pay heed to the finding that small and medium-sized businesses located in urban centres were among the biggest beneficiaries of this federal stimulus. The reason is that small independent enterprises tended to operate in local Canadian markets and as such were not heavily exposed to the turmoil in international markets.[13] Similarly, the federal government's provincial equalization payments and income support programs help protect the purchasing power of many lower-income Canadians, who then spend a greater proportion of their dollars in small, independent local shops in cities throughout the country.

Another factor not to be underestimated is the federal government's responsibility for immigration, which it increasingly delivers in collaboration with the provinces. Immigration is vital to meeting the needs of our labour market and expanding our economic base through the creation of new market opportunities and the formation of business start-ups. Consequently, it's troubling to hear, as reported in several news outlets, that promising young entrepreneurs are nowadays drawn to Australia, which is aggressively promoting itself to this demographic.[14] Canada eliminated its entrepreneur-class immigration program many years ago and only recently has returned to "studying how to attract and retain innovative entrepreneurs."[15]

What Can Provincial Governments Do?

The provinces and the municipalities, of course, play a critical part in undertaking investments and managing programs that directly affect the quality of our human, physical, and social infrastructure. On the human side of the ledger, there are the broader economic benefits of public institutions like schools, universities, and hospitals, which help to create and sustain a skilled and healthy workforce that contributes to the growth of businesses, big and small. Then there's the hugely vital research and innovation function played by the country's post-secondary institutions, which, since 1999 have fostered the creation of 1,242 spin-off companies.[16]

With respect to physical infrastructure, we know how integral transportation systems are to productivity by enabling people and goods to be moved efficiently across great distances. Nonetheless, as a range of studies have pointed out, Canada urgently needs to upgrade its aging intra- and inter-urban transportation systems. Traffic congestion, poorly maintained roads, and inadequate public transportation systems have a profoundly negative effect on the competitiveness of our businesses. In Montreal, for example, the overall cost of congestion in the metropolitan area is estimated at $1.4 billion or 1 per cent of GDP.[17]

What Can Local Governments Do?

Meanwhile, at the municipal level, we have the example of the Greater Toronto Area, which arguably has the worst traffic congestion of any major urban centre in the developed world, with the costs of lost productivity resulting from congestion pegged at $3.3 billion per year by the OECD.[18] Incredibly, notwithstanding such grim figures, some local politicians are actually proposing cuts in basic bus and streetcar service, with little regard for the negative impact on already under-serviced enterprises and poorer neighbourhoods located in the far reaches of the city's east and west ends.

Improving the Quality of Urban Life

Municipal governments can have an enormous influence on the social well-being and quality-of-life aspects of urban life. As Boston and New York demonstrate, key elements in the revival of these two cities in the late 1990s was the success of local governments in improving the day-to-day experience of ordinary citizens through effective strategies to reduce crime and other social ills such as homelessness, gang culture, and substance abuse. Without such efforts, businesses and people would not have moved back into neighbourhoods like Harlem or Jamaica Plain, once so emblematic of American urban decay.

Though Canada's major cities have never experienced a degree of social breakdown and economic decline like that observed in some U.S. cities, there are worrying signs of increasing inequality, homelessness, and poverty in our major urban centres.[19] Combating these challenges requires cities to deliver a range of services – from policing to parks to public health clinics to after-school programs – to enhance the quality of life and social infrastructure of communities. Again, it is worth remembering that such amenities, in addition to being socially progressive, also help attract the best and brightest people and entrepreneurs to cities.

Zoning and By-Law Modernization

Another significant policy instrument available to our provinces and municipalities is the urban planning system and local zoning by-laws that affect the size and location of businesses. We know that planning regimes favouring increased density and mixed-use development not only produce environmental benefits but also generate higher levels of economic growth and innovation and reduce the costs of paying for government services and infrastructure.

For example, in Toronto in the early 1990s, a small by-law change allowing for live-work accommodation helped attract creative entrepreneurs into abandoned industrial buildings, transforming them and revitalizing whole neighbourhoods once thought of as in permanent decline. Cities looking to maintain and grow their stock of small and medium-sized enterprises, particularly in retail and related services, need to look carefully at how granting zoning approval for big-box stores affects the existing retail mix and its supply chains and social capital in the surrounding community.

Government Subsidies and Tax Credits

Finally, a policy dialogue on small-scale enterprise promotion would not be complete without a consideration of the plethora of business support programs directed at this sector by all levels of government. In one respect, such support should be viewed in a positive light, as a sign that governments "get" how important new business formation and SMEs are to the economy. Indeed, few would find fault with efforts to streamline business regulations, reduce red tape, and generally make it easy to start a business. More contentious, however, is whether and to what extent SMEs should be directly supported through interest-free loans, grants, and tax credits.

If we are sceptical about supporting larger corporations in this way, we should also question whether small economic players should receive such government largesse. An obvious pitfall of such support is the perceived inability of bureaucrats to "pick winners," since, unlike private investors, they have few incentives to carefully select investment prospects.[20] An oft-cited example is the experience of Japan's Ministry of International Trade and Investment (MITI), which despite being staffed with Japan's best minds and trumpeted as part of Japan's early postwar economic success, generally picked losers.[21] This government practice is especially galling for successful firms that do not receive direct subsidies yet have to pay for these failed ventures through their taxes. Others suggest that providing such financial support to small business does not produce long-term success, as firms pop up around certain sector-based programs but quickly fizzle out once the subsidies cease.[22]

Another complaint about government support programs for SMEs is that they are often weakened by too many "soft" policy or politically motivated goals rather than strictly commercial ones. For example, the obsession with growing particular sectors, whether ICT or bio-sciences, ignores the fact that productive, profitable, and innovative small-scale entrepreneurs can emerge in any sector, from services to retail to manufacturing. Moreover, many independent owners operate in supply chains that interact with a myriad of different industries simultaneously.

The alternative to direct grants or loans, the tax credit, also comes in for damning criticism. Several independent reports commissioned by the federal government in 2010 point to the failure of its R&D tax-credit program to generate much in the way of investment in new technologies, innovation, or R&D. Readers may conclude that the best option for government is to get out of the subsidy and business support game entirely, leaving the private sector with the responsibility for providing consulting support and financing for small independent firms. Under such a minimalist model, the government's main role, from a business-promotion perspective, is to create a sound regulatory system, which, among other things, encourages a competitive banking and investment sector that facilitates the financing needed for the formation of new firms and the expansion of existing SMEs.

It is beyond dispute that a solid regulatory framework is the bedrock of the market system, but it is too easy to be a libertarian purist and just say "no to all subsidies." The sad reality is that, despite the free-trade rhetoric of politicians the world over, all Canada's major trading competitors – the United States, Germany, South Korea, and China, to name a few – provide direct support to stimulate exports, R&D, and capital investment by SMEs.

With that in mind, there might be a case for better targeting existing business support funding to sustain and create more "high growth" SMEs, a view recently expressed by a 2012 Martin Prosperity Institute report. One simple action would be to simply redirect a significant portion of the nearly $5 billion cost of R&D tax credits[23] to postsecondary research programs and on-campus commercialization and business spin-off activity. A considerable body of economic research clearly shows the strong relationship between economic growth, levels of innovation, and public R&D investments in universities. It is relevant to note as well that in the United States more than half of private sector patents originate in university research.[24] The presence of world-class universities and colleges in all of Canada's major urban centres creates a unique environment for potentially fruitful partnerships linking SMEs and universities, through activities such as internships and cooperative work programs, mentoring of young entrepreneurs, and applied R&D.

An early 2001 international (including Canada) analysis of best practices for promoting SME growth and competitiveness made the intriguing case that some business support should be directed to what are defined in the report as "high-growth SMEs" (i.e., firms with ten or more employees and an average annualized growth in employees or turnover greater than 20 per cent a year). [25] The report's authors contend that, given the empirical evidence for the importance of high-growth SMEs in creating jobs, it makes sense to leverage the positive impact of these enterprises.[26]

To use a sporting analogy, we perhaps require a business support version of Canada's successful "Own the Podium" program, which put Canada high in the gold medal rankings at the 2010 and 2014 Winter Olympics in Vancouver and Sochi. Instead of spreading sport funding equally across all disciplines, regardless of performance and medal prospects, the program targeted those athletes most likely to compete at a truly elite level. If governments are to continue playing the subsidy game, an approach that encourages SMEs to expand, when feasible, and become more competitive merits consideration. In this vein, tax rules that penalize SMEs when their revenues grow also need to be discouraged.

What All Levels of Government Can Do Right Now

Invest in Cities and Reverse the Rhetorical Love Affair with Lowering Taxes

While Glaeser and Kerr may be correct in asserting that there are no downsides from providing "too much quality of life," this does not appear to be the view of many governments around North America. Even as this book was being written, municipal, provincial, state, and federal governments were busy drafting budgets that would, among other measures, see the closure of public art galleries and museums and of wading pools for toddlers and the cessation of funding for a school breakfast program geared to young children in deprived areas. So much for the notion of the "high-amenity city."

But in defence of our current political leaders, they do have supporters, and they are merely reflecting well over two decades of elite consensus about the need to cut taxes, loosen regulations, and rein in government spending. If this were done, it has been argued, Canada (like other countries jumping on the austerity bandwagon) would lead the world in productivity and innovation, factors unquestionably critical to growth in wages and wealth creation. Regrettably, the outcomes say otherwise. A widely cited report by former TDCanada Trust economics chief Don Drummond paints a sobering picture of Canadian economic performance over this period of tax cuts and restrained public investment.[27] Here's a sampling:

- Labour productivity growth in Canada's business sector has been in decline since the 1970s and "has slowed to a crawl" since 2000. It is a trend not mirrored in other developed countries, and it's taking a toll on Canada's international economic clout.[28]
- Between 1990 and 2008, Canada's GDP per capita slipped from fifth to eleventh among OECD countries.[29]
- In 1970, Canada was the fifth most efficient economy out of twenty-four OECD countries. By 2009, it had fallen to fifteenth.[30]

While admitting that the arsenal of existing policies (fiscal discipline, price stability, lower corporate taxes, free trade, globalization, etc.) "hasn't done the trick," Drummond searches deeply for the causes of Canada's "productivity puzzle," trying to peer into what has mysteriously been described in the classic growth studies of the 1960s as the "black box" of productivity. But, as economist Andrew Jackson notes in a comment on Drummond's paper, the strait-jacket of rigid economic orthodoxy makes any analysis incapable of considering some slightly more interventionist policies that might actually help us in arresting the decline so vividly described in Drummond's report.[31]

Indeed as endogenous growth theory beginning in the 1990s has shown, how productivity is generated is not a "black box," but rather an open book.[32] Just think of all the positive spin-offs we could derive from having the kind of progressive economic policies, growth, and more or less full employment of the early 1970s when, as Drummond notes, Canada was near the top of the economic performance tables. It's just an educated guess, but perhaps we'd have firms operating at full capacity and thus forced to invest in capital and skills, as well as a much tighter employment market, which would in turn boost labour productivity.[33] The knock-on effects of this sort of growth today would be nothing short of nirvana for the country's small enterprises. However, this does involve some strategic micro-economic interventions and, more importantly, much more expansionary macro-economic fiscal policies, with full employment as a central target. This (even after years of economic stagnation) appears to be anathema to modern-day policy makers and to even the most progressive of industry economists such as Drummond.

Embracing Smart Revenue Generation, Long-Run Investment, and Small-Scale Innovation

In the end, the domestic and global success of firms big and small does not occur in a vacuum. Our options are therefore clear. We can, on the one hand, continue to muddle along with our current suite of warmed-over supply-side interventions, continuing in slow decline and ever more dependent on our non-renewable resource sector to maintain our standard of living. Or we can embrace an ambitious pro-growth agenda that would expand and diversify our economic base.

Such an agenda would touch on the following key themes:

- investments in human, physical, and social capital, especially in our major urban centres where much of our country's economic activity increasingly takes place;
- targeted support for SMEs and the promotion of entrepreneurialism;
- big investments in R&D activity in our postsecondary institutions; and
- maintenance, as in much of the postwar era, of a high-growth economy supported by expansionary macro-economic and monetary policies.

A supportive policy and fiscal environment, as just described, doesn't develop on the cheap. If we are serious about making a quantum leap in our economic performance, we need to have a serious discussion about how we pay for the kind of productivity-enhancing investments just described. Inevitably, this would require increased income and consumption taxes, user fees, road-tolls, and other revenue-generating instruments. Just as Alex Ling had to persuade his fellow business owners to pony up if they wanted to save their main street, so must politicians engage citizens and business leaders in a serious dialogue about the role of shared public investment in halting the decay of our urban transportation systems and aging public infrastructure.

And finally, it should be stressed, such revenues need to be derived from a broad base in a fair and equitable fashion, not just from big corporations or high-income earners, as some on the left seem to believe. Collectively, all Canadians and sectors of the economy have a contribution to make to our future well-being and to shaping an environment in which the creativity and entrepreneurial spirit of our residents can flourish.

Summary of Main Street Public Policy: Emphasizing the Small, to Big Effect

In closing, if there is one thing that we wish to assure our readers of it is that in modern globalized economies, small, locally owned enterprises rooted in neighbourhoods matter a great deal.

Economic writers and journalists in major news publications who deride the value of small independent enterprise, as well as those who focus on the evils of modern capitalism, all seem to agree on one thing

– that large enterprises are all that matter in the modern economy. Such arguments greatly miss the mark. This mistaken view is most common among those who (wrongly) see corporations as having everywhere and always achieved their success via innovation and hard-won market competition.

While this may be the case in some instances, we should not overlook the possibility that some of these large companies have grown by subverting political leadership in an effort to sidestep market competition and have indeed become "too big to fail." The effect of propping up large enterprises on the assumption that they hold the key to economic success has been tragic, insofar as it has misled policy makers into seeking growth by subsidizing mature Western enterprises rather than by enabling the historically proven Western practice of growth through local experiment with a variety of (initially at least) small, independently owned firms.

Because such small, independent firms tend to congregate in dense urban environments that are as open to new ideas as they are to newcomers, we need to push for urban economic initiatives that preserve urban amenities such as good schools, parks, and culture, for it is these amenities that attract the talent pool within which entrepreneurs are born.

The urban economic agenda has to preserve space for small business to set up shop and eventually grow. This means preserving a stock of commercial and retail space of a size (500 to 2,500 square feet) that is conducive to small-scale entrepreneurship. In practice this requires policy makers to ensure that before they approve regulations that allow major tracts of inner-city and inner-suburban built forms to be gentrified or demolished for some new condo development, they give serious consideration to the viability of what was there before (in the case of the city centre, small two- and three-story buildings with storefronts at street level, and in the case of the early postwar suburbs, the strip mall with its profusion of small shops and office space above). Any new-built forms should be required to provide space to accommodate small, locally owned enterprises.

Land-use regulations may seem like urban arcana remote from the concerns of modern industrial policy, but these rules matter because they shape local urban structures, which can either enable small-scale enterprises to flourish or doom them to perish.

Urban land use and structure shape how we live – often in unexpected ways. Consider that our survey of BIA members found that most of the owner operators commuted less than twenty minutes to work and that most of their customers were drawn from the local neighbourhood. Is it any wonder that the evidence shows that large, dense cities with nearby amenities produce significantly lower levels of carbon emissions than smaller, more spread-out suburban environments? This may also explain why life expectancy in dense urban environments is higher; people in New York City (the densest city in North America) live nearly two years longer, on average, than in the nation as a whole.[34]

As national economies around the globe struggle to regain their economic strength, planners and politicians would do well to note the economic research showing that denser urban environments are also far more productive and offer better pay than less urbanized regions. New technologies and globalization that seemingly allow knowledge workers to work anywhere have actually put a premium on living in a handful of urban centres with plentiful amenities and easy access to interconnected airport hubs. New labour market entrants, whether young or foreign-born, also gain disproportionately by living and working in cities. Young workers find it easier to gain the skills required in a competitive market-place where many diverse enterprises are located close together, and migrant entrepreneurs are often more able and willing than larger firms to cater to small but growing niche tastes.

Such benefits depend on the availability, in cities like Halifax, Toronto, and Vancouver, of spaces for new local enterprises to set up shop and flourish. The main streets of our cities, with their street-level storefronts and inner suburban strip malls, enable human interactions that are at the heart of social cohesion, economic innovation, and sustainable living. We need to do everything in our collective power to preserve them.

9 Recommendations for Making Small-Scale Enterprise a Transformative Force

Throughout this book we have advanced recommendations and offered policy advice aimed at enabling small-scale enterprise to achieve its potential. We have also tried to raise awareness of the power that small economic actors can exert when they begin to act in concert, both internally (through the BIA movement) and externally (with governments, communities, and yes, even large businesses). Some of our recommendations have been directed at governments, while others, as seen in chapter 6, are focused on BIA best practices. Along the way we offered findings from observations in the field, theory, empirical data, and academic research to support our recommendations.

Here now is a summary of the most important recommendations to emerge from our analysis.

Drop the Bias in Favour of Bigness

The supports provided to business by most governments as well as the attention of many media outlets and research funding bodies are disproportionately directed towards major corporate players. This is understandable, for as Mancur Olsen reminds us in the *Logic of Collective Action*, large corporations are ideally placed to maximize the benefits of size and to capitalize on the lower coordination costs associated with being few in number.

But other institutions, including local businesses, also matter, even if their voices and message are diffuse. The fact that local economies are best placed to withstand the vagaries of global economic meltdowns or stock market crashes should make policy makers stop and think.

An interesting thought experiment is the following: what could North America's cities and local business associations have done with the billions in bail-out money handed to the country's biggest banks and car makers? Would it have made a tangible difference in people's lives and spurred a faster economic recovery? We suspect so, but until we refocus our gaze towards alternative, city-based strategies for economic development that perhaps require more time and patience to pay off, we simply won't know.

Encourage Independent, Local, and Small-Scale Private Action

The need for collective, not necessarily government, action to respond to the complexity and diversity of our cities was a theme that emerged in our opening chapters. One way of dealing with this level of complexity is to empower people and institutions at the level where issues and problems can best be identified and where solutions can best emerge.

The BIA movement began with just such a need to resolve a local problem. The fact that its financing was institutionalized in order to ensure its efficacy, and did not depend only on voluntary commitments, goes some way to explain its success. Empowering local resident associations – in effect, creating (at the neighbourhood level) representative councils with some statutory control over central city-hall planning – would make for investments that are better tailored to public needs and ultimately reduce the amount of NIMBYism and knee-jerk opposition commonly faced by development proposals in most cities.

While not all business owners agree with their BIA's spending priorities, BIAs at least offer increased transparency and opportunity for debate at a very local level. Being one voice out of 200 is certainly better odds than one vote in a million.

In Canada, Provinces Need to Empower Cities

There is a huge imbalance between the needs of Canadians for responsive government, which is to say local government, and the power cities have been given to finance and respond to those needs.

When we enumerate all the things that "government" does, we find that what the federal government does has very little impact on our daily lives; that provincial governments have a little more; and that local governments have the most. Absent a major military invasion, our local governments determine nearly everything, from whether there is a local pool or library in a neighbourhood to the quality of the drinking water. And yet, the role of cities is not recognized in the federal constitution. Cities, perhaps to the surprise of most Canadians, are subject to the provisions of provincial government charters, which, as was seen in the case of Halifax's and Toronto's tragic amalgamation experiences, can be rescinded to devastating effect. Indeed, as noted by economic geographer Meric Gertler, "given the ... centrality of cities to the ... prosperity of the country ... all the great social policy questions of the day – education, health, poverty, housing and immigration – become urban policy questions."[1]

De-amalgamate Some City Governance Structures and Move Other Decision-Making Powers Up a Level

People (entrepreneurs or customers) do not make locational decisions about where to live or set up a business by analysing the degree of decentralized governance at a municipal level. Rather the effect is more indirect, flowing from the consequences of destroying either a higher order of "city-wide" governance (known in North America as "metropolitan governance") or by eviscerating local representation and decision-making powers.

A resident of London, England, between 1999 and 2008 – what some have termed London's new golden age – would have been able to observe local neighbourhood councils making improvements to curbsides, rezoning long vacant industrial lands for commercial and retail purposes, and hosting neighbourhood cultural events, among many other positive initiatives.

The former cities of Metro Toronto (which included the City of Toronto, Scarborough, Etobicoke, North York, East York, and York) historically performed much of what local councils were doing in London during this period. These functions all ended in 1998, when, against the wishes of a majority of voters (with the highest opposition not in downtown Toronto but in the suburban cities of Scarborough, North York, and Etobicoke), then provincial Premier Mike Harris destroyed what was, up to then, a metro governance structure emulated around the world.

It is interesting to note that the period of London's recent ascent (during which it was featured on the covers of *Newsweek* and *Time* magazines) follows the move in the mid-1980s by British Prime Minister Margaret Thatcher to eliminate the Greater London Council (GLC), fearing that its then left-leaning government headed by Ken Livingston would undo her conservative pro-market reforms.[2] Flash forward to early 2000, and London re-elects Ken Livingston as its first mayor in seventeen years. The problems plaguing London at the time of the new city-wide elections were coordination problems that had not been fully addressed because no single body was responsible for solving them. Congestion (there were reports at the time that traffic conditions in London had deteriorated to those of horse-and-buggy days) and transport reliability issues were the largest items on the to-do list.

One of the first actions taken by the newly elected mayor was to impose a congestion fee for entering London and plough back revenues into improved public transit. This had two noticeable effects: congestion in central London immediately fell, as more people biked or took buses to work; and, with the transport system receiving a greater share of funding, public transit started becoming more reliable.

Some may point to the global financial system and New Labour's "light touch" regulatory system as the fuel that powered London's (and to a great extent Britain's) economy during those years. But the question remains why so many urban professionals and firms unconnected to finance moved to London at a time when other jurisdictions (Frankfurt or Singapore) were offering similar inducements? And, in the aftermath of the financial collapse, why was London able to bounce back when similar economic centres did not? Part of the answer, we contend, lies in the indirect benefits gained when cities agree to govern a complex urban agglomeration using multiple tools and governing arrangements. It is, arguably, these changes that enabled London to reverse a three-decades-long slide in its economic and social fortunes.

Both centralized systems of local governance (as in present-day Halifax and Toronto) and models that lack an overarching governance structure and rely exclusively on smaller city governments or city councils to do the heavy lifting of civic building and public maintenance are flawed. What one needs instead is a dual local governance system or what in North America we know as the metropolitan form of government, whereby a supra-elected authority deals with issues that cross urban boundaries – e.g., traffic congestion – and a local city council deals with issues that literally reside closer to home such as a lack of functioning waste bins on "Main Street."

Do Not Design Away Urban Hubs of New Business Formation

They may not be very pretty, but the disused warehouses in older city neighbourhoods and the equally bland forms of our early postwar suburban industrial parks and strip malls nevertheless constitute the economic equivalent of a Petri dish, in which new ideas can spring forth and be tested in local markets.

Some of these ideas may remain local, such as the local fitness gym, but others may expand to a 275 fitness club empire with one in every forty-five Canadians as members. Such is the story of Goodlife Fitness, which in Canada began in a small nondescript strip mall in London, Ontario.

All Levels of Government Need to Return to Investing in Urban Infrastructure

Since the recession of the early 1990s, our urban infrastructure has been starved of the investment needed to keep it healthy. The mid-1990s federal claw-back in transfer funding, along with other cuts in many provincial budgets, left our cities with a huge backlog of much-needed repairs to roads and electrical grids. As well, in cities like Vancouver and Toronto, a significant expansion of public transit is long overdue. The irony is that the 1990s stalled what was once the best program for the maintenance and expansion of infrastructure in the world. It was no accident that as late as 1991 Toronto was referred to in the *Economist* as "New York run by the Swiss."

Without renewed investment, our cities will fail to keep up. As tired workers and weary drivers attest, we can no longer delay much-needed updates in the things that allow all businesses, big and small, to survive. The first three years of the minority federal government's Action Plan (2008–10), spurred by one of the worst macro-economic catastrophes of the last 100 years, was by most accounts a well-managed public investment vehicle that offered an excellent shot in the arm to communities across Canada. Our cities desperately need the good work started in 2008 to continue.

Local Amenities Attract Talented People ... so Maintain Their Functionality and Enhance Their Beauty

We are still not accustomed in North America to talking about the "look" and "feel" of a particular building or urban development. Perhaps this is because we think these elements are trivial by comparison with the vital and overriding goal of "improving economic GDP." But this kind of thinking actually runs counter to a growing mountain of evidence suggesting that *how* our cities structure access to the daily necessities of life matters more than almost anything else. This is because the businesses that are increasingly drawn to cities (software developers, new media, business services, etc.) could in fact be performing their work almost anywhere. This raises the obvious point about the need to lower taxes to attract business. But this is a myopic view of what entrepreneurs, as citizens at least, truly value. As an overall net benefit calculation, the value of your location, so long as taxes and fees are not unduly onerous, is the most important determinant of whether a business stays or goes.

Cities that fail to understand that aesthetics matter are doomed to decline. Detroit, Rochester, and Buffalo provide compelling examples of what not to do. Lowering taxes to zero and offering zero rents (as Detroit is now doing) will not put Humpty Dumpty back together again.

The BIA Mandatory Levy Should Be Extended to Other Community Groups

The growth of the business improvement area (BIA) movement and the connections between the organizing of BIAs and union organizing tell us a great deal about success in small retail and related service industries.

The success of the BIA movement in Canada, and particularly in Ontario, is no accident, we believe. The BIA movement borrowed the "agency shop" model of the Rand Formula, whereby every business/ property owner benefiting from BIA activity is forced to pay a levy (the equivalent of union dues). In 1948, Justice Rand of the Ontario Supreme Court ruled that "automatic dues check off" for workers covered by a collective agreement was legal, even though it infringed on some personal freedom, because it eliminated the "free rider effect." This is not the case in many U.S. states, where "right to work laws" are in place and union membership is consequently very low. The same principle applies to the BIA movement – that is, where BIAs are not allowed to charge compulsory levies, the number of BIAs is lower (i.e., in Quebec as compared to Ontario) and their effectiveness is limited.

It is no accident that the organizing and growth of BIA membership parallels the early growth of the union movement. As quoted in Dave Meslin's Fourth Wall exhibit on improving democratic access to local government, we argue that, "Toronto's BIA model is ... a great example of how support from City Hall [simply in the form of enabling legislation to collect dues payments] can help local grassroots groups flourish.

It would be great to see the same level of support going to our residents' associations. And imagine what these two sets of groups could do for our neighbourhoods if they were working together."[3]

Summary

We have seen that there is no guarantee, even in Toronto, the birthplace of the BIA movement with the largest concentration of BIAs in the world, that the future of independent business is secure. (We might also ask whether it *should* be secure, since if a better form or mode of solving problems and offering services to people emerges, we should embrace it.)

However, we also need to guard against assuming that the growth of, say, contemporary large-scale retail formats "proves" the lack of efficiency or quality of small, locally owned enterprises. The reality is that the success of a particular business form is profoundly affected by policy decisions, and, in the small business case, hinges on how cities zone and plan for urban economic development. Municipal governments can literally "design away" areas of the city that would otherwise host an active small-business and independent start-up culture. New ideas and distributed (as opposed to centralized) control of economic decision making have allowed Western industrialized society to grow for not just the last 50 years but for over 500 years, since the breakdown of feudalism and the start of the Industrial Revolution.

By ensuring that small-scale, locally based, and independently owned entrepreneurs still have a place in our major cities, we are giving ourselves more (not less) choice and also keeping open the possibility that the next half-millennium will produce as many innovations as the centuries that have preceded us.

10 Conclusion: Cities, Small Business, and Distributed Decision Making

What It Takes to Win Big ... When You're Small

How often do we, as consumers, patronize a store, sometimes for years, where the staff have never bothered to learn our names or even acknowledge us as repeat customers? I venture to say that we all feel that way more often than not. But it doesn't have to be that way. In the preceding chapters, we have seen plenty of examples of small business that rejected the pressure to become big and chose instead to become great.[1]

In a book published almost a decade ago, *Small Giants*, Bo Burlingham recounts the story of restaurateur Danny Meyer, who owns several restaurants in New York City, including the Gramercy Tavern, which was voted the third-best restaurant in Manhattan several years ago. Meyer's business philosophy can be summed up in one word: "soul." It is his belief that all successful companies must have a soul and that traditional customer service – such as promptness, getting food orders right, and cleaning up properly afterwards – is a *technical* skill that can be taught. Not surprisingly, he invests in these behaviours early on when an employee is hired. However, Meyer also wants his people to deliver something more. He wants them to make customers feel that they are on *their* side. Meyer considers this an *emotional* skill. This attention to a hard-to-observe worker quality means that although he is the owner of a "small business empire," Meyer adopts big-league selection and recruitment techniques in order to find and hire people who already have the capacity to be empathic. As Burlingham attests in his book, you can't *instil* empathy; nor can you *make* people sensitive to the way their actions affect others. As a result, if you are a small business owner and you want your employees to go that extra mile for your customers, you have to hire for those hard-to-teach emotional abilities, and then train for everything else. It's a brilliant and seemingly easy-to-replicate formula.

So why aren't more companies with far greater resources doing the same thing? There are many reasons; the first and most obvious is that you need a business owner like Meyer who *cares* about great service in the first place. Sadly, many companies and their owners do not. Second, it's *hard* work to hire people in such a way, whereas it is relatively easy to ensure that people have the requisite experience on a résumé and to verify the accuracy of some paper qualifications. Lastly, businesses, large and small, often don't have to worry about being the "best" in order to be profitable. So long as competition is not an issue, bad service can persist alongside tidy profits. Bad service only costs companies when there are viable alternatives for consumers to choose from. In New York's fiercely competitive hospitality sector, however, if you lack a big name brand you need to be better than "good enough" in order to survive.

So what does such an empathic business philosophy look like in practice? At Meyer's restaurants, when waiters see customers having trouble deciding between two items on a menu, they sometimes bring both, with the second one on the house. One of Meyer's managers once returned a handbag by sending it by courier (at the restaurant's expense) instead of just holding it for the customer at the restaurant. One employee, without prompting, put a flower on a specific table for a couple before they arrived, knowing they always sit there on their anniversary. As Terry O'Reilly noted in a recent episode of his radio program *Under the Influence*, in which Burlingham's book and Meyer's story were recounted for listeners, "None of these acts of customer service are earth-shattering. Just beautifully unusual."[2]

When small businesses go on to do great things, it is because the owners universally want customers to leave not just satisfied, but happy. As noted by O'Reilly, "That's a step beyond good service. It requires the company to develop an emotional connection with their customers through individual, one-on-one contact."

In Part I, our city chapters on Halifax, Vancouver, and Toronto described examples of a similar sense of emotional connection, but one that ventured beyond the customer to encompass the community as a whole. The formation of the first ever BIA in a west-end neighbourhood of Toronto known as Bloor West Village was not an accidental innovation, nor did it emanate from an R&D department, nor was it the brainchild of a well-staffed government ministry. It was the outcome of hard work by a small but dedicated core of small business owners, led by the charismatic Alex Ling. There is no doubt that enabling legislation from at least two levels of government helped institutionalize the local innovation. Allowing for a mandatory levy that could be applied to all business owners in a neighbourhood who were benefiting from local investments ensured the success of the BIA and the adoption of the concept by other neighbourhoods and jurisdictions. The presence of large anchor tenants – typically, well-known branded companies – also helped attract foot traffic, reinforcing the success of the BIA model and helping to ensure the survival of small independent firms alongside big-name chains on city main streets.

But we must not forget that the source and wellspring of the BIA movement was and still is small-scale, locally based, and independently owned enterprises. This brings us to the overarching observation that links ideas about city viability to recent visions of economic success.

Mass Flourishing, Distributed Intelligences, and Other "Complex" Phenomena

Christopher Kennedy's book *The Evolution of Great World Cities* ends with his observation that cities should be considered "complex systems," by which he means that they are made up of self-organizing adaptive agents. Cities are more "biological" than they are "rational," which means in practice that grand centralized decision making for cities can only take you so far. If cities do well, they do so because of the actions of many actors, not just one.

Such was the "luck" that Toronto had when the first BIA was created forty years ago in what was then the City of Toronto, which itself was part of a larger metropolitan Toronto area that encompassed three other cities and two boroughs: five local jurisdictions in all, coordinated by a metropolitan form of governance. The enabling legislation was enacted into law by the then Progressive Conservative provincial government of Bill Davis, since cities are incorporated under provincial law in Canada. Under the legislation, the government of the time wisely mandated municipalities henceforth to create BIA-type legislation in their own jurisdictions without the need for further provincial approval. This initiative demonstrates how diverse actors – both public and private, and both small and large – have a role and can exert a positive influence inside urban environments. There is always room for coordinated and well-planned decision making, but this is not the result of centralization and is instead created by distributing decision making to the lowest possible level wherever possible.

Of particular interest is how similar ideas, whether under the guise of "mass flourishing" or "distributed intelligence,"[3] emerge in accounts of economic growth from historical and macro-economic perspectives. Edmund Phelps – one of the most influential and respected economists of his generation, and the recipient of the 2006 Nobel Prize in economics for his work in reshaping macro-economics – argues in *Mass Flourishing: How Grassroots Innovation Created Jobs, Challenge, and Change* that innovation is the driver of the "dynamic economy." Furthermore, he points out that innovation emerges *de bas en haut* from a decentralized system of individualistic decision making in a competitive market environment. In Phelps's view there is no need to direct this "flourishing" by either a public or a private centralizing authority, and this is where a deep connection to work on complex systems and our own study comes in.

If this does not sound all that earth shattering, then consider this: Phelps prefers an innovative society to a traditionally wealthy one as measured by things like greater GDP. He suggests that wealth maximization has poisoned most Western economies and lured a generation away from "voyages of creativity and discovery."

In this we agree with Phelps. Productivity growth is an "abstraction," especially in societies that are already materially wealthy. In such cases it is surely better to focus on a "spirit" of bottom-up dynamism premised on acts of local consumption and innovation. And the place to find this dynamism, consumption, and innovation is the city, the only location where distributed sets of actors can foster such interchanges at relatively low cost and with a sufficiently big pay-off – assuming the presence of such public goods as a safe environment, solid transport, relatively affordable housing, good quality education, and locally responsive governance structures.

The Importance of Small-Scale Business and City Life: Three Takeaways

We are so accustomed to thinking of economies generally, and our own North American economy especially, as dominated by large enterprises and central governments that there may be a certain novelty in the idea that small-scale "mass flourishing" is the key to our long-term collective success. This supposed pre-eminence of large corporations also raises the question "Why, then, does most of our economic system consist of relatively small enterprises?"

The simple answer is that the main trend in large organizations is towards the use of either high technology or outsourcing or both. This approach has been "successful" insofar as most of the labour force is now employed outside of corporations. There are roughly two-and-a-half million sole proprietorships and partnerships in Canada, which means that almost twice as many people work in small-scale enterprises than as employees of industrial giants. The belief that large enterprises are crucial for the long-term viability of our economic system is simply mistaken, at least as it relates to where most of the "work" of producing and distributing goods and services gets done.

Three conclusions emerge from these final observations.

First, experiments with new ways of doing things are almost always best conducted on a small scale, at least in the initial stages, in order to test the viability of an idea. In fact, a focus on small scale-experimentation pervades the literature associated with the sources of Western development, suggesting that it should also be linked to discussions of urban dynamism and economic growth.

Our second observation is that cities should continue to be places where smallness is preserved as a function of urban design – places where spaces with small footprints (2,500 square feet or less) are valued and preserved for small-scale enterprise. Cities that do a good job of ensuring that these spaces exist and that local decision making is kept strong, while maintaining overall regional or cross-boundary investments in things like transportation, also will likely ensure that conditions are ripe for small-scale "mass flourishing."

Finally, to the extent that decentralized decision making is reflected in the organization of economic activity at all levels, we should not be surprised by statistics showing the important role small-scale enterprise actually plays in our societies. The strength of small-scale entrepreneurship is chronically underestimated, judging by the inducements given to attract large, established economic actors to a jurisdiction or in encouraging them to stay.

If we have learned anything from the research for this volume, it is that small, local, and independently owned firms not only are better economic citizens in the sense of employing more of us in full-time jobs than larger enterprises do; they also perform a vital social and cultural function. They define and delineate neighbourhoods and give cities their unique flavour – qualities no one could ever have imagined or precisely planned. Our book is not a clarion call for anarchy – far from it. It is a resounding and emphatic tribute to the benefits of power distributed among many stakeholders rather than only a few and to the shared belief that, as cities grow and evolve, decision making is best coordinated rather than controlled and power is best distributed rather than closely held.

Afterword[1]: Or …Why Staying Small, Local, and Independent Matters to City Life

At the beginning of this book we asked, "How do small, independent, locally operated businesses survive?" We hope we have provided some answers to that question while also addressing other important issues in the life of cities and the small businesses that increasingly are becoming champions in preserving locally resilient and diversified economies.

It seems appropriate to end *Small Business and the City* with one more story about how locally based enterprises manage to hang on, stubbornly in many cases, in our urban centres. These final thoughts will be filtered through the lens of personal memory and commentary by an author who is himself the son of a small-scale entrepreneur. These are lessons that only dawned upon this author once the book was nearly completed – insights that folded back on his early experiences of learning about the role of independent business from his father, the proprietor of a small business that survives in its original location to this day.

This story, we hope, will reveal some important general truths about what makes cities incubators for small-scale entrepreneurship, and likewise what makes small businesses vital to keeping large cities socially cohesive and dynamic places to live. We end this book, then, with a personal journey that starts by taking readers back to where "it" (the BIA movement and this book) all began.

Standing in the Place Where You Live

The city I now live in is also the city in which I was born. It is the place where I spent the first years of my young adult life, before leaving for London, England, and what was my first real academic job. That entire twenty-six-year period – from birth to adolescence to young adulthood – was spent in the same neighbourhood, in the same apartment, and among many of the same friends I had made as a child. That probably explains why, even when living far from my home, I always felt connected to my Scarborough neighbourhood and to my city, Toronto.

But something did change while I was living abroad; I developed a new appreciation for, and understanding of, the urban environment in which I had grown up. The strip malls that lined the main streets of Wexford in west Scarborough, in what is now east Toronto, were a taken-for-granted part of the environment sometimes disparaged as undistinguished or unattractive by me and my friends.

But this all began to change once the distance between me and my all-too-familiar landscape began to really sink in. At first, in my initial visits back home, I saw the small, eclectic shops and strip malls, with their noisy and clashing signage and built forms, as a blight and would tell anyone who could stand listening to my rants that this kind of low-rise wasteful development would not last a day in a "real, world-class" city like London. Gradually, however, in subsequent visits home, my view of the old neighbourhood and its storefronts began to change.

The Strip Malls of the Inner Suburbs as Bastions of Indigenous Local Culture

The strip malls of Scarborough and other inner suburbs built between the 1950s and the early 1980s were actually quite exotic when compared to the patterns and forms of life I had seen in European cities or to the Warholesque-replica shopping centres of North America's suburbs. Indeed, the sheer number of independent businesses that line a street like Lawrence Avenue as you travel east from the Don Valley Parkway is unique probably in the entire Western world. You may find such density of independent activity in the favelas of Sao Paolo or in the streets of Mumbai or in a city like Tokyo that has actively worked to preserve its independent entrepreneurs, but not in a North American suburb or in a city as young as Toronto. Indeed, not many modern cities have been able to preserve these bastions of independent ownership, most often for the newly arrived, in the way that Canada's largest city has done. Most North American cities of comparable size have morphed into a long indistinguishable parade of chain stores, franchises, and corporate mega-store outlets.

Indeed, just south of where I grew up, along Eglinton Avenue East in what was formerly known as the Golden Mile, the birthplace of Canada's war munitions effort and Scarborough's postwar manufacturing base, the area has been turned into a five-kilometre stretch of geographically, environmentally, and architecturally depressing retail mono-culture. The power centre, as we have seen in this book, is the retail form that most North American communities have adopted in the past two decades, and Eglinton Avenue East is a perfect example. Interestingly, though, only a few kilometres north, in my little corner of east Toronto, the scene is completely different. Why?

One answer can be gleaned from the spate of obituaries written about the architect Oscar Niemeyer who died in late 2012. One of the buildings – "areas," actually – of Sao Paolo (Brazil) that he was responsible for was the Copan, built in 1966.[2] At the time of writing, it is nearly fifty years old (close to the age of our Toronto strip malls); but, unlike the one-storey mall, the Copan is nearly forty storeys tall and houses 1,600 apartments within its massive structure. What is interesting from our perspective is that, around its base, there are dozens of small, independently owned and operated businesses catering to almost every need of the estimated 5,000 residents who call the Copan their home. There are clothing stores, salons, repair shops, and restaurants all bustling with life and business. According to Globe and Mail "City Space" columnist Lisa Rochon, "the place crackles with the imperfect raw energy of humanity [not by some accident of fate, but because] Niemeyer made room for that."

Affordable, easily accessible, well-designed, and appropriately sized spaces that provide for anybody and almost any use – tenants, shopping, or tourism – are the lifeblood of dynamic and interesting cities and the places where independent business thrives. Sitting on a sidewalk terrace in Toronto and looking around, I notice well-dressed businessmen sitting next to parents whose children arrive after school for a snack, and at a nearby cafe table I notice a former leader of Canada's Liberal Party.

As noted by Jane Jacobs, who lived just up the road from this coffee shop, these interactions are both random and planned. They are planned in the sense that the provision of an urban but liveable mini-city (i.e., a neighbourhood with space for most local amenities) still works wonderfully to set up these seemingly chance encounters that not only make our lives a little more interesting but that also foster social connectivity and the distribution of ideas and valuable local knowledge.

At this point, I remembered that, in my very first published article, in the Canadian Journal of Economics, I had in fact found a relationship between the places where self-employed people set up shop and the health of their businesses.[3] Using a crude statistic from the census, I and my co-author, Eric Santor, found that businesses located in areas of the city where a majority of the built form was completed prior to 1960 were in fact more successful (as measured by net revenue) than small-scale entrepreneurs located in newer suburbs.

In North America, neighbourhoods constructed before the 1960s contain a compact gathering of houses, apartment buildings, corner groceries, main-street shops, and offices, all within walking distance of one another.[4] This type of urban design, we hypothesized, facilitates the individual or personal harnessing of social capital. Where population density is high and urban design favours pedestrian traffic, information is more easily spread and transportation costs are lower, both of which make it easier for small-scale owners to inform and retain local customers.

Why Such an Abundance of Independent Businesses in Some Areas of the City?

So there were clues as to where and why small business is likely to survive in a city. But I was still left with my original question of why so many mom-and-pop shops survived in my stretch of Scarborough but not just down the road? I was puzzled. A more important question is what makes it possible for so many small businesses across the country to compete with the major chains, despite a lack of marketing budgets, large-scale capital, and human resource management systems?

Small Business as an "Experiential Good"

The answers to these questions eluded me for most of the time spent writing this book. Then I remembered the story told by my father to my brother and me many years before. The story (or parable, as it became with many retellings) was about a Canadian car repair franchise that in the late 1970s and early 1980s had aggressively advertised in major media outlets and was slated to do to independent garages what McDonald's had done to the local greasy spoon – make them obsolete.

But something else happened along the way to car repair domination. Not long after their much-publicized launch, the franchise empire folded, hounded by allegations of consumer fraud. The chain's mechanics were found to have lied to customers about needed repairs and in some cases to have sabotaged car engines so that customers would return for more repairs later on. The lesson drilled home by my father was simple: in his business (he was also a mechanic and owner of a small independent garage) honesty and word-of-mouth referrals always trumped flashy advertising. In fact, he would claim that it was his customers who paid all his insurance and advertising bills, because they would tell others of his honest repairs and fair pricing.

Flash forward fifteen years and I was learning a similar lesson in my industrial economics class at university. What my father was talking about was the difference between *experience* and *search*. In an experiential world, you pay first and learn about quality later. Think of things like a haircut or a medical procedure. We don't "try on our surgeon" first or "sample the best hairdresser" before choosing the one we like. We have to pay on the assumption that we "trust" who is delivering the service and we are agreeing to pay the owner before the true quality of his or her work is revealed. For something small and not too costly, like a movie or a book – classic "experiential purchases" – this is a risk that many are willing to take even if the reviews are bad. But costly car repairs are not typically done on "faith" alone or after a bad review. Most people want to bridge that quality-knowledge gap with a positive personal reference. The value of an endorsement from someone you trust is what the big auto repair chain forgot to include in its expensive marketing equation.

It is these intertwined elements of my own life – the city and neighbourhood that had been my home for those formative years and my own experience as the son of a small business owner – that are the fundamental inspirations for the writing of this book. My father, working alone, apart from the occasional summers when my brother and I (my brother more than me) would join him at the garage, somehow managed to pay off a mortgage, pay college tuition fees for both of us, and still have enough left over for his own retirement and that of my mother, who stayed at home to keep the accounts for the business and to care for us.

How was all that possible? How did the many small businesses that I began noticing all around me manage to survive in the same way my father's small business did?

Why Being Local and Independently Owned Sometimes Wins Out

The Case of Olive Garden and the City of Toronto

Again, for an answer I recalled another case that illustrates the importance of experiential factors, space and location, and a third aspect that epitomizes the city I call home. The relevant story is of the restaurant chain Olive Garden, which is noticeably absent from the Toronto hospitality market. But this was not always the case. It made an appearance here in the 1980s and early 1990s. In fact, I remember as a kid going in and seeing the free garlic bread and thinking "How could this go wrong?!" But go wrong it did, and the restaurant chain closed its Toronto-based locations by the end of the decade. The reason, according to head office – perhaps in an effort to placate worried investors – was very specific to the Toronto market. There were too many Italians living in the city. That is, there was already too much competition in the Toronto region from good, reasonably priced, authentic Italian restaurants. So the American chain quietly packed its bags and said "*Ciao*" to selling pasta north of the forty-ninth parallel.

The Olive Garden example brings to light another element that makes a city like Toronto unique: its cultural and ethnic diversity. For its size, Toronto is the most ethnically and linguistically diverse city in the world. It has as many languages as New York, with one-quarter of the population. Since the late 1960s, thanks to favourable immigration policies and an openness and tolerance for diversity, Toronto – which for most of its history trailed Montreal as the immigrant magnet – has slowly but steadily acquired a reputation as a welcoming community. It is now the home of many little countries and towns. There are little Italys, Portugals, Indias, Lebanons, Polands, Jamaicas – even a little Malta – as if the island wasn't small enough – and there are Koreatowns, Greektowns, and at least three Chinatowns. There are authentic Jewish delis and Mongolian grills. This global diversity has been backstopped by a healthy postwar immigration from Western Europe and the British Isles and recent immigration from the Caribbean, Asia, and Eastern Europe. We have a virtual United Nations of authentic ethnic entrepreneurship that is surprisingly open to new customers and accessed (crucially) by customers from other ethnic communities.

The Case of Gomez Auto Service (1970–1995)

Again I point to the case of my father's car repair shop, Gomez Auto Service (see exhibit A.1), which he opened with his brother in 1970. It served customers for more than twenty-five years, a significant proportion of his clients being of Latin American origin (many of them fleeing civil unrest and upheaval in places like Chile, Argentina, and Columbia). My father, who had immigrated to Toronto from Spain almost a decade earlier than most of these newer Spanish-speaking immigrants, also acquired a base of non-ethnically linked local customers.

Exhibit A.1. Photo of Gomez Auto Service. The sign was painted by my uncle, Nicolas Gomez. Acrylic on canvas. *Image courtesy of Pat Dumas-Hudecki © 2008*

This is (paradoxically) crucial to sustaining entrepreneurial ethnic enclaves. As anyone who has looked at the washed-out signage of an old commercial brick building knows, an ethnic customer base first clusters around low-rent areas and easy-to-access housing; but less than half a generation later, many of these customers move to more affluent neighbourhoods. They will always come back to the original shops, of course, but not as often, so new customers have to come from somewhere else. The nice thing about Halifax, Vancouver, and Toronto is that everyone seems to be (and truly "feels") welcome in ethnically homogeneous business zones. Why this should be and why this is not really the case in a city like Paris or in many places south of the border is an interesting question, one that I hope has been credibly answered in this book.

Final Thoughts

My father had one important phrase that he often liked to repeat, this one borrowed from the practical wisdom of Confucius: "If a man can't smile he shouldn't be in business." Small-scale entrepreneurs have been found to be overly optimistic, in the sense that, if they really followed a rational course of action (i.e., knowing how much more likely they are to fail than succeed and how long it may take them to recoup their investments in time and money), they would never go into business for themselves. Yet they plough ahead – irrationally, according to standard economic logic.

But this seems like an odd way of ending our story, especially given our thousand-year-old Chinese proverb. As citizens first and consumers second, we value unique experiences and we still want the honest dealing and personal service provided by the small-scale entrepreneur. More importantly, perhaps, the genuine smile that comes from recognizing a long-time customer and friend is something that no Wal-Mart greeting will ever replace.

About the Authors

Rafael Gomez is an associate professor of employment relations at the University of Toronto. He holds a cross-appointment at Woodsworth College and the Centre for Industrial Relations and Human Resources. He received a BA in economics and political science from York University (at Glendon College), and an MA in economics and a PhD in industrial relations from the University of Toronto. He has taught at the London School of Economics as a senior lecturer in management and at Glendon College, York University. He has been invited to conduct research and lecture at universities and research institutes around the world, including in Madrid, Moscow, Munich, and Zurich. In 2005 he was awarded the Labor and Employment Relations Association's John T. Dunlop Outstanding Scholar Award for exceptional contributions to international and comparative labour and employment research.

Andre Isakov is the manager of Park Planning and Design with the City of Coquitlam, British Columbia. While writing the book he was the manager of Planning and Community Services for the village of Harrison Hot Springs. Previously, Andre was the executive director of Business Improvement Areas of British Columbia (BIABC). He has also worked for several BIAs in British Columbia. Andre has a BA in political science and communication and a Master of Urban Studies degree from Simon Fraser University, where his studies focused on community development and on BIAs and their popularity as economic development tools. Andre is interested in the practical and theoretical questions related to the use of public space, governance, public policy, municipal service delivery, and economic development that BIAs raise. He is actively involved in his community and has served on numerous municipal and provincial committees and boards.

Matt Semansky is an award-winning journalist based in Dartmouth, Nova Scotia. His work has appeared in publications such as *This Magazine*, the *National Post*, the *Halifax Chronicle Herald*, and *The Coast and Marketing*. His education includes a journalism degree from Ryerson University (2006) and a BA from the University of Western Ontario (1998). He has reported on issues of urban revitalization and is interested in how BIAs function as a tool of economic and social transformation within cities.

Notes

Foreword

1 Glaeser and Kerr, "What Makes a City Entrepreneurial?"
2 Ibid.
3 Jacobs, *The Death and Life of Great American Cities*.

1 Introduction: Small Business and City Life

1 Adam Smith was a notable contrarian on this topic. He felt that the "joint stock company" – what we now refer to as the "corporation" or public company – was an inferior corporate model to the independent owner-operated firm. The "attention of the manager when his [own] capital is employed," argued Smith, "is much more acute than that of the appointed trustee (i.e., manager)." In addition, a closer reading of even Karl Marx and Joseph Schumpeter shows that they in fact had a lot of admiration for "true capitalists," prompting one scholar even to ask, "Is there a Marxian entrepreneur?" For more, see Hollander, *The Economics of Karl Marx*.
2 The famous example of Disney's first-mover investment in New York's Times Square revitalization plans in the early 1990s is a case in point. Disney's first store built outside the magical kingdom proved to be the spur that caused a "cascade" of further investment by other parties.
3 Doucet and Jones, "The Big Box, the Flagship, and Beyond." These ideas were brought to my attention by an excellent student essay by Jesse Rudy titled "The Destruction of the Stockyards Industrial District," which appeared in the 2011 edition of VOX, published at Woodsworth College, University of Toronto.

4 Accessed from Chrysler corporate website: http://www.chryslergroupllc
.com/company/AboutUs/CCI/Pages/AboutUs-CCI.aspx.
5 This is an idea borrowed from the evolutionary economics school. See
Nelson and Winter, *An Evolutionary Theory of Economic Change*. The connection this work has with cities is explored by Christopher Kennedy in *The
Evolution of Great World Cities*.
6 This is much like a coral reef on the ocean floor that depends on the symbiotic relationship between the bottom of the food chain and the larger
predators above. Knocking out the coral kills the entire food chain above.
7 Kennedy, *Evolution of Great World Cities*, 13.
8 Telecommunications, entertainment and media, and banking and finance
are prominent industries whose companies are exempt from NAFTA/
World Trade Organization trade rules and other free-trade regulations.
9 Starbucks cafes range in size from 1,000 to 1,500 square feet and are mostly
located in office buildings, downtown and suburban retail centres, airport
terminals, university campus areas, or busy neighbourhood shopping
areas convenient to pedestrian foot traffic. While similar materials and
furnishings are used to keep the look consistent and expenses reasonable, no two cafes end up being exactly alike. See Thompson and Gamble,
"Starbucks Corporation."
10 The ratings are based on a survey of 16,519 *Consumer Reports* subscribers who reported on 27,612 appliance-purchase experiences in the 2010
Consumer Reports "National Research Centre Shopper Satisfaction Survey."
11 Marketing experts are aware of this deficiency owing to scale and have
created "customer-relationship" marketing strategies for large corporations fearing loss of consumer goodwill. These include systems that
recognize customer first names when they phone help lines or cards that
are mailed on customer birthdays.
12 Smith, *Wealth of Nations* (Digireads.com, 2009), 439.
13 According to Blais (*Perverse Cities*), big-box stores are defined as stores that
are several times larger than the average store in the same category. They
range from 20,000 square feet to over 150,000 square feet. Power centres
are defined as three or more big boxes with a shared parking lot, along
with smaller ancillary retail outlets such as banks or restaurants. The average power centre has 380,000 square feet of floor space and can occupy up
to eighty acres of land. Recently "power nodes" have entered the scene,
and they are defined as extended clusters of big boxes and power centres
located within one kilometre of another power centre or major mall.
14 Ibid., 67–8.

15 Blais, *Perverse Cities, Hidden Subsidies, Wonky Policies, and Urban Sprawl*, 67–8.
16 Ibid.
17 Given the gridlock in our major cities, coupled with the future of oil prices and what this may mean for the car as the dominant mode of transport in our cities (see Rubin, *The End of Growth*), there are signs that this retail model may have reached its nadir in North America. Best Buy, a pioneer in large box store electronics retailing, has, since 2010, closed down nearly 100 of its major retail outlets in North America and in their place opened up smaller (customized) mini-Best Buys in local neighbourhoods. See Gruley and McCracken, "The Battle for Best Buy."
18 Lehrer, "Re-placing Canadian Cities: The Challenge of Landscapes of 'Desire' and 'Despair,' " 442.
19 Infantry, "Bank of Montreal to Open Condo-Sized Branches."
20 Duany, Plater-Zyberk, and Speck, *Suburban Nation*.
21 Blais, *Perverse Cities*, 69.
22 Fleming and Goetz, "Does Local Firm Ownership Matter?"
23 Ontario College of Family Physicians, "The Health Impacts of Urban Sprawl Information Series." Downloaded at: http://ocfp.on.ca/docs/committee-documents/urban-sprawl---volume-4---social-and-mental-health.pdf?sfvrsn=5.
24 Boer, Zheng, Overton, Ridgeway, and Cohen, "Neighborhood Design and Walking Trips in Ten U.S. Metropolitan Areas," 302.
25 Ibid.
26 Owen, *Green Metropolis.*
27 Hume, "More Density Downtown Will Cut Down on Gridlock." Available on-line at: http://www.thestar.com/news/gta/2013/12/01/more_density_downtown_will_cut_down_on_gridlock_hume.html.
28 Saunders, *Arrival City.*
29 Knight, *Risk, Uncertainty, and Profit*.
30 An excellent 2014 documentary, whose title riffs on the same quip, is *The Unknown Known* by filmmaker Errol Morris. For more about what this phrase really means see Peter Osnos's article "The True Subject of Errol Morris's Donald Rumsfeld Doc: Smugness" in *The Atlantic*. Downloaded at: http://www.theatlantic.com/entertainment/archive/2014/04/the-true-subject-of-errol-morriss-donald-rumsfeld-doc-smugness/360344/.
31 Hall, *Cities in Civilization*, 5.
32 See Florida, *Cities and the Creative Class*.
33 See "The Dronefather."

2 The BIA Movement: Setting the Stage for Main Street Revitalization

1 There is a deep irony here. Yorkdale was modelled on the success of Southdale Center in Endina, Minnesota (a suburb of Minneapolis). Southdale Center was completed in 1956 and was trumpeted as the world's first indoor shopping centre. It was designed by Victor Gruen, an Austrian immigrant with socialist beliefs who detested the suburban life-style of 1950s America and wanted to design a structure that would bring people together and create a sense of community. He sought to do this by providing a meeting place that traditional towns used to have but modern American suburbs lacked. People would come together to shop, drink coffee, and socialize. He modelled Southdale on the arcades in European cities – arcades that were located centrally around residential and working areas of the city. See Gruen and Smith, *Shopping Towns USA.*

2 Underground stations, not surprisingly, were (and still are) more expensive to build than above-ground street-car stops, so the subway line built beneath Bloor Street had relatively few of them.

3 See Fogelson, *Downtown: Its Rise and Fall.*

4 As pointed out by Foster, these systems were actually privately funded by real estate development companies. Most of these private lines went bankrupt and were handed over to public transit authorities to run. See Foster, *From Streetcar to Superhighway.*

5 Duany, Plater-Zyberk, and Speck, *Suburban Nation.*

6 Burayidi, *Downtowns.*

7 The iconic Simpsons department store (now Hudson's Bay), located on Toronto's Queen Street, was completed in 1929. The original Eaton's Toronto flagship building was completed in 1930. The ill-fated tower was never built, because of the Great Depression.

8 Thanks to the efforts of, what else? – a downtown BIA – in 2007 the Higbee corner window and front area of the department store reopened as a Visitor Center and the headquarters for Positively Cleveland, the city's convention and visitors' bureau.

9 One of Bill Clinton's most impressive but often overlooked legacies was the active role played by the federal government, which worked directly with more than 200 city governments on both major (Boston's "big dig") and minor projects. Henry Cisneros, who served as the tenth secretary of Housing and Urban Development (HUD) from 1993 to 1997, initiated and most importantly found funds for the revitalization of many of the nation's downtown cores.

10 Symes and Steel, "Lessons from America."

11 It turns out something as mundane as a proper sidewalk can have a significant impact on a local economy. See the 2010 paper by Navarro-Gonzalez and Quintana-Domeque, "Paving Streets for the Poor."

12 Yang, "The Birthplace of BIAs Celebrates 40 Years." Retrieved on 12 December 2012.

13 Mumford, *The City in History*, xi.

14 Ville Radieuse, or the Radiant City, is an unrealized urban masterplan by Le Corbusier, first presented in 1924 and published in a book of the same name in 1933.

15 See the exhibit's web page, at http://www.urbanspacegallery.ca/exhibits/heart-our-cities-ontarios-downtown-malls-and-their-transformations.

16 Ibid.

17 De Botton, *The Architecture of Happiness*, 246–7.

18 Gertler, "Tacit Knowledge and the Economic Geography of Context, or the Undefinable Tacitness of Being (There)," 75.

19 Unsourced quotations are from personal interviews conducted during research for the book.

20 It is interesting to note that Hirschman's book was published only one year after the Bloor West Village BIA was formed. There was clearly something in the air. See Hirschman, *Exit, Voice, and Loyalty.*

21 Epple and Nechyba, "Fiscal Decentralization."

22 Hoyt and Gopal-Agge. "The Business Improvement District Model," 947–8.

23 One of the largest and growing expenditures by BIAs is on private security. See Vindevogel, "Private Security and Urban Crime Mitigation."

24 This idea appeared in a public talk given by Kelly Pike entitled "CSR & Labour in Developing Countries: ILO's Better Work Programme as New Governance Form (a Ryerson CSR Institute talk)." It was held on Thursday, 31 January 2013, at the Ted Rogers School of Management, Ryerson University, 55 Dundas West, 9th floor, room 3-099. See: http://www.ryerson.ca/csrinstitute/key_dates/event_archive.html.

25 Brooks and Strange, "The Micro-Empirics of Collective Action."

3 The View from Main Street Halifax:
The Challenge of Being *the* Big Fish in a Small Pond

1 The primary research and writing of this chapter were carried out by Matt Semansky, who, though hailing from Toronto's North York, now lives and writes in Dartmouth, Nova Scotia.

2 A metropolitan area is identified by its census metropolitan area (CMA) or census agglomeration (CA) as defined by Statistics Canada, "Population

and Dwelling Counts, for Census Metropolitan Areas and Census Agglomerations, 2011 and 2006 Censuses."

3 Hachey left this position in 2013, after primary reporting for this chapter was completed.

4 Facing a funding shortfall, The Hub downsized in 2014, moving to a new office space and significantly reducing services (Source: Halifax *Chronicle-Herald*).

5 Bernard Smith left NEBA in 2013. His successor, David Fleming, announced his resignation a year later. At the time of writing, NEBA was looking for a new executive director.

4 The View from Main Street Vancouver: A City Region with an Emerging Sense of Place

1 The primary research and writing of this chapter were carried out by Andre Isakov, who hails from Vancouver's Coquitlam area, and who has lived and worked in beautiful Harrison Hot Springs, British Columbia.

2 See Jenkins, *Social Identity*, 4.

3 Ibid.

4 A list of the fastest-growing jurisdictions in Canada was published by Statistics Canada: http://news.nationalpost.com/2012/02/08/canada-census-2011-see-which-cities-and-towns-have-grown-the-most/. In North America a list was recently published by *Forbes* magazine and can be found on-line at http://www.forbes.com/2010/10/07/cities-austin-texas-calgary-opinions-columnists-joel-kotkin.html.

5 See Royer, *Time for Cities*, 41.

6 "Global factors" generally refers to globalization and other global changes, including climate change. Local factors include local identity, work ethics, and traditions, as well as cultural and natural environments, which can and do have an impact on the economic and social life of a community. In terms of population dynamics, in- and out-migration of populations can significantly affect the cultural, social, environmental, and economic conditions of an area. The ability of these factors to influence local economic conditions depends on local power structures and interplays of competing interests. See Organization for Economic Cooperation and Development, *Territorial Indicators of Employment*.

7 An active literature has emerged on this issue. See Terluin, "Differences in Economic Development in Rural Regions of Advanced Countries," and Rodríguez-Pose and Palavicini-Corona, "Does Local Economic Development Really Work?"

8 Terluin, "Differences in Economic Development in Rural Regions of Advanced Countries," 328.

9 For example, no metropolitan Vancouver community grows bananas, but many produce blueberries. Therefore, metropolitan Vancouver imports bananas and exports blueberries.

10 See Royer, *Time for Cities*, 85.

11 See Jacobs, *The Green Economy*.

12 Barca, McCann, and Rodríguez-Pose, "The Case for Regional Development Intervention."

13 Centre for Sustainable Community Development, Simon Fraser University: http://www.sfu.ca/cscd.html.

14 See Isakov, *Going Local*.

5 The View from Main Street Toronto: The Bottom-Up, Top-Down Conundrum

1 The primary research and writing of this chapter were carried out by Rafael Gomez.

2 From CBC TV's "The Way It Is" program, circa 1969, urbanist and author Jane Jacobs compares late 1960s Toronto and Montreal on how they have been planned and built, while condemning major highways planned for GTA. See http://video.google.com/videoplay?docid=4918908210204767118#.

3 The Maria biscuit was originally created by an English bakery, Peek Freans, in London, England, in 1874 to commemorate the marriage of the Grand Duchess Maria Alexandrovna of Russia to the Duke of Edinburgh. It became popular throughout Europe, particularly in Spain. Following the Spanish Civil War, the biscuit was called the Maria and became a symbol of Spain's economic recovery after bakeries produced mass quantities to consume a surplus of wheat.

4 Typical of this movement has been the hugely successful Jane's Walk program started by Jane Farrow in honour of Jane Jacobs. The walk is held in more than 100 neighbourhoods in the City of Toronto on Jane Jacobs's birthday in June. Books on a similar theme have followed, with titles such as *Stroll: Psychogeographic Walking Tours of Toronto,* as have dedicated websites, such as the *Torontoist,* that straddle the border between city news and insider city-boosterism.

5 For the full review see *Now* magazine's website: http://www.nowtoronto.com/food/story.cfm?content=175351.

6 See http://www1.toronto.ca/wps/portal/contentonly?vgnextoid=8b3ba d51a40ea310VgnVCM10000071d60f89RCRD.

7 As the company website proudly boasts, "Today you can find us in our wonderful and inspiring 15,000 square foot showroom at 3313 Danforth Avenue at Pharmacy. Toronto East-Enders will recognize this location as the original 'Mansion House.' Even though we're 7 times larger than our humble beginnings, we haven't forgotten what has gotten us here – our ever-growing 'Frontier family,' loyal customers who have become friends. Their referrals and recommendations to their families and friends make us proud of the quality of product and service that we provide. Together with their ever growing team, Dan and Renee continue to strive to keep grandma Grace's vision of an eco-friendly business for generations to come."

8 Margaret Mead's most famous quotation about the power of thoughtful individuals coming together to foster change often overshadows her other thoughtful comments on urban life: "A city is a place where there is no need to wait for next week to get the answer to a question, to taste the food of any country, to find new voices to listen to and familiar ones to listen to again."

9 It is interesting to note that in Halifax the new amalgamated city left the downtown core feeling alienated. What is common in both cases, however, is that a new centralized city structure was not wholly well-received and suffered from a lack of attention to local needs.

10 The levy is the name given to the property tax bump that is paid by all commercial property owners along a BIA strip.

11 The 40-minute number (one way) is the Toronto Board of Trade figure that includes the Greater Toronto Area (GTA). Statistics Canada reports the one-way commute in Toronto as being only 33 minutes. See Turcotte, "Commuting to Work: Results of the 2010 General Social Survey."

12 An excellent starting point for those interested is the audio walking tour put together by Dave LeBlanc in collaboration with Heritage Toronto. In it, Dave LeBlanc, columnist for the *Globe and Mail,* guides listeners through the development of this unique modernist community, with contributions from those who designed it, including Macklin Hancock, Douglas Lee, and Henry Fliess. See http://heritagetoronto.org/discover-toronto/itours/don-mills-itour.

13 The original co-owners sold their portion of the business in 2013 to focus on starting their own family and to possibly pursue further expansion of the brand in other corners of the city.

14 There are indeed several large apartment blocks built in the 1970s that house many people, often new arrivals, in an affordable fashion and close to public (albeit bus only) transit.

6 The "Art and Science" of Small Business Survival: Lessons in BIA Practice

1 See White, "As Layoffs Near 160,000, Banks May Shrink for Good."
2 According to economic historian Roman Studer, "The idea that the reach of the market is associated through the division of labour with the level of economic development, and that the expansion of markets, that is, the process of market integration, leads to economic growth, has made Adam Smith one of the best known economists of all time." See Studer, "Does Trade Explain Europe's Rise?"
3 This was a feature found to be true in local construction industries. See Chad Syverson's cleverly titled paper "Market Structure and Productivity: A Concrete Example."
4 Glaeser, Kolko, and Saiz, "Consumer City," 32.
5 See Waldfogel, "The Median Voter and the Median Consumer."
6 This mirrors work done in macro-economics on country size and growth. Alesina and his colleagues have found that a country's size can positively affect economic performance and can influence everything from per-capita patent generation to weaker preferences for free trade. See Alesina, Spolaore, and Wacziarg, "Trade, Growth and the Size of Countries."
7 See Schiff, "Cities and Product Variety."
8 See ibid.
9 World Bank, "What Is Social Capital?"
10 To explain the large differences in labour productivity across U.S. states, Antonio Ciccone and Robert Hall proposed two models – one based on local geographical externalities and the other on the diversity of local intermediate services – where spatial density results in aggregate increasing returns. Both models lead to a positive relation between county employment density and productivity at the state level. Using data on gross state output, the authors find that a doubling of employment density increases average labour productivity by around 6 per cent. This means that more than half of the variance of output per worker across states can be explained by differences in the density of economic activity. See Ciccone, and Hall, "Productivity and the Density of Economic Activity."
11 Meslin's exhibit addresses a variety of issues, including the need for a budget process that allows citizen participation, introducing better civics education for students, and redesigning the city's website in order to highlight opportunities to run for office and get involved. The Fourth Wall illustrates just how much the current bureaucratic approach and political system discourage participation; they often cater to those in power

rather than the citizens they actually serve. Many of the proposals aren't all that drastic, but might have a great impact. Why, Meslin asks, doesn't the city hold elections on weekends, when more people would be able to participate? After all, as one chart illustrates, other city events that depend on public participation – Nuit Blanche, Pride, Doors Open, Caribana – are held on the weekend. Fourth Wall is tapping into a hunger for increased citizen participation in local politics among people who are currently alienated from the process – something Meslin has built a career on as the founder of the Toronto Public Space Committee, the Toronto Cyclists Union, the election-participation contest City Idol, and the electoral reform group RaBIT. See http://thefourthwall.ca/proposals.htm.

7 Of People, Profits, and Place: Lessons in Local Economic Development

1 Knighton, "Why White People Should Oppose Whole Foods."
2 Moynihan, "Whole Foods Fight in Boston."
3 Knighton, "Why White People Should Oppose Whole Foods."
4 Ibid.
5 Allen, "Bristol City Council Must Support the Community and Reject Tesco."
6 Ibid.
7 Ibid.
8 James, "Waterfront Rebuff First of Many for Ford?" http://www.thestar. com/news/gta/2011/09/21/james_waterfront_rebuff_first_of_many_ for_ford.html.
9 Ibid.
10 Kingsworth, "This Economic 'Crisis of Bigness.' "
11 Kohr, *The Breakdown of Nations*, 1.
12 Ibid., chapters 5 and 6.
13 Woodhouse, ed., *International Encyclopedia of the Social Sciences*.
14 Morgenson, "How Mr Volcker Would Fix It."
15 Ibid.
16 Dalmia, "Still Government Motors."
17 Farfan, "Retail Store Closings Roundup."
18 See Davis, Merriman, Samayoa, Flanagan, Baiman, and Persky, "The Impact of an Urban Wal-Mart Store on Area Businesses."
19 Ibid.
20 Ibid.
21 Ibid.

22 Ibid.
23 Industry Canada, Office of Consumer Affairs (OCA), Chapter 2 – "Consumers and Changing Retail Markets."
24 Ibid.
25 Ibid.
26 Ibid.
27 Glaeser and Kerr, "What Makes a City Entrepreneurial?" In a recent working paper, "Small Business, Entrepreneurship, and Innovation," Roger Martin argues that not all smaller businesses are the same. Our economy would be better served if public policy focused on assisting the relatively small number of entrepreneurial high-growth, high-impact firms that will drive innovation, productivity, and prosperity. Thus, the emphasis in taxation and broader economic policy should shift from smaller to growing firms. The authors admit that this is a challenge and that identifying and supporting these firms is not easy – and there is no special formula for achieving it.
28 Holm, "Key Lesson from Iceland Crisis Is 'Let Banks Fail.'"
29 See "Cracks in the Crust."
30 Ibid.
31 McInroy and Longlands, "Productive Local Economies."
32 Ibid.
33 Ibid.
34 Leonhardt, "The Depression."
35 National Small Business Association, "Testimony of Scott Hague to US Subcommittee on Small Business."
36 See Stangler "The Economic Future Just Happened."
37 Industry Canada, "The Growth Process in Firms."
38 "Financing, CFIB Makes Its Case to Ontario."
39 Ibid.
40 Ibid.
41 Grant, "Small Businesses Key to Job Creation."
42 Martin Prosperity Institute, et al., "From the Ground Up: Growing Toronto's Cultural Sector."
43 Bolgar, "Foreign Investors Flock to Europe's Economic Motor."
44 Ibid.
45 Texas Perspectives Inc., "Big Box Retail and Austin."
46 Ibid.
47 Goetz and Rupasingha, "Wal-Mart and Social Capital."
48 Ibid.
49 Ibid.

50 Ibid.
51 Leung and Rispoli, "The Contribution of Small and Medium-Sized Businesses to Gross Domestic Product."
52 Chang, "Anti-capitalist? Too Simple."
53 Glaeser and Kerr, "What Makes a City Entrepreneurial?"
54 Ibid.
55 Ibid.
56 Ibid.
57 Ibid.
58 S. Mitchell, "Study Finds Local Businesses Key to Income Growth."
59 See Fleming and Goetz, "Does Local Firm Ownership Matter?"
60 Ibid.
61 Ibid.
62 See Flavelle, "Why Do We Pay More in Canada?"
63 Olive, "Small Business, the Romance Is Over."
64 Dotan, "Urban Thinkers Line Up against Ford's Waterfront Plan."
65 Kaminer, "A Low-Slung Piece of Toronto Gains Casual-Hip Cachet."
66 Hopper, "Fewer Americans, More Europeans: Toronto's 2010 Tourism Numbers."
67 Glaeser, Kolko, and Saiz, "Consumer City."
68 Ibid.
69 Ibid.
70 Ibid.
71 Civic Economics, "The San Francisco Retail Diversity Study."
72 Ibid.
73 Ibid.
74 Ibid.
75 Ibid.
76 Ibid.
77 See Hamermesh and Biddle, "Beauty and Labor Market."
78 Martin Prosperity Institute, et al., "From the Ground Up."
79 Ibid.
80 Bolgar, "Foreign Investors Flock to Europe's Economic Motor."
81 Ibid.
82 Mofid, "Small Is Beautiful: The Wisdom of E.F. Schumacher."
83 Ibid.
84 Ibid.
85 Ibid.
86 Ibid.
87 Jacobs, *Dark Age Ahead*, 161–2.

88 Ibid.
89 Goetz and Rupasingha, "Wal-Mart and Social Capital."
90 Curran, "Challenging the Sprawl of Big Box Retail."
91 Industry Canada, Office of Consumer Affairs (OCA), "Consumers and Changing Retail Markets."
92 Ibid.
93 Ibid.
94 Ibid.
95 See Goetz and Rupasingha, "Wal-Mart and Social Capital."
96 Ibid.
97 Ibid.
98 Ibid.
99 Ibid.
100 Ibid.
101 Ibid.
102 See Erlanger, "A Paris Plan, Less Grand Than Gritty."

8 Small Business and the Main Street Agenda: Lessons in Public Policy

1 See Acs and Audretsch, *Innovation and Small Firms.*
2 In retrospect, quite far-sightedly, *Wikinomics: How Mass Collaboration Changes Everything,* by Tapscott and Williams, clearly showed how some organizations, at little or no cost, used mass collaboration and open-source technology to succeed. Since the Tapscott and Williams book, many have followed suit with similar titles, including the authors themselves with *Macrowikinomics: New Solutions for a Connected Planet.*
3 The fact that there are many small coastal firms operating successfully in a highly decentralized way (in contrast to the largely bankrupt, big, state-owned enterprises of China's interior) shows the error of attributing Chinese success to centralized state action. See Adams, Gangnes, and Shachmurove, "Why Is China so Competitive?" and Keane, "Great Adaptations: China's Creative Clusters and the New Social Contract."
4 Wren and Storey, "Evaluating the Effects of Soft Business Support upon Small Firm Performance."
5 We need to qualify this statement with the usual *ceteris paribus* proviso about operating in highly competitive sectors where barriers to entry are low and hence, one would assume, open to many new players. Otherwise, we know very well that in the absence of competition – i.e., as a result of regulation or natural monopoly forces – firms can remain large market leaders without much innovation.

6 Smith, *Wealth of Nations* (Digireads.com, 2009), 62.
7 Monck, Porter, Quintas, Storey, and Wynarczyk, in *Science Parks and the Growth of High-Technology Firms,* made an early comparison between the performance of firms in greenfield (largely suburban) science parks and a comparable sample of firms located elsewhere. Remarkably, they found that the firms located in science parks generated fewer jobs than did comparable firms located on main streets and in urban centres. There is debate over what this may mean, as some contend that we need to account for the "make-up" of entrepreneurs on and off park sites. See also Lindelof and Loftsen, "Science Park Location and New Technology Based Firms in Sweden."
8 Owen, *Green Metropolis*, 43–5.
9 The fastest-growing fast-food outlet in Sweden is Max, an independently owned burger franchise that has built its success by offering locally sourced meals with transparency about the source of all ingredients.
10 A fact duly noted by John Sewell in *The Shape of the Suburbs*, 208.
11 Gertler, "Rules of the Game."
12 Glaeser and Kerr, "What Makes a City Entrepreneurial?"
13 See Government of Canada, "The Stimulus Phase of Canada's Economic Action Plan: A Final Report to Canadians."
14 Grant, "Attracting the Entrepreneurial Immigrant."
15 Ibid.
16 Association of Universities and Colleges of Canada, "The Value of University Research."
17 Board of Trade of Metropolitan Montreal, "Public Transit: At the Heart of Montréal's Economic Development."
18 Canadian Broadcasting Corporation, "Traffic Jams Cost Toronto $3.3B per Year."
19 See Hulchanski, *The Three Cities within Toronto.*
20 "Should Government Invest in Private Companies?"
21 Glaeser and Kerr, "What Makes a City Entrepreneurial?"
22 "Should Government Invest in Private Companies?"
23 Creutzberg, "Canada's Innovation Underperformance."
24 Association of Universities and Colleges of Canada, "The Value of University Research."
25 Lilischkis, "Policies in Support of High-Growth Innovative SMEs."
26 Ibid.
27 Drummond, "The Productivity Puzzle."
28 Ibid.
29 Ibid.

30 Ibid.
31 Jackson, "Canada's Productivity Problem."
32 The work of Charlotte Mellander in her native Sweden clearly demonstrates the role played by attracting creativity and talent in fostering productivity gains. Mellander and Florida, "Creativity, Talent, and Regional Wages in Sweden."
33 Ibid.
34 Owen, *Green Metropolis*.

9 Recommendations for Making Small-Scale Enterprise a Transformative Force

1 Gertler, "Economy and Society in Canada," 128.
2 The Greater London Council (GLC) was the top-tier local government administrative body for Greater London from 1965 to 1986.
3 See Fourth Wall, The Exhibit, at http://thefourthwall.ca/downloads.htm.

10 Conclusion: Cities, Small Business, and Distributed Decision Making

1 I owe this observation to an episode of CBC Radio's *Under the Influence*, hosted by the brilliantly erudite Terry O'Reilly. See http://www.cbc.ca/undertheinfluence/season-3/2014/03/28/tales-of-customer-service-2/.
2 Ibid.
3 The term used in *Wikinomics* by Don Tapscott and Anthony Williams to describe the success of the "Wiki" economy over the organized and planned innovations of Microsoft and other big economic actors.

Afterword: Or ... Why Staying Small, Local, and Independent Matters to City Life

1 The writing of this chapter was carried out by one of the authors from personal experience. He is the son of the mechanic referred to in the Afterword.
2 Rochon, "City Space."
3 Gomez and Santor, "Membership Has Its Privileges."
4 Jacobs, *The Death and Life of Great American Cities*.

References

Acs, Z., and D. Audretsch. *Innovation and Small Firms*. Boston, MA: MIT Press, 1990.

Adams, F., B. Gangnes, and Y. Shachmurove. "Why Is China so Competitive? Measuring and Explaining China's Competitiveness." *World Economy*, 29 (2006): 95–122.

Allen, S. "Bristol City Council Must Support the Community and Reject Tesco." *Guardian*, 22 April 2011. Available on-line at http://www.theguardian.com/commentisfree/2011/apr/22/bristol-riot-tesco.

Alesina, A., E. Spolaore, and R. Wacziarg. "Trade, Growth and the Size of Countries." In P. Aghion and S. Durlauf, eds, *Handbook of Economic Growth*, 1st ed., vol. 1: 1499–1542. Amsterdam: Elsevier, 2005.

Association of Universities and Colleges of Canada (AUCC). "The Value of University Research." 2011. Available on-line at http://www.canada123.org/wp-content/uploads/2011/05/The-Value-of-University-Research.pdf.

Barca, F., P. McCann, and A. Rodríguez-Pose. "The Case for Regional Development Intervention: Place-Based versus Place-Neutral Approaches." *Journal of Regional Science*, 52, 1 (2012): 134–52.

Baraness, M. *Toronto Places: A Context for Urban Design*. Toronto: University of Toronto Press, 1992.

Beckert, S. *The Monied Metropolis: New York City and the Consolidation of the American Bourgeoisie, 1850–1896*. Cambridge: Cambridge University Press, 2001.

Berke, P.R., and D. Godschalk. *Urban Land Use Planning*. 5th ed. Urbana: University of Illinois Press, 2006.

Blais, P. *Perverse Cities, Hidden Subsidies, Wonky Policies, and Urban Sprawl*. Vancouver: University of British Columbia Press, 2010.

Block, R. "BIA Backlash: Why Small Business Wants Out." *Metropolitan Toronto Business*, 76, 10 (1986): 10–12.

Board of Trade of Metropolitan Montreal. "Public Transit: At the Heart of Montréal's Economic Development." November 2010. Available on-line at: http://www.btmm.qc.ca/~/media/Files/News/2010/10_11_26_ccmm_etude-transport_en.pdf.

Boer, R., Y. Zheng, A. Overton, G.K. Ridgeway, and D.A. Cohen. "Neighborhood Design and Walking Trips in Ten U.S. Metropolitan Areas." *American Journal of Preventive Medicine,* 32, 4 (April 2007): 298–304. Available at: doi: 10.1016/j.amepre.2006.12.012.

Bolgar, C. "Foreign Investors Flock to Europe's Economic Motor." *Wall Street Journal.* 2010. Available on-line at http://online.wsj.com/ad/article/germany-economy.html.

Bolton, R. " 'Place' as 'Network': Applications of Network Theory to Local Communities." In Å.E. Andersson, W.P. Anderson, and B. Johansson, eds, *The Economics of Disappearing Distance (Essays in Honor of T.R. Lakshmanan),* 115–31. Burlington, VT: Ashgate, 2003.

Bolton, R., and H. Westlund. "Local Social Capital and Entrepreneurship." *Small Business Economics* (21 September 2003): 77–113.

Brooks, L., and W. Strange. "The Micro-Empirics of Collective Action: The Case of Business Improvement Districts." *Journal of Public Economics,* 95, 11–12 (2011): 1358–72.

Brugmann, J. *Welcome to the Urban Revolution: How Cities Are Changing the World.* London: Bloomsbury Press, 2009.

Budd, J.W. *Employment with a Human Face: Balancing Efficiency, Equity, and Voice.* Ithaca, NY: ILR Press, 2004.

Burayidi, M. *Downtowns: Revitalizing the Centers of Small Urban Communities.* New York: Routledge, 2001.

Burlingham, B. *Small Giants: Companies That Choose to Be Great Instead of Big.* New York: Portfolio, 2005.

Canada Newswire. "Canadian Small and Medium-Sized Business Buck Recession Trend: CIBC." 5 October 2009. Available on-line at http://www.newswire.ca/en/story/560835/canadian-small-and-medium-sized-business-buck-recession-trend-cibc.

Canadian Broadcasting Corporation (CBC). "Traffic Jams Cost Toronto $3.3B per Year: OECD Report." 10 November 2009. Available on-line at http://www.cbc.ca/news/canada/toronto/traffic-jams-cost-toronto-3-3b-per-year-oecd-1.811427.

Chang, H. "Anti-capitalist? Too Simple. Occupy Can Be the Catalyst for a Radical Rethink." 15 November 2011. Available on-line at http://www.theguardian.com/commentisfree/2011/nov/15/anti-capitalist-occupy-pigeonholing.

Chappell, K. "Business Improvement Areas Find New Voice, Funding, at City Hall." *Ottawa Business*, 16, 5 (2011): 26.

Ciccone, A., and R.E. Hall. "Productivity and Density of Economic Activity." *American Economic Review*, 86, 1 (March 1996): 54–70.

Civic Economics. "San Francisco Retail Diversity Study." 1 May 2007. Available on-line at http://community-wealth.org/content/san-francisco-retail-diversity-study-report-prepared-san-francisco-locally-owned-merchants.

Cohen, P., and M. Rustin, eds. *London's Turning: Thames Gateway – Prospects and Legacy*. Design and the Built Environment Series. Aldershot, Hants, and Burlington, VT: Ashgate, 2008.

Collins, W. *Slum Clearance and Urban Renewal in the United States*. National Bureau of Economic Research, Working Paper Series. No. w17458. Cambridge, MA: National Bureau of Economic Research, 2011.

"Cracks in the Crust." *Economist*, 11 December 2008. Available on-line at http://www.economist.com/node/12762027.

Creutzberg, T. "Canada's Innovation Underperformance: Whose Policy Problem Is It?" Mowat Centre, 14 October 2011. Available on-line at http://mowatcentre.ca/canada-innovation-underperformance/.

Curran, D. "Challenging the Sprawl of Big Box Retail." January 2002. Available on-line at http://smartgrowth.bc.ca/Portals/0/Downloads/Challenging%20the%20Sprawl%20of%20Big%20Box%20Retail.pdf.

Dahl, D. "Top Companies Started during a Recession." *AOL Small Business*, 10 May 2010. Available on-line at http://www.huffingtonpost.com/.2010/05/10/top-companies-started-during-a-recession_n_923853.html.

Dalmia, S. "Still Government Motors." *Forbes*, 23 May 2010. Available on-line at http://www.forbes.com/2010/04/23/general-motors-economy-bailout-opinions-columnists-shikha-dalmia.html.

Davies, M.S. "Business Improvement Districts." *Journal of Contemporary Law*, 52 (1997): 187–210.

Davis, J., D. Merriman, L. Samayoa, B. Flanagan, R. Baiman, and J.Persky. "The Impact of an Urban Wal-Mart Store on Area Businesses." Loyola University, Center for Urban Research and Learning. Chicago, December 2009. Available on-line at http://ecommons.luc.edu/cgi/viewcontent.cgi?article=1002&context=curl_pubs.

De Botton, A. *The Architecture of Happiness*. Toronto: McClelland and Stewart, 2006.

Dotan, H. "Urban Thinkers Line Up against Ford's Waterfront Plan." 15 September 2011. Available on-line at http://torontoist.com/2011/09/urban-thinkers-line-up-against-fords-waterfront-plan/.

Doucet, M., and K. Jones. "The Big Box, the Flagship, and Beyond: Impacts and Trends in the Greater Toronto Area." *Canadian Geographer,* 45 (2001): 494–513.

"The Dronefather." *Economist,* 1 December 2012. Available on-line at http://www.economist.com/news/technology-quarterly/21567205-abe-karem-created-robotic-plane-transformed-way-modern-warfare.

Drummond, D. "The Productivity Puzzle: Why Is the Canadian Record So Poor and What Can Be Done about It?" 2010. Available on-line at http://www.td.com/document/PDF/economics/special/td-economics-special-ab0610-productivity.pdf.

Duany, A., E. Plater-Zyberk, and J. Speck. *Suburban Nation: The Rise of Sprawl and the Decline of the American Dream: Can Our Neighborhoods Be Saved?* 10th anniversary edition. New York: North Point Press, 2010.

Edensor, T., D. Leslie, S. Millington, and N. Rantisi, eds. *Spaces of Vernacular Creativity: Rethinking the Cultural Economy.* London: Routledge, 2009.

Epple, D., and T. Nechyba. "Fiscal Decentralization." In J.V. Henderson and J-F. Thisse, eds, *Handbook of Urban Economics,* vol. 4: 2423–80. Amsterdam: North Holland Press, 2004.

Erlanger, S. "Paris Plan, Less Grand Than Gritty." *New York Times.* 10 June 2009. Available on-line at http://www.nytimes.com/2009/06/11/world/europe/11paris.html?pagewanted=all&_r=0.

Evans, R. *Regenerating Town Centres,* Manchester: Manchester University Press, 1997.

Farfan, B. "Retail Store Closings Roundup: U.S. Retailers Closing or Liquidating Stores." *About.com,* 19 October 2011. Available on-line at http://retailindustry.about.com/od/storeclosingsandopenings/a/2011-US-Retail-Industry-Store-Closings-Liquidations-Roundup-Chains-Going-Out-Business.htm.

Feehan, D., and M. Feit, eds. *Making Business Districts Work: Leadership and Management of Downtown, Main Street, Business District, and Community Development Organizations.* New York: Routledge, 2006.

Filion, P. "Growth and Decline in the Canadian Urban System: The Impact of Emerging Economic, Policy and Demographic Trends." *Geojournal* 75 (2010): 517–38.

Filion, P. "Reorienting Urban Development? Structural Obstruction to New Urban Forms." *International Journal of Urban and Regional Research,* 34 (2010): 1–19.

Filion, P. "Toronto's Tea Party: Right-Wing Populism and Planning Agendas." *Planning Theory and Practice,* 12 (2011): 464–9.

"Financing, CFIB Makes Its Case to Ontario." *Globe and Mail,* 2 February 2010. Available on-line at http://www.theglobeandmail.com/report-on-business/small-business/start/financing/cfib-makes-its-case-to-ontario/article1453691/.

Flavelle, D. "Why Do We Pay More in Canada? Our Retailers Are Less Competitive, Says Carney." *Toronto Star*, 2 November 2011. Available on-line at http://www.thestar.com/business/2011/11/02/why_do_we_pay_more_in_canada_our_retailers_are_less_competitive_says_carney.html.

Fleming, D., and S. Goetz. "Does Local Firm Ownership Matter?" *Economic Development Quarterly* 25, 3 (2011): 277–81. Available at http://resolver.scholarsportal.info/resolve/08912424/v25i0003/277_dlfom.

Florida, R. *Cities and the Creative Class*. London: Routledge, 2005.

Florida, R. *The Rise of the Creative Class: And How It's Transforming Work, Leisure, Community and Everyday Life*. New York: Basic Books, 2003.

Florida, R., and C. Mellander. "There Goes the Metro: How and Why Artists, Bohemians and Gays Affect Housing Values." *Journal of Economic Geography*, 10, 2 (2010): 167–88.

Florida, R., C. Mellander, and K. Stolarick. "From Music Scenes to Music Clusters: The Economic Geography of Music in the U.S., 1970–2000." *Environment and Planning* A, 4 (2010): 785–804.

Florida, R., C. Mellander, and K. Stolarick. "Talent, Technology and Tolerance in Canadian Regional Development." *Canadian Geographer*, 54, 3 (2010): 277–304.

Fogelson, R. *Downtown: Its Rise and Fall, 1880–1950*. New Haven, CT: Yale University Press, 2001.

Foot, David K. *Boom, Bust & Echo: How to Profit from the Coming Demographic Shift*. Toronto: Macfarlane Walter & Ross, 1996.

Foster, M. *From Streetcar to Superhighway: American City Planners and Urban Transportation, 1990–1940*. Philadelphia: Temple University Press, 1981.

Friedman, T. *Hot, Flat, and Crowded: Why We Need a Green Revolution – and How It Can Renew America*. New York: Farrar, Straus and Giroux, 2008.

Gertler, M. "Economy and Society in Canada: Flows of People, Capital and Ideas." *Isuma: Canadian Journal of Policy Research*, 2, 3 (2001): 119–30.

Gertler, M. "Tacit Knowledge and the Economic Geography of Context, or the Undefinable Tacitness of Being (There)." *Journal of Economic Geography*, 3, 1 (2003):75.

Glaeser, E., and W. Kerr. "What Makes a City Entrepreneurial?" Rappaport Institute for Greater Boston, Harvard Kennedy School. February 2010. Available online at http://www.hks.harvard.edu/var/ezp_site/storage/fckeditor/file/pdfs/centers-programs/centers/taubman/PB_Glaeser_Kerr_entrepreneurs.pdf.

Glaeser, E.L., J. Kolko, and A. Saiz. "Consumer City." *Journal of Economic Geography*, 1, 1: 27–50. doi:10.1093/jeg/1.1.27. Available on-line at http://resolver.scholarsportal.info/resolve/14682702/v01i0001/27_cc.

Goetz, S., and A. Rupasingha. "Wal-Mart and Social Capital." *American Journal of Agricultural Economics*, 88, 5 (2006): 1304–10.

Gomez, R., and E. Santor. "Membership Has Its Privileges: The Effect of Social Capital and Neighbourhood Characteristics on the Earnings of Microfinance Borrowers." *Canadian Journal of Economics / Revue canadienne d'Economique*, 34, 4 (November 2001): 943–66.

Government of Canada. "The Stimulus Phase of Canada's Economic Action Plan: A Final Report to Canadians." Available on-line at http://actionplan.gc.ca/en/page/stimulus-phase-canada-s-economic-action-plan-final-report-canadians.

Grady, W. *Toronto the Wild: Field Notes of an Urban Naturalist*. Toronto: Macfarlane, Walter, and Ross, 1995.

Grant, T. "Attracting the Entrepreneurial Immigrant." *Globe and Mail*, 31 July 2011. Available on-line at http://www.theglobeandmail.com/news/national/time-to-lead/attracting-the-entrepreneurial-immigrant/article2115786/page1/.

Grant, T. "Small Businesses Key to Job Creation." *Globe and Mail*, 3 February 2010. Available on-line at http://www.theglobeandmail.com/report-on-business/small-business/start/talent/small-businesses-key-to-job-creation/article1454510/.

Gross, J. "Business Improvement Districts in New York City's Low-Income and High-Income Neighborhoods." *Economic Development Quarterly*, 19, 2 (2005):174–89.

Gruen, V., and L. Smith. *Shopping Towns USA: The Planning of Shopping Centres*. Philadelphia: Reinhold Press, 1967.

Gruley, B., and J. McCracken. "The Battle for Best Buy: Incredible Shrinking Big Box." *Business Week*, 18 October 2012. Available on-line at http://www.businessweek.com/articles/2012-10-18/the-battle-for-best-buy-the-incredible-shrinking-big-box.

Hall, P.V. *Cities in Civilization*. London: Pantheon Books, 1998.

Hall, P.V., and M. Hesse, eds. *Cities, Regions and Flows*. London: Routledge, 2013.

Hamermesh, D., and J. Biddle. "Beauty and Labor Market." *American Economic Review*, 84, 5 (1994): 1173–94.

Hirschman, A. *Exit, Voice, and Loyalty: Responses to Decline in Firms, Organizations, and States*. Cambridge, MA: Harvard University Press, 1970.

Hollander, S. *The Economics of Karl Marx*. Cambridge: Cambridge University Press, 2010.

Holm, H. "Key Lesson from Iceland Crisis Is 'Let Banks Fail.' " *Agence France-Presse*, 6 November 2011. Available on-line at https://au.finance.yahoo.com/news/key-lesson-iceland-crisis-let-023854916.html.

Hopper, T. "Fewer Americans, More Europeans: Toronto's 2010 Tourism Numbers." *National Post*, 6 June 2011. Available on-line at http://news

.nationalpost.com/2011/06/06/fewer-americans-more-money-torontos-2010-tourism-numbers/.

Houstoun, L. *Business Improvement Districts*. Washington, DC: Urban Land Institute, 1997.

Hoyt, L. *The Business Improvement District: An Internationally Diffused Approach to Revitalization*. Cambridge, MA: MIT Press, 2003.

Hoyt, L. "Planning through Compulsory Commercial Clubs: Business Improvement Districts." *Economic Affairs*, 25 (2005): 24–7.

Hoyt, L., and D. Gopal-Agge. "The Business Improvement District Model: A Balanced Review of Contemporary Debates." *Geography Compass*, 1 (2007): 946–58.

Hulchanski, D. *The Three Cities within Toronto: Income Polarization among Toronto's Neighbourhoods, 1970–2005*. Toronto: Cities Centre, University of Toronto, 2010. Available on-line at http://www.urbancentre.utoronto.ca/pdfs/curp/tnrn/Three-Cities-Within-Toronto-2010-Final.pdf.

Hume, C. "More Density Downtown Will Cut Down on Gridlock." *Toronto Star*, 1 December 2013. Available on-line at http://www.thestar.com/news/gta/2013/12/01/more_density_downtown_will_cut_down_on_gridlock_hume.html.

Hvidt, M. "Private-Public Ties and Their Contribution to Development: The Case of Dubai." *Middle Eastern Studies*, 43, 4 (2007): 557–77.

Hyman, R. *Understanding European Trade Unionism: Between Market, Class and Society*. London: Sage, 2001.

Immergluck, D., and G. Smith. "How Changes in Small Business Lending Affect Firms in Low- and Moderate-Income Neighborhoods." *Journal of Developmental Entrepreneurship*, 8, 2 (2003): 153–75.

Industry Canada. "The Growth Process in Firms: Job Creation." *Firm Age*. Available on-line at http://www.ic.gc.ca/eic/site/061.nsf/eng/h_rd02114.html.

Industry Canada, Office of Consumer Affairs (OCA). "Consumers and Changing Retail Markets." *Consumer Trends Report*, chapter 2. Available on-line at http://www.ic.gc.ca/eic/site/oca-bc.nsf/eng/ca02096.html.

Infantry, A. "Bank of Montreal to Open Condo-Sized Branches." *Toronto Star*, 6 May 2013. Available on-line at http://www.thestar.com/business/2013/04/29/bank_of_montreal_to_open_condo_sized_branches.html.

Inman, R., ed. *Making Cities Work: Prospects and Policies for Urban America*. Princeton, NJ: Princeton University Press, 2009.

Isakov, A. *Going Local: Inspirational Stories of Local Government and Local Economy in British Columbia*. Vancouver: Centre for Civic Governance, 2009.

Jackson, A. "Canada's Productivity Problem." *The Progressive Economics Forum*, 28 July 2010. Available on-line at http://www.progressive-economics.ca/2010/07/28/canadas-productivity-problem/.

Jacobs, J. *Dark Age Ahead*. New York: Random House, 2004.

Jacobs, J. *The Death and Life of Great American Cities*. New York: Modern Library, [1961]1993.

Jacobs, M. *The Green Economy: Environment, Sustainable Development and the Politics of the Future*. Vancouver: University of British Columbia Press, 1993.

James, R. "Waterfront Rebuff First of Many for Ford?" *Toronto Star*, 21 September 2011. Available on-line at http://www.thestar.com/news/article/1057658--james-waterfront-rebuff-first-of-many-for-ford.

Jenkins, R. *Social Identity*. New York: Routledge, 2005.

Jennings, J. "The Empowerment Zone in Boston, Massachusetts, 2000-2009: Lessons Learned for Neighborhood Revitalization." *Review of Black Political Economy*, 38, 1 (2011): 63–81.

Judd, R., and R. McNeil. "Large Firms and Small Firms: Job Quality, Innovation and Economic Development." *Journal of American Business Review*, 1, 1 (2012): 157–64.

Kaminer, M. "A Low-Slung Piece of Toronto Gains Casual-Hip Cachet." *New York Times*, 9 October 2011. Available on-line at http://www.nytimes.com/slideshow/2011/10/09/travel/20111009-surfacing.html.

Keane, M. "Great Adaptations: China's Creative Clusters and the New Social Contract." *Continuum*, 23, 2 (2009): 221–30.

Kennedy, C. *The Evolution of Great World Cities*. Toronto: Rotman-UTP Publishing, 2012.

Kingsworth, P. "This Economic 'Crisis of Bigness.' " *Guardian*, 25 September 2011. Available on-line at http://www.guardian.co.uk/commentisfree/2011/sep/25/crisis-bigness-leopold-kohr.

Klosterman, R. *Community Analysis and Planning Techniques*. Lanham, MD: Rowman and Littlefield Publishers, Inc., 1990.

Kohr, L. *The Breakdown of Nations*. London: Routledge and Kegan Paul, 1957.

Knight, F. *Risk, Uncertainty, and Profit*. Boston, MA: Hart, Schaffner & Marx; Houghton Mifflin Co., 1921.

Knighton, C. "Why White People Should Oppose Whole Foods." *Boston Indymedia*, 2011. Available on-line at http://boston.indymedia.org/feature/display/212710/index.php.

Le Corbusier. *The City of Tomorrow and Its Planning*. London: Architectural Press, 1971 (originally published as *Urbanisme*, 1929).

Le Corbusier. *The Radiant City: Elements of a Doctrine of Urbanism to Be Used as the Basis of Our Machine-Age Civilization*. New York: Orion Press, 1967 (originally published as *La Ville Radieuse*, 1933).

Lehrer, U. "Re-placing Canadian Cities: The Challenge of Landscapes of 'Desire' and 'Despair.'" In T. Bunting and P. Filion, eds, *Canadian Cities in*

Transition: Local through Global Perspective, 3rd ed., 439–49. Don Mills, ON: Oxford University Press, 2006.

Leibovitz, J. "Institutional Barriers to Associative City-Region Governance: The Politics of Institution-Building and Economic Governance in 'Canada's Technology Triangle.' " *Urban Studies*, 40 (2003): 2613–42.

Leonhardt, D. "The Depression: If Only Things Were That Good." *New York Times*, 8 October 2011. Available on-line at http://www.nytimes.com/2011/10/09/sunday-review/the-depression-if-only-things-were-that-good.html?pagewanted=all.

Leung, D., and L. Rispoli. "The Contribution of Small and Medium-Sized Businesses to Gross Domestic Product: A Canada–United States Comparison." *Statistics Canada*, June 2011. Available on-line at http://publications.gc.ca/collections/collection_2011/statcan/11F0027M/11f0027m2011070-eng.pdf.

Levy, P. "Paying for the Public Life." *Economic Development Quarterly*, 15, 2 (2001): 124–31.

Lilischkis, S. "Policies in Support of High-Growth Innovative SMEs." *Inno-Grips*. Policy Brief No. 2, Version 1.5. June 2011. Available on-line at http://ec.europa.eu/enterprise/policies/innovation/support/pro-inno/index_en.htm.

Lindelof, P., and H. Loftsen. "Science Park Location and New Technology Based Firms in Sweden – Implications for Strategy and Performance." *Small Business Economics*, 20 (2003): 245–58.

Lloyd, M., J. McCarthy, S. McGregal, and J. Berry. "Business Improvement Districts, Planning and Urban Regeneration." *International Planning Studies*, 8 (2003): 295–322.

Martin, R. "Small Business, Entrepreneurship, and Innovation." Institute for Competitiveness & Prosperity Working Paper Number 15, 23 February 2012. Available on-line at http://www.competeprosper.ca/work/working_papers/small_business_entrepreneurship_and_innovation.

Martin Prosperity Institute, University of Waterloo, University of Toronto at Scarborough, OCAD University, E.R.A. Architects Inc., Wavelength/Music Gallery Independent Designer. "From the Ground Up: Growing Toronto's Cultural Sector." *City of Toronto*, 2011. Available on-line at http://martinprosperity.org/2011/10/11/from-the-ground-up-growing-torontos-cultural-sector-2011/.

Massey, D. "Liveable Towns and Cities: Approaches for Planners." *Town Planning Review*, 76, 3 (2005): i–vi.

McCarthy, J. "Regeneration of Cultural Quarters: Public Art for Place Image or Place Identity?" *Journal of Urban Design*, 11 (2006): 243–62.

McInroy, N., and S. Longlands. "Productive Local Economies: Creating Resilient Places." *Centre for Local Economic Strategies*, December 2010. Available on-line at http://www.cles.org.uk/wp-content/uploads/2011/01/Resilience-for-web1.pdf.

McKinnie, M. *City Stages: Theatre and Urban Space in a Global City (Cultural Spaces)*. Toronto: University of Toronto Press, 2007.

Mead, M. "Famous Sayings." Number 4. Available on-line at http://www.ranker.com/list/a-list-of-famous-margaret-mead-quotes/reference.

Mellander, C. "Creative and Knowledge Industries: An Occupational Distribution Approach." *Economic Development Quarterly*, 23, 4 (2009): 294–305.

Mellander, C., and Florida, R. "Creativity, Talent and Regional Wages in Sweden." *Annals of Regional Science*, 46, 3 (2009): 637–60.

Mellander, C., R. Florida, and K. Stolarick. "Inside the Black Box of Regional Development." *Journal of Economic Geography*, 8 (2008): 615–49.

Meslin, D., C. Palassio, and A. Wilcox. *Local Motion: The Art of Engagement in Toronto*. Toronto: Coach House Press, 2010.

Mitchell, J. *Business Improvement Districts and the Shape of American Cities*. State University of New York Series on Urban Public Policy. Albany, NY: State University of New York Press, 2008.

Mitchell, S. "Study Finds Local Businesses Key to Income Growth, New Rules Project." 17 August 2011. Available on-line at http://www.ilsr.org/study-finds-local-businesses-key-income-growth/.

Mofid, K. "Small Is Beautiful: The Wisdom of E.F. Schumacher." 11 April 2011. Available on-line at http://www.gcgi.info/news/128-small-is-beautiful-the-wisdom-of-ef-schumacher.

Monck, C., B. Porter, P. Quintas, D. Storey, and P. Wynarczyk. *Science Parks and the Growth of High-Technology Firms*. London: Croom Helm, 1988.

Morcol, G., L. Hoyt, J. Meek, and U. Zimmermann, eds. *Business Improvement Districts: Research, Theories, and Controversies*. Boca Raton, FL: CRC Press, 2008.

Morgenson, G. "How Mr Volcker Would Fix It." *New York Times*, 23 October 2011. Available on-line at http://www.nytimes.com/2011/10/23/business/volckers-advice-for-more-financial-reform.html.

Mowat Centre. "Canada's Innovation Underperformance." Available on-line at http://mowatcentre.ca/canada-innovation-underperformance/.

Moynihan, M.A. "Whole Foods Fight in Boston." 16 April 2001. Available on-line at http://online.wsj.com/news/articles/SB100014240527487046284045 76264531346066192.

Mumford, L. *The City in History*. San Diego, CA: Harcourt Inc., 1961.

"National Research Centre Shopper Satisfaction Survey." *Consumer Reports*, 2010. Available on-line at http://www.consumerreports.org/cro/

magazine-archive/2010/july/shopping/retail-stores/overview/index.htm.

National Small Business Association. "Testimony of Scott Hague to US Subcommittee on Small Business." 6 May 2009. Available on-line at http://www.nsba.biz/docs/testimony_of_scott_hauge.pdf.

Navarro-Gonzalez, M., and C. Quintana-Domeque. "Paving Streets for the Poor: Experimental Analysis of Infrastructure Effects." IZA Discussion Paper 5346. November 2010.

Nelson, R., and S. Winter. *An Evolutionary Theory of Economic Change.* Cambridge, MA: Harvard University Press, 1982.

Neubert, A. *Business Improvement Districts – ein Modell fur Deutschland.* Saarbrucken: VDM Verlag, 2008.

Now magazine website. "Top 5 Toronto Pizza." Available on-line at http://www.nowtoronto.com/food/story.cfm?content=175351.

Olive, D. "Small Business, the Romance Is Over." *Toronto Star,* 20 October 2011. Available on-line at http://www.thestar.com/business/2011/10/20/olive_small_business_the_romance_is_over.html.

Ontario College of Family Physicians. "The Health Impacts of Urban Sprawl Information Series: Volume Four: Social and Mental Health." (September 2005). Downloaded at http://ocfp.on.ca/docs/committee-documents/urban-sprawl---volume-4---social-and-mental-health.pdf?sfvrsn=5.

Organization for Economic Cooperation and Development (OECD). *Territorial Indicators of Employment: Focus on Rural Development.* Paris: OECD, 1996.

Olson, M. *The Logic of Collective Action: Public Goods and the Theory of Groups.* Cambridge, MA: Harvard University Press, 1977.

Osbaldeston, M. *The Option of Urbanism: Investing in a New American Dream.* Washington, DC: Island Press, 2007.

Osbaldeston, M. *Reinventing Los Angeles: Nature and Community in the Global City.* Cambridge, MA: MIT Press, 2007.

Osbaldeston, M. *Unbuilt Toronto: A History of the City That Might Have Been.* Toronto: Dundurn, 2008.

Osnos, P. "The True Subject of Errol Morris's Donald Rumsfeld Doc: Smugness." *The Atlantic,* 9 April 2014. Downloaded at http://www.theatlantic.com/entertainment/archive/2014/04/the-true-subject-of-errol-morriss-donald-rumsfeld-doc-smugness/360344/.

Owen, D. *Green Metropolis: Why Living Smaller, Living Closer, and Driving Less Are the Keys to Sustainability.* New York: Riverhead Books, 2009.

Peel, D., and M. Lloyd. "Re-generating Learning in the Public Realm: Evidence Based Policy-Making and Business Improvement Districts in the UK." *Public Policy and Administration,* 23 (2008): 189–205.

Phelps, E.S. *Mass Flourishing: How Grassroots Innovation Created Jobs, Challenge, and Change*. Princeton, NJ: Princeton University Press, 2013.

Rankin, K.N. "Commercial Change in Toronto's West-End Neighborhoods." Research Paper 214. Toronto: Cities Centre, University of Toronto, 2008.

Ratcliffe, J., B. Williams, and S. Branaugh. *Managing and Financing Urban Regeneration: A Preliminary Study in the Prospective Use of Business Improvement Districts and Tax Increment Finance Districts in Ireland*. Dublin: Dublin Institute of Technology, 1999.

Rentfrow, J., C. Mellander, and R. Florida. "Happy States of America: A State-Level Analysis of Psychological, Economic, and Social Well-Being." *Journal of Research in Personality*, 43, 6 (2009): 1073–82.

Rochon, L. "City Space." *Globe and Mail*, 8 December 2012.

Rodríguez-Pose, A. "Economists as Geographers and Geographers as Something Else: On the Changing Conception of Distance in Geography and Economics." *Journal of Economic Geography*, 11, 2 (2011): 347–56.

Rodríguez-Pose, A., and E.I. Palavicini-Corona. "Does Local Economic Development Really Work? Assessing LED across Mexican Municipalities." *Geoforum*, 44 (2013): 303–15.

Rosson, P., and C. McLarney. "Industry Clusters in Peripheral Regions: A Biotechnology Case Study." In R. MacGregor and A. Hodgkinson, eds, *Small Business Clustering Technologies: Applications in Marketing, Management, IT and Economics*, 99–125. Hershey, PA: Idea Group Publishing, 2006.

Royer, G. *Time for Cities: Canadian Towns and Cities Are Going Broke! Strategies for a Sustainable Future*. Port Moody, BC: Self Published, 2007 (2013 updated edition). Available on-line at http://www.timeforcities.ca/read-online.html.

Rubin, J. *The End of Growth*. 1st ed. Toronto: Random House Canada, 2012.

Rubin, J. *Why Your World Is about to Get a Whole Lot Smaller: Oil and the End of Globalization*. Toronto: Random House Canada, 2009.

Rudy, J. *The Destruction of the Stockyards Industrial District*. VOX, Woodsworth College, University of Toronto, 2011.

Saunders, D. *Arrival City: The Final Migration and Our Next World*. Toronto: Knopf Canada, 2010.

Saxenian, A. *Regional Advantage: Culture and Competition in Silicon Valley and Route 128.* Cambridge, MA: Harvard University Press, 1994.

Schiff, N. "Cities and Product Variety." University of British Columbia Sauder School of Business Working Paper. January 2012. Available on-line at http://www.sauder.ubc.ca/Faculty/Research_Centres/Centre_for_Urban_Economics_and_Real_Estate/~/media/Files/Faculty%20Research/Urban%20Economics/Working%20Papers/Schiff-dd_May_2013.ashx.

Searle, G., and P. Filion. "Planning Context and Urban Intensification Outcomes: Sydney versus Toronto." *Urban Studies*, 48 (2011): 1419–38.

Senor, D., and S. Singer. Start-Up Nation: The Story of Israel's Economic Miracle. Washington, DC: Twelve Books, 2009.

Sewell, J. *The Shape of the Suburbs: Understanding Toronto's Sprawl*. Toronto: University of Toronto Press, 2009.

"Should Government Invest in Private Companies?" *Globe and Mail*, 11 November 2011. Available on-line at http://www.theglobeandmail.com/report-on-business/small-business/sb-money/business-funding/should-government-invest-in-private-companies/article2232210/.

Smith, Adam. *An Inquiry into the Nature and Causes of the Wealth of Nations*. London: J.M. Dent, (1776) 1910; Digireads.com Publishing (1776), 2009.

Smith, N. *The New Urban Frontier: Gentrification and the Revanchist City*. London and New York: Routledge, 1996.

Smith, P.J., and K. Stewart. "Local Government Reform in British Columbia, 1991–2005: One Oar in the Water." In J. Garcea and E.C. LeSage, Jr, eds, *Municipal Reforms in Canada: Reconfigurations, Re-empowerment, and Rebalancing*, 25–56. Toronto: Oxford University Press, 2005.

Smith, P.J., and K. Stewart. "Local Whole-of-Government Policymaking in Vancouver: Beavers, Cats, and the Mushy Middle Thesis." In R. Young and C. Leuprecht, eds, *Canada: The State of the Federation 2004: Municipal-Federal-Provincial Relations Canada*, 251–72. Montreal: McGill-Queen's University Press, 2006.

Smyth, H. *Marketing the City: The Role of Flagship Developments in Urban Regeneration*. London and New York: E. & F.N. Spoon, 1994.

Stangler, D. "The Economic Future Just Happened." Ewing Marion Kauffman Foundation (2009). Available on-line at http://www.kauffman.org/~/media/kauffman_org/research%20reports%20and%20covers/2009/06/theeconomicfuturejusthappened.pdf.

Statistics Canada. "Population and Dwelling Counts for Census Metropolitan Areas and Census Agglomerations, 2006 and 2001 Censuses." Available on-line at http://www12.statcan.gc.ca/census-recensement/2006/dp-pd/hlt/97-550/Index.cfm?TPL=P2C&Page=FLTR&LANG=Eng&T=303&GK=CMA.

Stokes, R. "Business Improvement Districts and Inner City Revitalization: The Case of Philadelphia's Frankford Special Services District." *International Journal of Public Administration*, 29, 1–3 (2006): 187–219.

Stroll, M. *Psychogeographic Walking Tours of Toronto*. Toronto: Coach House Books, 2010.

Studer, R. "Does Trade Explain Europe's Rise? Geography, Market Size and Economic Development." *LSE Economic History Working paper, No. 129/09*. Available on-line at http://www.lse.ac.uk/economichistory/pdf/wp129.pdf.

Svensson, P., M. Klofsten, and H. Etzkowitz. "An Entrepreneurial University Strategy for Renewing a Declining Industrial City: The Norrköping Way." *European Planning Studies,* 20, 4 (2012): 505.

Symes, M., and M. Steel. "Lessons from America: The Role of Business Improvement Districts as an Agent of Urban Regeneration." *Town Planning Review,* 74, 3 (2003): 301–13.

Syverson, C. "Market Structure and Productivity: A Concrete Example." *Journal of Political Economy,* 112, 6 (December 2004): 1181–222.

Tapscott, D., and A.D. Williams. *Wikinomics: How Mass Collaboration Changes Everything.* 2nd ed. New York: Penguin Books, 2008.

Terluin, I. "Differences in Economic Development in Rural Regions of Advanced Countries." *Journal of Rural Studies,* 19 (2003): 327–44.

Texas Perspectives Inc. "Big Box Retail and Austin." City of Austin, Texas, 1 June 2004. Available on-line at http://www.gatewayplanning.com/BIG%20BOX/Big%20Box.Austin.final1.pdf.

Texeira, C. *Immigrant Entrepreneurship in Kelowna, B.C.* Vancouver: Metropolis British Columbia, Beaconsfield, QC: Canadian Electronic Library, 2012.

Thompson, A., and J. Gamble. "Starbucks Corporation: Starbucks: A Case Study." Available on-line at http://www.mhhe.com/business/management/thompson/11e/case/starbucks-2.html.

"Torontoist." Available on-line at http://torontoist.com/.

Tossell, I. "Should Government Invest in Private Companies?" *Globe and Mail,* 11 November 2011. Available on-line at http://www.theglobeandmail.com/report-on-business/small-business/sb-money/business-funding/should-government-invest-in-private-companies/article2232210/.

Travers, T. *The Politics of London: Governing an Ungovernable City.* Basingstoke, Hants: Palgrave Macmillan, 2003.

Trono, A., and M. Zerbi. "Milan: The City of Constant Renewal." *GeoJournal,* 58, 1 (2008): 65–72.

Turcotte, M. "Commuting to Work: Results of the 2010 General Social Survey." Statistics Canada Catalogue no. 11–008-X. August 2011. Available online at http://www.google.ca/search?hl=en-CA&source=hp&q=Commuting+to+work%3A+Results+of+the+2010+General+Social+Survey&gbv=2&oq=Commuting+to+work%3A+Results+of+the+2010+General+Social+Survey&gs_l=heirloom-hp.13..0.2137.2137.0.3953.1.1.0.0.0.0.100.100.0j1.1.0...0.0...1c.1.s5e5O4va5ds.

Turner, C. *The Leap: How to Survive and Thrive in the Sustainable Economy.* Toronto: Random House Canada, 2011.

Underhill, P. *Why We Buy: The Science of Shopping.* New York: Simon & Schuster, 1999.

Urban Task Force. *Towards an Urban Renaissance: Final Report of the Urban Task Force*. Chaired by Lord Rogers of Riverside. London: Department of the Environment, Transport and the Regions, 1999.

Vaughan, M. "Introduction: Henri Bergson's Creative Evolution." *SubStance*, 36 (2006): 7-24.

Vindevogel, F. "Private Security and Urban Crime Mitigation: A Bid for BIDs." *Criminology and Criminal Justice*, 5, 3 (2005): 233-55.

Waldfogel, J. "The Median Voter and the Median Consumer: Local Private Goods and Population Composition." *Journal of Urban Economics*, 63, 2 (2008): 567-82.

Ward, K. "Policies in Motion, Urban Management and State Restructuring: The Translocal Expansion of Business Improvement Districts." *International Journal of Urban and Regional Research*, 30 (2006): 54-75.

Webman, J. *Reviving the Industrial City*. New Brunswick, NJ: Rutgers University Press, 1982.

Wheeler, K. "Business Improvement Districts." *Economic Development Today*, 42 (2002): 21-3.

White, S. "As Layoffs Near 160,000, Banks May Shrink for Good." *Financial Post*, 12 November 2012. Available on-line at http://business.financialpost.com/2012/11/16/as-layoffs-near-160000-banks-may-shrink-for-good/.

Whitzman, C. *Suburb, Slum, Urban Village: Transformations in Toronto's Parkdale Neighbourhood, 1875-2002*. Vancouver: University of British Columbia Press, 2009.

Wilcox, A., and J. McBride, eds. *Utopia: Towards a New Toronto*. uTOpia series. Toronto: Coach House, 2005.

Woodhouse, E., ed. *International Encyclopedia of the Social Sciences*. 2nd ed. Available on-line at http://homepages.rpi.edu/~woodhe/docs/Lindblom%20in%20Intl%20Ency%20Soc%20Sci.pdf.

World Bank. "What Is Social Capital?" Available on-line at http://web.worldbank.org/WBSITE/EXTERNAL/TOPICS/EXTSOCIALDEVELOPMENT/EXTTSOCIALCAPITAL/0,,contentMDK:20185164~menuPK:418217~pagePK:148956~piPK:216618~theSitePK:401015,00.html.

Worldwatch Institute. *State of the World 2007: Our Urban Future (State of the World)*. New York: W.W. Norton, 2007.

Wren, C., and D. Storey. "Evaluating the Effects of Soft Business Support upon Small Firm Performance." *Oxford Economic Papers*, 54 (2002): 334-65.

Yang, J. "The Birthplace of BIAs Celebrates 40 Years." *Toronto Star*, 18 April 2010. Available on-line at http://www.thestar.com/news/gta/2010/04/18/the_birthplace_of_bias_celebrates_40_years.html.

Index